The Compositional Process of J. S. Bach

VOLUME I

NUMBER FOUR IN
THE PRINCETON STUDIES IN MUSIC

The Compositional Process of

J. S. Bach

A Study of the Autograph Scores
of the Vocal Works

VOLUME I

By Robert Lewis Marshall

PRINCETON UNIVERSITY PRESS

1972

To Arthur Mendel

PREFACE

DURING ONE of the discussions at the Leipzig Bach Festival of 1950 the question was raised whether the Bach autographs could contribute to an understanding of his creative process. The problem was briefly considered at that time but apparently has not been seriously investigated since, although the Leipzig Congress initiated a period of vigorous philological activity which has subjected the available source material to an intensive scrutiny and has resulted in the establishment of a new chronology of Bach's vocal compositions, and continues to date with a new edition of the complete works.

Now it is not difficult to understand why a large-scale study of Bach's creative process has never been undertaken. An empirically oriented era of humanistic scholarship like the present one is reluctant to be drawn into the seemingly metaphysical realms of genius, inspiration, fantasy, and so on, which seem to belong more properly in the domain of the psychologist if not that of the poet and philosopher. Indeed, in the case of Bach the would-be investigator of the creative process is discouraged very early in his pursuit. For one realizes soon enough that Bach was a remarkably "clean" worker, and that, while his compositions rarely seem to have sprung forth fully grown from the head of their creator, the manuscripts contain few traces of the genesis of the compositions notated in them.

This was all evident to Philipp Spitta, who was apparently convinced of the futility of an attempt to gain insight into Bach's creative process. He remarks in his biography of Bach:

> Bach's scores do not give the impression that he made many sketches or experimented with the basic ideas in advance, as did, for example, Beethoven. The appearance of the scores suggests that they were written after the work concerned was thought out internally by the composer thoroughly and extensively, but not to such an extent that the composer did not conceive any further during the act of writing. The cases in which he rejected the entire original layout of a piece are relatively rare; corrections of details, on the contrary, are frequent (II, 180).

And, in his essay "Beethoveniana" Spitta writes:

> We know that Sebastian occasionally made jottings in advance for a planned composition. In general the creative act was for him, too, [as it was for Mozart] an internal one; only it seems to have come to fruition more slowly, although with the same steadiness as in Mozart's case. Despite the great complexity

of [Bach's] music, we know of few cases where the layout of a piece was rejected once it had been worked out. Nor did he often falter while working out the details. Sometimes he made changes when he took up a work again at a later date; but for an understanding of the way it was formed in the beginning, the evidence provided by such changes tells us nothing (p. 181).

Who would rush in where Spitta feared to tread?

THE PRESENT study was originally planned to embrace only the surviving manuscripts for the vocal works written through Bach's first year as Thomas Cantor in Leipzig, the hope being to trace the development of Bach's compositional routine in his "formative" years and into the maturity of the Leipzig period. This plan was quickly shattered. The early works are preserved overwhelmingly in fair copies or in what will be called "revision copies" in the present study. As copies they reveal, of course, nothing "of the way it was in the beginning." And as Spitta observed, the Leipzig scores, taken individually, disclose few secrets. One manuscript may reveal a number of insights into, say, the formation of melody, and the next one nothing about melody but quite a bit perhaps about Bach's understanding of the continuo. It became clear, therefore, that to stop the survey after the last manuscript in the first Leipzig cantata *Jahrgang* entailed the risk that new—and perhaps crucial—clues contained in the next manuscript would remain undiscovered, and this risk would exist at any arbitrary cutoff point. The only approach assured of any degree of success, then, was to consider all the surviving autographs. On such a scale the totality of the "relatively rare" rejected drafts and the "frequent" corrections of details would begin to form a picture of Bach's compositional process.

Along with the scope of the study it was necessary to clarify its goal. Was the subject of the investigation the "creative process" or the "compositional process" or the "compositional procedures" of Johann Sebastian Bach? This may be only a question of terminology, but a number of misunderstandings could arise if the wrong term were applied.

"Creative process" evokes those notions of inspiration, genius, imagination, qualities which remain hidden from any reasonably objective analysis. "Procedure" on the other hand, as "a way of doing something," suggests a relatively mechanical act. Such acts as ruling paper, correcting parallel fifths, or determining the proper scansion of a text were certainly to be considered in the study as part of its hoped-for objectivity and sober foundation in the tangible evidence of the autographs. But it seemed that the observation of these individual acts, taken together, resulted in a picture of a "process"—a "continuing development involving many changes"—governed by an active and critical intelligence. The awareness of a musical personality eventually emerges, with its likes and dislikes, its hierarchy of values, and its flexible response to various musical situations and problems. Insofar as the study was able to follow the interplay of mind and matter, it could be said to be dealing with the *process* of musical composition.

The degree to which the study was able to throw light on the way a work was "formed in the beginning" is admittedly limited, and the extent of this limitation depends, of course, on how close to "the beginning" one insists on penetrating. Whether the evidence considered here tells us much, little, or nothing may be decided by each reader.

I WISH to express my gratitude to a number of individuals and institutions for their assistance: to the United States State Department and Educational Commission (Fulbright Commission) and the Martha Baird Rockefeller Fund for Music for their generous grants and financial assistance which have enabled me to spend a total of three years in Germany conducting research and a year at Princeton University preparing the draft of the study; to the staffs of the music divisions of the Berliner Staatsbibliothek, the Westdeutsche Bibliothek, Marburg, the Universitätsbibliothek and Musikwissenschaftliches Institut, Tübingen, the Hessische Landes- und Hochschulbibliothek, Darmstadt, the Bibliothèque Nationale, Paris, the Library of Congress, the New York Public Library, the Pierpont Morgan Library, New York, and the Kunstsammlungen auf der Veste Coburg for their willingness to allow me to work with their priceless collections of Bach autographs and to provide me with microfilms of many of these manuscripts; to Dr. Alfred Dürr of the Johann-Sebastian-Bach-Institut, Göttingen, and Professor Werner Neumann of the Bach-Archiv, Leipzig, for the opportunity to examine their photocopies of Bach manuscripts; to Dr. Dürr once again, and to Professor Georg von Dadelsen, Mr. William H. Scheide, Mr. Richard Sherr, Dr. Ulrich Siegele, Professors Edward E. Lowinsky and Kenneth J. Levy, and my wife Traute for their many helpful suggestions and their interest in this project; to my wife again for her patience and willingness to prepare both the final typescript and the index; to Eve Hanle for her attention to countless editorial details of greater and lesser magnitude; to Mr. Laurence Libin for his assistance in the reading of proof; and finally to Professor Arthur Mendel for his active interest and encouragement at every stage in the history of this project, for his unfailingly wise and constructive criticism of the entire manuscript, and for the example of his own dedicated scholarship.

CONTENTS

VOLUME I

VOLUME II

LIST OF FACSIMILES

VOLUME I

VOLUME II

ABBREVIATIONS

BG   *Johann Sebastian Bach's Werke.* Complete edition of the Bach-Gesellschaft. 46 vols. Leipzig, 1851–1900.

BJ   *Bach-Jahrbuch,* Leipzig and Berlin, 1904—.

BWV   Wolfgang Schmieder. *Thematisch-systematisches Verzeichnis der musikalischen Werke von Johann Sebastian Bach. Bach-Werke-Verzeichnis.* Leipzig, 1950.

NBA   *Johann Sebastian Bach. Neue Ausgabe sämtlicher Werke.* Edited by the Johann-Sebastian-Bach-Institut, Göttingen, and the Bach-Archiv, Leipzig. Kassel, Leipzig, 1954—.

NBA . . . KB   Critical reports (*Kritische Berichte*) of the NBA.

NBG   Publications of the Neue-Bach-Gesellschaft. Leipzig, 1900—.

Other bibliographical references are usually given in an abbreviated form consisting of the last name of the author and the year of publication. A key to these abbreviations appears in the bibliography. A number of musical abbreviations are explained in the introduction to Volume II.

The Compositional Process of J. S. Bach
VOLUME I

CHAPTER I

The General Nature of the Bach Autographs:
Manuscript Types and Their Combinations

THE GERMAN Bach literature since Spitta and the BG has traditionally distinguished two types of autograph score: The *Reinschrift* or fair copy, and the *Konzeptschrift* or composing score. Although one understands intuitively what is meant by these terms, it is virtually impossible to create any infallible, unambiguous criteria which would serve to relegate every manuscript either to one group or the other.

In the clearest and most extreme cases, one can indeed recognize *Reinschriften* with considerable certainty by their meticulous calligraphic script and by the virtual absence of any corrections that cannot be interpreted as slips of the pen or momentary lapses of attention. On the other hand, a typical composing score reveals, through a relatively hasty handwriting, an often large number of formative corrections,[1] and the occasional presence of sketches and drafts, that Bach most probably wrote these manuscripts while conceiving the music contained in them.

The appearance of an autograph score, however, can be affected by such unknowable biographical factors as the degree of "inspiration" and patience at the command of the composer at the moment he penned a particular manuscript or composition. When Bach's invention was flowing most freely, he was capable of composing an almost flawless score; and, if he wished, he could set it down in a careful calligraphic hand, so that an observer can hardly determine whether the manuscript is a fair copy or a composing score. Conversely, Bach at times copied from a preexistent source in an inattentive, hasty manner that produced a score that was neither calligraphic nor free of corrections.[2]

The two ideal types should therefore be considered the extremes of a veritable continuum of gradations formed by the 170 extant autograph scores which represent every degree of calligraphy and every variation in the density and significance of corrections. For the entire composing and/or music-writing process was subject to the vagaries of inspiration and the moods of the composer.

Georg von Dadelsen has suggested that it is therefore desirable to introduce

---

[1] For the definition of "formative" correction and other classifications of correction types used in this study, see pp. 34–36 below.

[2] The evidence for these statements will be presented below.

four terms into the discussion of autograph types.[3] He proposes to use the terms *kalligraphische Schrift* and *Gebrauchsschrift* when only handwriting criteria are being considered (as in his study) and to reserve the terms *Reinschrift* and *Konzeptschrift* for a description of what he calls the *Quellen-Charakter*. How the "character of the source" is to be determined is not explained by von Dadelsen except in general terms of the "hasty" (*flüchtig*) or "final" (*endgültig*) appearance of the manuscript. But since he excluded the particulars of script-type here, he presumably has in mind also the evidence supplied by the presence of corrections and sketches.

It is helpful to present von Dadelsen's terminology schematically as follows:

1. HANDWRITING CRITERIA[4]
    a) Calligraphic: careful horizontal and vertical placement of all symbols; upright stems; evenly and rationally spaced note-heads and symbols, often varying in size according to temporal value (i.e., whole notes are larger than the heads of half-notes, quarter-notes larger than eighth-notes, etc.)
    b) Non-calligraphic (*Gebrauchsschrift*): tilted stems; irrationally, unevenly spaced note-heads and symbols; frequently ambiguous placement of symbols (especially crucial in regard to pitch)
2. COMPOSITIONAL CRITERIA
    a) Fair copy (*Reinschrift*): very few or no formative corrections; corrections usually limited to rectifying copying errors or slips of the pen; no sketches or drafts
    b) Composing score (*Konzeptschrift*): relatively numerous corrections of a formative nature, plus the presence of sketches and drafts.

The comments above should make it evident that either member of each group can be combined—theoretically and in fact—with either member of the other group. The most common and typical combinations are, as one would expect, 1a–2a, the calligraphic fair copy, and 1b–2b, the hasty composing score.

In addition to the variety of fair copies and composing scores, one clearly "intermediate" manuscript type appears often enough to merit a specific designation here. Many manuscripts of the early cantatas, and again those of the 1730's and '40's, reveal a calligraphic penmanship and contain comparatively few corrections. Those corrections present are for the most part minor—concerned perhaps with text underlaying—or "grammatical" in nature. Furthermore, they are usually concentrated in particular lines—the voice parts, say—or in particular sections of movements, e.g., either the A or B section of a da-capo aria. These features suggest that in his early period (particularly the pre-Cöthen years) Bach

[3] Dadelsen 1958, pp. 71–72.   [4] See Dadelsen 1958, pp. 58–72, and Schünemann 1936[1], pp. 17–19.

worked a great deal from preliminary drafts which may have been subsequently destroyed, and they confirm our knowledge that the composer made extensive use of earlier material in his compositions of the 1730's and '40's. The autographs of all these works can perhaps best be described as "revision copies," reflecting a stage in the compositional process more advanced than that observed in the composing scores of the Leipzig church cantatas of the 1720's, but hardly to be classified together with the famous calligraphic *Reinschriften* of, say, the Brandenburg Concertos or the *Well-Tempered Clavier*. In the Weimar and Mühlhausen cantatas one often has the impression that the invention of themes and overall design of many movements had been worked out in advance and that only the final touches were then added in the revision copy. In at least two instances[5] the preliminary drafts or scores were apparently so complete that Bach had a copyist write out large portions of the final manuscripts. We may assume that Bach's slower pace in Weimar—the church cantatas were mostly written at four-week intervals between 1714 and 1716[6]—in comparison with the weekly production of his first three years in Leipzig,[7] encouraged a relatively leisurely routine and consequently a more conscientious penmanship. By the same token his slower routine in Leipzig after 1727 and his increasing use of preexistent material in the cantatas of this period, occasionally enabled him to employ the services of a copyist to write out large portions of a score. In the score of BWV 174 (1729), for example, a copyist wrote out most of the string parts in the opening sinfonia (which is based on the first movement of the Brandenburg Concerto No. 3), while Bach composed and wrote in only the new wind and continuo parts.[8]

While the introduction of the term "revision copy" will often explain the appearance of a particular score and the type of corrections it contains better than the terms "fair copy" and "composing score," there remain nonetheless a number of elegant, carefully penned autographs, particularly from the pre-Cöthen period but also from later years, which elude any attempt at such classification. A particular manuscript may be a highly "inspired" composing score, a revision copy, a rather careless fair copy, or a fair copy that had been subjected to yet further revision. In the case of such problematic manuscripts there can rarely be any certainty that one of these designations any more than the others accurately reflects the biographical circumstances surrounding the production of the scores.

These reservations should be kept in mind as the reader considers the following tabulation of the manuscripts that form the basis of this study. The chronological

[5] Cantata 61 (P 45/6) and Cantata 185 (P 59).
[6] See Dürr 1951, pp. 52–55.
[7] See the findings of Dürr 1957 and Dadelsen 1958.

[8] There are several other scores in which the string parts are fair copy and the woodwind or brass parts newly composed. These will be considered below.

source list that follows makes no attempt to place each manuscript into one category. Such an exclusive categorization would not only be impossible for the reasons already mentioned, but also because separate portions of the same manuscript are often clearly representative of different autograph types. The existence of such combinations within a single manuscript—or even within a single movement—testifies to some remarkable idiosyncrasies in Bach's working habits which will be considered later.

EXPLANATORY NOTES ON THE CHRONOLOGICAL SOURCE LIST

DATE. Unless there is a footnote to the contrary, dates of the pre-Leipzig cantatas are based on the findings of Dürr 1951; those of the Leipzig cantatas on Dürr 1957 and Dadelsen 1958.

BWV. This column presents the number of the work assigned in the standard *Bach-Werke-Verzeichnis* by Wolfgang Schmieder, with the following additions: a superscript Arabic numeral following the BWV number indicates whether the MS preserves the first or second version of the work concerned (e.g., BWV 118^1); a superscript Roman numeral refers to the section of the work contained in the MS (e.g., BWV 232^I); the number following a stroke is the number of the movement contained in the MS, when the MS is a fragment (e.g., BWV 199/8); the letter "R" indicates that the autograph is a later revision or fair copy of a work known to have been composed at an earlier date (e.g., BWV 66R).

LOCATION. Where the call number alone is given preceded by P or St (*Partitur* or *Stimmen*) the manuscript belongs to what was originally the collection of the Berlin Staatsbibliothek. These manuscripts are catalogued in Kast 1958. The abbreviations employed there to indicate the postwar location of each manuscript—Tb: Universitätsbibliothek Tübingen; Mbg: Westdeutsche Bibliothek, Marburg—are no longer valid. The Tübingen and Marburg MSS are now in the Staatsbibliothek, Stiftung Preussischer Kulturbesitz (West) Berlin, and are designated in the present list as follows:

WB: West Berlin
No initial: Deutsche Staatsbibliothek, Berlin, German Democratic Republic
AMB: Amalienbibliothek (i.e., the library of Princess Anna Amalie of Prussia), now part of the Deutsche Staatsbibliothek

Other Abbreviations
Cambridge: Fitzwilliam Museum, Cambridge
Darmstadt: Hessische Landes- und Hochschulbibliothek, Darmstadt
LC: Library of Congress, Washington, D. C.

Morgan, NY: The Pierpont Morgan Library, New York

NYPL: New York Public Library

Paris: Bibliothèque Nationale, Paris

PP: Score in private possession

Asterisks. All sources have been studied in the original except those whose location name here is followed by an asterisk. For these the photocopies of the Johann-Sebastian-Bach-Institut, Göttingen, have been consulted. The manuscript of BWV 135 was examined in the facsimile edition only. Surviving scores that could not be seen by the present writer either in the original or in photocopy are indicated by a double asterisk.

Parentheses. Single parentheses: the MS is mainly autograph, with some non-autograph sections. Double parentheses: the MS is mainly non-autograph, with some autograph sections.

TYPE. The abbreviations FC (fair copy), RC (revision copy), CS (composing score) always refer to the compositional type rather than script type. They are occasionally modified by parentheses or by hyphens to suggest that the manuscript described bears the characteristics of, or wavers between, two types and cannot properly be attributed to one category.

+: different movements of the MS belong to different categories;

/: distinct portions of a single movement belong to different categories.

STRUCTURE. This column refers to the fascicle structure of the MSS, a subject that will be discussed in Chapter III. The meanings of the symbols used are:

1: single leaf (half-sheet)

I: single sheet; II: binio; III: ternio, etc.

I·I: a binio with a single leaf inserted in it; 3 × II + I in I, etc.: three biniones followed by a single sheet, all placed within a single sheet which serves as a folder, usually with a title page.

EXTANT AUTOGRAPH SCORES OF THE BACH VOCAL WORKS IN CHRONOLOGICAL ORDER

Date	*BWV*	*Location or Call No.*	*Type*	*Structure*
		MÜHLHAUSEN		
1707–1708	131	PP*	FC(-RC)	II + II
2/4/1708	71	P 45/1	FC(-RC)	III + II

EXTANT AUTOGRAPH SCORES OF THE BACH VOCAL WORKS IN CHRONOLOGICAL ORDER (*cont'd*)

Date	BWV	Location or Call No.	Type	Structure
		WEIMAR		
2/23/1713?[9]	208	P 42/3	CS	2 × II + I
3/25/1714	182	(P 103) WB	FC + RC + CS	2 × II + I
4/22/1714	12	P 44/7 WB	FC + RC + CS	III
8/12/1714	199	Royal Library, Copenhagen*	RC + CS	[not seen]
2nd pre-Leipzig performance[10]	199/8	P 1162	CS	1
12/2/1714	61	(P 45/6)	FC	III
12/30/1714	152	P 45/3	RC + CS	II + I
7/14/1715	185	((P 59)) WB	FC	III
11/24/1715	163	P 137 WB	RC + CS	III
12/22/1715	132	P 60 WB	(FC) + RC + CS	III
1/19/1716	155	P 129	CS	II
12/20/1716[11]	147	P 102 WB	(FC)-RC + CS	IV + II
		CÖTHEN		
12/10/1717?[12] (1722?)	173a	P 42/2	CS	3 × II + I in I
1/1/1719	134a	Paris, MS 2	CS	6 × I
		LEIPZIG		
2/1723?	23	P 69 WB	RC + CS	2 × II + I
2/7/1723	22	P 119	(FC) + RC	2 × II + I
5/16/1723?	59	P 161 WB	CS	III
Before 7/2/1723	237	P 13/4	CS	2 × I

[9] See NBA I/35, KB, pp. 39–43, for the arguments based on documentary, notational, and watermark evidence favoring an assignment to the year 1713 rather than the previously accepted date 1716.

[10] See the edition of C. A. Martienssen, NBG Jg. XIII, Heft 2 (Leipzig, 1913), p. iv.

[11] Only the first movement was entered in the score at this time. The remainder of the score was written in Leipzig between 1728 and 1731. See Dürr 1957, pp. 59 and 106.

[12] See the most recent summary of the arguments regarding the date of this composition in NBA I/35, KB, pp. 132–133.

EXTANT AUTOGRAPH SCORES OF THE BACH VOCAL WORKS
IN CHRONOLOGICAL ORDER (*cont'd*)

Date	BWV	Location or Call No.	Type	Structure
		JAHRGANG I: 1723 (*cont'd*)		
5/30/1723	75	P 66 WB	(RC)-CS	I + 4 × II
6/6/1723	76	P 67	CS	3 × II + I
6/20/1723	24	P 44/4 WB	CS	2 × II + I
7/18/1723	136	St 20 WB	CS	2 × 1
7/25/1723	105	P 99	CS	5 × I
8/8/1723	179	P 146 WB	CS	3 × I
8/22/1723	77	P 68 WB	CS	3 × I + 1
8/30/1723	119	P 878 WB	RC + CS	2 × III + II
9/5/1723	138	P 158 WB	CS	4 × I + 1
10/3/1723	48	P 109	CS	3 × I in I
10/17/1723	109	P 112	CS	5 × I
11/2/1723	194	P 43/3	FC + RC + CS	7 × I
11/14/1723	90	P 83	CS	3 × I
12/25/1723	243a	P 38	CS	8 × I
12/25/1723	238	P 13/5	CS	I
12/26/1723	40	P 63	CS	5 × I
		JAHRGANG I: 1724		
1/1/1724	190	P 127 WB	CS	2 × I
1/6/1724	65	P 147	CS	4 × I
1/30/1724	81	P 120	CS	4 × I
2/6/1724	144	P 134	CS	2 × I
4/16/1724	67	P 95	CS	5 × I
5/14/1724	86	P 157	CS	2 × I in I
5/21/1724	44	P 148	CS	3 × I
		JAHRGANG II: 1724		
6/11/1724	20	PP	CS	6 × I
6/18/1724	2	PP	CS	3 × I
6/25/1724	135	Bach-Archiv, Leipzig*	CS	4 × I
7/2/1724	10	LC	CS	4 × I in I
8/6/1724	94	P 47/2	CS	4 × I
8/20/1724	113	PP	CS	4 × I
9/3/1724	33	PP	CS	5 × I
9/29/1724	130	PP*	CS	5 × I

EXTANT AUTOGRAPH SCORES OF THE BACH VOCAL WORKS
IN CHRONOLOGICAL ORDER (*cont'd*)

Date	BWV	Location or Call No.	Type	Structure

JAHRGANG II: 1724 (*cont'd*)

Date	BWV	Location or Call No.	Type	Structure
10/1/1724	114	PP	CS	4 × I
10/8/1724	96	P 179	CS	5 × I
10/15/1724	5	PP*	CS	4 × I?
10/22/1724	180	PP*	CS	5 × I
11/5/1724	115	Cambridge*	CS	3 × I
11/19/1724	26	P 47/1	CS	4 × I
11/26/1724	116	Paris, MS 1	CS	4 × I
12/3/1724	62	P 877 WB	CS	4 × I
12/25/1724	91	P 869 WB	CS + FC	4 × I
12/25/1724	232III	P 13/1	CS	5 × I
12/27/1724	133	P 1215	CS	5 × I
12/31/1724	122	P 868 WB	CS	3 × I

JAHRGANG II: 1725

Date	BWV	Location or Call No.	Type	Structure
1/1/1725	41	P 874 WB	CS	(8)7 × I
1/7/1725	124	P 876 WB	CS	4 × I
1/14/1725	3	PP**		
1/28/1725	92	P 873 WB	CS	6 × I
2/11/1725	127	P 872 WB	CS	5 × I
4/2/1725	6	P 44/2 WB	CS(+RC?)	4 × I in I
4/8/1725	42	P 55	RC + CS	5 × I
4/15/1725	85	P 106	CS	3 × I
4/22/1725	103	P 122	CS	5 × I
4/29/1725	108	P 82	CS	3 × I + 1
5/6/1725	87	P 61	CS	3 × I
5/10/1725	128	PP*	CS	4 × I
5/13/1725	183	P 149	CS	3 × I
5/22/1725	175	P 75	CS + RC	3 × I
5/27/1725	176	P 81	CS	3 × I
Apr./May 1725	36c	P 43/2	CS	7 × I

JAHRGANG III?: 1725

Date	BWV	Location or Call No.	Type	Structure
7/29/1725	168	P 152	CS	3 × I
8/3/1725	205	P 173	CS(+RC?)	19 × I
8/26/1725	164	P 121 WB	CS	4 × 1
10/31/1725	79	P 89	CS	6 × I

EXTANT AUTOGRAPH SCORES OF THE BACH VOCAL WORKS
IN CHRONOLOGICAL ORDER (*cont'd*)

Date	BWV	Location or Call No.	Type	Structure
		JAHRGANG III: 1725		
12/25/1725	110	P 153	RC + CS	10 × I
12/26/1725	57	P 144	CS	5 × I
12/27/1725	151	Kunstsammlung Veste Coburg	CS	3 × I
12/30/1725	28	P 92	RC + CS	6 × I
		JAHRGANG III: 1726		
1/1/1726	16	P 45/7	CS	4 × I in I
1/13/1726	32	P 126	CS	4 × I
1/20/1726	13	P 45/4	CS	3 × I
1/27/1726	72	P 54	CS	5 × I
Feb. 2 to May 19: Performance of Works by Johann Ludwig Bach and Reinhard Keiser				
5/30/1726	43	P 44/6 WB	CS	5 × I
6/23/1726	39	P 62	CS	6 × I
7/21/1726	88	P 145 WB	CS	5 × I
7/28/1726	170	P 154 WB	CS	3 × I
8/4/1726	187	P 84	CS	5 × I + 1
8/11/1726	45	P 80	CS	5 × I
8/25/1726	102	P 97	CS	5 × I
9/8/1726	35	P 86 WB	FC + CS	7 × I
9/22/1726	17	P 45/5	CS	5 × I
9/29/1726	19	P 45/8	CS	5 × I
10/6/1726	27	P 164 WB	CS	4 × I
10/13/1726	47	P 163	CS	5 × I + 1
10/20/1726	169	P 93 WB	RC + CS	4 × I
10/27/1726	56	P 118 WB	CS	3 × I
11/3/1726	49	P 111	FC + CS	5 × I + 1 + I
11/10/1726	98	P 160 WB	CS	3 × I
11/17/1726	55	P 105 WB	CS + FC (or RC)	2 × I + 1
11/24/1726	52	P 85 WB	FC + CS	4 × I
		1726 to 1730		
12/11/1726	207	P 174 WB	RC + CS	11 × I
1/1/1727?	225	P 36/2 WB	CS	5 × I
1726 or 1727	204	P 107	CS	5 × I
1/5/1727	58	P 866 WB	FC + RC + CS	3 × I

EXTANT AUTOGRAPH SCORES OF THE BACH VOCAL WORKS
IN CHRONOLOGICAL ORDER (cont'd)

Date	BWV	Location or Call No.	Type	Structure
		1726 to 1730 (cont'd)		
2/2/1727	82	P 114 WB	CS	4 × I
2/9/1727	84	P 108	CS	4 × I
10/17/1727	198	P 41/1	CS	10 × I
c. 1728	188	P 972 and various fragments*	RC + CS	? × I?
c. 1728	197a	Morgan, NY	CS	I
1/1/1729?	171	PP*	RC + CS	4 × I
6/6/1729	174	(P 115) WB	FC/CS + CS	10 × I
10/24/1729	226	P 36/1 WB	RC + CS	II + I + I
probably c. 1729	120a	P 670 WB	FC/CS + CS	3 × I
probably c. 1729	201	P 175 WB	CS	13 × I
9/17/1730	51	P 104	FC(-RC) + CS	4 × I
		1731 to 1733		
4/8/1731	112	Morgan, NY	RC + CS	3 × I
8/27/1731	29	P 166	FC/RC + CS	II + 3 × I
12/2/1731	36²	P 45/2	FC + RC + CS	6 × I
1728–31	243	P 39	FC(-RC)	6 × II + I
1728–31	117	PP*	CS(+RC?)	5 × I
7/6/1732	177	P 116	CS	6 × I
4/21/1733?¹³	232ᴵ	P 180 WB	FC-RC?	12 × II in I
9/5/1733	213	P 125	CS + RC	6 × I + II + II
12/8/1733	214	P 41/2	CS	8 × I
		1734 to 1735		
10/5/1734	215	P 139	FC/RC + CS	11 × I
1734	97	NYPL	CS + FC(-RC?)	
12/25/1734	248ᴵ	P 32 WB	RC + CS	IV + II
12/26/1734	248ᴵᴵ	P 32 WB	RC + CS	3 × II
12/27/1734	248ᴵᴵᴵ	P 32 WB	RC + CS	2 × II + I
1/1/1735	248ᴵⱽ	P 32 WB	FC + RC + CS	IV + II
1/2/1735	248ⱽ	P 32 WB	RC + CS	II + 4 × I

[13] The speculation that Bach may have written the *Missa* for the festivities surrounding the visit of Friedrich August II to Leipzig on this date was put forth in Schering 1936[1] and retained as a possibility in Dürr 1957 and Dadelsen 1958.

EXTANT AUTOGRAPH SCORES OF THE BACH VOCAL WORKS
IN CHRONOLOGICAL ORDER (*cont'd*)

Date	BWV	Location or Call No.	Type	Structure
				1734 to 1735 (*cont'd*)
1/6/1735	248^{VI}	P 32 WB	RC + CS	III + IV + 1
1/30/1735	14	P 879	CS	$5 \times$ I
4/11/1735	66R	P 73	FC + RC + CS	$7 \times$ I in I
4/12/1735	134R	P 44/3 WB	FC(-RC) + RC	$7 \times$ I in I
5/19/1735	11	P 44/5 WB	FC + RC + CS	IV + III + I
c. 1732–35	9	LC	CS	$4 \times$ I + 1
c. 1732–35	100	P 159	FC(-RC) + CS	$2 \times$ II + 1 + I(+1?)
c. 1732–35	211	P 141	CS	$6 \times$ I
c. 1732–35	249^2	P 34 WB	FC-RC	$2 \times$ IV + III
				1735 to 1750
10/7/1736[14]	206	P 42/1	CS	$11 \times$ I
9/28/1737	30a	P 43/1	CS	V + III + 1
1736–37?[15]	118^1	PP	CS	I + 1
c. 1735–42[16] (1737–38?)	234	Darmstadt	RC	$2 \times$ IV
c. 1735–42 (1737–38?)	236	Darmstadt	RC	$2 \times$ IV + 1
1738–42	30	P 44/1 WB	FC-RC + CS	$2 \times$ IV
c. 1735–42	197	P 91	FC-RC + CS	$7 \times$ I
8/30/1742	212	P 167 WB	CS + RC	$4 \times$ I + ½
after 1735	244R	P 25	FC(-RC)	$7 \times$ V + VI + 1
after 1735	239	P 13/3	FC	1
after 1735?	240	P 13/2	RC	I
1742–45	191	P 1145	FC/RC	IV + IV
1742–45	200	PP*	CS	1
c. 1742	245R	((P 28)) WB	FC	II + $5 \times$ IV + I
1742–45	34	(AMB 39)	FC	IV (or $4 \times$ I?)
1740–49	118^2	PP*	FC	I
after 1746	195R	((P 65))	FC + CS	$3 \times$ III + II
1746–49	232^{II-IV}	P 180 WB	FC + RC + CS	IV + $2 \times$ IV + II IV III + II

[14] See the discussion in NBA I/36, KB, pp. 166–168.

[15] *Ibid.*, p. 166, which states that BWV 118^1 uses the same paper as Cantata 206. Bach's use of the paper has been limited to the years 1736–37.

[16] The alternative dates of 1737–38 in this entry and the one that follows are based on the hypothesis in Schering 1936^1, p. 30, that Bach wrote the short Masses for F. A. von Sporck, who died in 1738.

This tabulation can be augmented with three autograph scores which have come to light in recent years. The manuscripts, which all date from the last decade of Bach's life, preserve arrangements of or insertions into works by other composers. The first score of this type to re-emerge contains a parody arrangement by Bach of Pergolesi's *Stabat mater*. (The autograph, in the possession of the Deutsche Staatsbibliothek—Mus. ms. 30 199—is discussed in Platen 1961. Alfred Dürr later discovered the original—non-autograph—parts for the arrangement. See Dürr 1968.) The parody text is a rhymed paraphrase of Psalm 51, beginning with the words "Tilge, Höchster, meine Sünden." The autograph is a short score in which Bach notated in full only the vocal parts and the (unfigured) continuo along with longer obbligato instrumental passages.

In 1962 Georg von Dadelsen published a study of a manuscript score (Mus. ms. 1160 WB) from Bach's possession and penned by one of his copyists containing six Mass settings by Giovanni Battista Bassani. Von Dadelsen calls particular attention to a sixteen-measure intonation, in Bach's handwriting, of the words *Credo in unum Deum* inserted on a separate leaf before the opening words *Patrem omnipotentem* of the fifth Mass. Bach's script has the character of a "calligraphic" composing score, and the intonation accordingly represents a previously unknown composition by J. S. Bach. (See Dadelsen 1962 and the transcription of the piece in Wolff 1968, pp. 202–203.)

Christoph Wolff, finally, in his investigation of Bach's personal collection of music by other composers written in the quasi-Palestrinian *stile antico* discovered an autograph page containing Bach's arrangement of the *Suscepit Israel* section from a *Magnificat* setting by Antonio Caldara. (The arrangement is now bound with the remainder of the work in the Deutsche Staatsbibliothek: Mus. ms. 2755.) In the arrangement Bach added two obbligato treble instruments to Caldara's scoring for four-voice chorus and continuo. (The movement is transcribed in Wolff 1968, pp. 204–209. A facsimile appears on p. 223 and a thorough discussion on pp. 21–23 of the same study.)

These three works could appear in a modification of the table above as follows:

Date	Work	Call No.	Type	Structure
	(not in BWV)			
c. 1740 (Wolff) (Dadelsen: 1736–40)	*Credo* Intonation in F major (for Bassani: Mass No. 5 in F)	Mus. ms. 1160 WB (f. 84v)	CS	1
c. 1740 (Wolff)	Caldara-Bach: *Suscepit Israel*	Mus. ms. 2755	CS/FC	1
c. 1741–46 (Platen, Dürr)	Pergolesi-Bach: *Tilge, Höchster, meine Sünden*	Mus. ms. 30 199	RC	

IF ONE APPLIES the criteria of the calligraphic fair copy rigorously, then it appears that hardly one of the extant manuscripts of the vocal works is both entirely autograph and a thoroughly flawless fair copy.[17] The only unambiguous exception to this observation is provided by the score for the one-movement Sanctus in D minor, BWV 239 (P 13/3), and this work is perhaps spurious.[18] The reorchestrated version of the one-movement motet, *O Jesus Christ mein's Lebens Licht*, BWV 118² (PP), is essentially a fair copy, but even here there are one or two corrections that may be compositional in nature.[19] It would seem that Bach did not have the patience or inclination—or ability—merely to copy any vocal work on a larger scale (the scores of which were for his own personal use only) in a purely mechanical manner without introducing—at least occasionally—improvements of detail. For copying meant literally writing music, which meant in turn for such a musical talent as Bach a constant stimulus to the critical imagination and fantasy. If Bach was absolutely certain that there was nothing more to be improved in a particular score, he delegated the copying task—at least in part—to a copyist.[20] It has already been mentioned that major portions of two Weimar fair copies, Cantatas 61 and 185, are in a copyist's hand. The first movement of BWV 61 (P 45/6) is primarily non-autograph,[21] while in BWV 185 (P 59) only Movement 5, mm. 26ff. and Movement 6 are in Bach's hand.[22]

Nevertheless, in the autograph scores of fifteen works one or several movements containing absolutely no formative corrections, or virtually none, appear in the company of revision copies or composing scores and can reasonably be considered fair copies. The following tabulation provides a brief description of these movements.

FAIR COPIES

BWV 91/5 and 6 (P 869). The movements are written on the fourth sheet (*Bogen*) of the score. This sheet, with a different watermark from the rest of the score ("two-headed eagle plus HR" instead of a half-moon), contains a late, nearly flawless revision of Movement 5 and a fair copy of Movement 6. (See NBA

---

[17] See in this connection Wackernagel 1955 for a list of the corrections found in the fair copy of the Brandenburg Concertos.

[18] See Dürr 1957, p. 116, and the literature mentioned in BWV.

[19] In m. 107, viola: [musical notation]

m. 18: [musical notation] unchanged. Measure 24, Violin 2: [musical notation] changed to [musical notation]; the alto has [musical notation] unchanged. In BWV 118¹ Trombone 1 and alto have [musical notation] unchanged. The manner of reproducing autograph corrections is explained in the Introduction to Volume II.

[20] The only exception to this rule—in principle—is the calligraphic autograph for the *St. Mat-*

thew Passion (P 25), but this score, too, is by no means a flawless autograph. The "O Mensch bewein" chorus, for example, is clearly a revision copy (see Mendel 1964). On the other hand, the rule is well illustrated by the score of the *St. John Passion* (P 28), which after the first twenty folios is in the handwriting of a copyist.

[21] See NBA I/1, KB, p. 10, for an exact description of Bach's role in the copying of this movement. There are, besides, a number of compositional corrections scattered throughout the autograph portions of Mvt. 1 as well as in Mvts. 4 through 6.

[22] See Dadelsen 1958, p. 77.

I/2, KB, pp. 125–126.) The cantata was originally composed for Christmas Day, 1724; the revision presumably dates from the mid 1730's.[23]

BWV 35/1 (P 86). The score of BWV 35/1 has almost no corrections except for the rectification of occasional transposition lapses in the organ part (notated in C minor) and a few changes in the chord-tone disposition in the inner string parts. The movement is based on the first movement of the Clavier Concerto in D minor, BWV 1059, only nine measures of which have been preserved.

BWV 35/5. Apparently all the visible corrections are concerned with copying errors. The movement may be based on the lost final movement of BWV 1059.

BWV 49/1 (P 111). The movement is based on the third movement of the Clavier Concerto in E major (BWV 1053). There are some transposition corrections in the *Chorton* organ part.

BWV 55/4 (P 105). In addition to the absence of corrections, the unusually careful alignment of text and music[24] suggests this is a fair copy.

BWV 52/1 (P 85). The sinfonia is based on Movement 1 of the first Brandenburg Concerto (BWV 1046). For the most part, the score contains no corrections, except for the clarification of ambiguous symbols. The one or two observable formative changes seem insufficient to classify the score as a revision copy.

BWV 58/2, 4, and 5 (P 866). Watermark evidence reveals that at some time between 1732 and 1735 Bach replaced the original second sheet of the manuscript with a new one containing a new setting of the third movement.[25] The procedure is reminiscent of Bach's revision of BWV 91/5 described above. Unlike the latter, though, the new movement here appears as a composing score. The remaining music notated on the sheet (Mvt. 2, mm. 15b to end, Mvt. 4, complete, and Mvt. 5, mm. 1–45), however, was simply recopied.

BWV 36/1, 3, and 7 (P 45/2). These movements are based on the corresponding movements (Nos. 1, 3, 9) of BWV 36c.

BWV 243 (P 39). The D major version of the *Magnificat* is based on an earlier version in E-flat major, BWV 243a. The small number of formative corrections in some movements of the work mostly involve improvements in voice leading or are concentrated in the lines of the newly composed flute parts in Movements 1, 4, 7, and 12. The presence of these corrections makes it impossible to consider the entire manuscript a fair copy, although it maintains a high degree of calligraphy throughout. Movements 10 and 12 are essentially fair copies; Movements 2 and 5 are flawless.

BWV 147/8 (P 102). While this movement is a fair copy, the remainder of the score must be regarded as a revision copy.

[23] See Dürr 1957, pp. 76–77.

[24] The composing scores of recitatives almost invariably contain indications that the text was written down before the music. See Chapter V below.

[25] See NBA I/4, KB, pp. 133, 135, 146, 148.

BWV 97/3 (NYPL). See the comments on BWV 55/4, above. In this instance it seems rather clear that the music was written down before the text: words and syllables are often crowded in order to obtain a proper alignment of text and music.

BWV 134 (P 44/3). The autograph, like that of BWV 243, is primarily a fair or revision copy. While P 44/3 was prepared in 1735, the cantata presumably was composed in 1724.[26] No movement is a flawless copy. Movements 2, 4, and 6 can be considered essentially fair copies; Movements 1, 3, and 5, containing a number of significant corrections, should be classified as revision copies.

BWV 11/1 (P 44/5). This parody score[27] could also be considered a revision copy, but with the exception of perhaps a half-dozen compositional corrections of chord-tone disposition, almost all of the very few corrections are explainable as slips of the pen, clarification of blots, or copying errors. The almost total absence of any trace of the parody underlaying process reveals how effortlessly Bach on occasion could prepare a parody work.[28] The only observable underlaying correction was the following in mm. 153–154, bass:

lo - bet   bet

and that was surely due to inattention, for these measures are a repetition of mm. 44–45, which have only the final reading.

BWV 11/10. This is surely a parody movement, but penned almost flawlessly.

BWV 34 (P AMB 39). The score, based on BWV 34a, is clearly a fair copy throughout. Movements 2 and 4 are flawless; the voices in Movements 1, 3, and 5 show no signs of parody revision. Movement 2, although musically not identical with Movement 2 of BWV 34a, is nonetheless a perfect fair copy. The voices and other revisions in these movements were presumably reworked in the lost (or discarded) score of BWV 34a and then simply copied into P AMB 39 together with the instrumental parts. There are few corrections in general, and almost all of them can be explained as the results of inattention. Like BWV 61 and 185, this score is not entirely autograph. Repeated sections and doubling instrumental parts in the last movement were not written out

---

[26] See Dürr 1957, pp. 68–69, 110.

[27] See Dürr 1962[1] for confirmation of Pirro's suggestion that the source for this movement was BWV Anhang 18, *Froher Tag, verlangte Stunden,* and refutation of Smend's proposal that the source was

Picander's text *Kommt ihr angenehmen Blicke,* from the cantata *Auf! zum Scherzen, auf! zur Lust.*

[28] Or it indicates that the new text underlay was worked out before P 44/5 was written. See the comments below to BWV 34.

but indicated with repeat signs or blank measures. The latter were filled in by Friedemann Bach.[29]

BWV 195/1, 3, and 5 (P 65). These movements are all written in a copyist's hand except for the first eleven measures (through m. 12 in the Violin 1 part) of Movement 3. The remaining movements of the work are autograph and presumably composing scores.

BWV 232[II, IV], *Credo, Agnus Dei, Benedictus, Dona nobis pacem* (P 180). The movements are almost flawless and written with an attempt at calligraphy in the hand of the aged Bach.

Revision copies constitute an intermediate category by definition, and it is consequently more difficult to determine when their limits simply disappear into the peripheries of the two other categories. It is hard not to treat this group as a convenient catch-all for classifying those manuscripts that are neither clearly fair copies nor composing scores. The characteristics of revision copies described above seem to be prominent enough in the following scores to permit a positive attribution.

BWV 131 (PP): throughout

BWV 71 (P 45/1): throughout

BWV 12/4–6 (P 44/7)

BWV 152/1, 2, 4, 6 (P 45/3)

BWV 163/1, 2 (P 137)

BWV 132/1 (P 60). This may be a calligraphic composing score. Movement 5 is quite clearly a calligraphic revision copy.

BWV 147 (P 102): throughout. Movement 8 seems to be a fair copy.

BWV 23/1 (P 69)

BWV 22 (P 119): throughout

BWV 194/1–3 (P 43/3)

BWV 42/1 (P 55). This sinfonia may be based on a lost instrumental work.

BWV 175/4, 6 (P 75). Movement 4 is a parody of BWV 173a/7; Movement 6 may be based on a lost work.[30]

BWV 110/1 (P 153). This movement, which is based on the first movement of the fourth Orchestral Suite in D major (BWV 1069), is written in a calligraphic hand. There are, however, a rather large number of revisionary corrections. On the other hand, the fifth movement of the cantata, while also based on an earlier composition (the *Virga Jesse floruit* movement, "Movement D," from the E♭ version of the *Magnificat*), was obviously written down hastily and is indeed more heavily corrected than the fourth movement, for which P 153 presumably was the composing score.

[29] See NBA I/13, KB, pp. 113, 115–116.   [30] See NBA I/14, KB, p. 211.

BWV 28/2 (P 92). The autograph score here was presumably copied from a set of parts, since there are separate staves for the doubling instruments—a rarity in Bach autograph scores for movements written in motet style.[31]

BWV 55/3 (P 105)

BWV 171/1, 4 (PP). The first movement is probably based on an instrumental composition. Movement 4 is a parody of BWV 205/9.[32]

BWV 226/1, 3 (P 36/1)

BWV 51/1 (P 104). Movements 2–5 are calligraphic but presumably composing scores.

BWV 112/1 (Morgan). The calligraphic script and the remarkable presence of autograph continuo figures on the first page of the score suggest that Bach may have intended this score to be a fair copy. The occasional presence of voice leading corrections, however, and a change in the heading of the movement (see Appendix I) justify an assignment as revision copy.[33]

BWV 36/5 (P 45/2)

BWV 243 (P 39). See the comments above, p. 16.

BWV 232^I (P 180). The opening four measures of *Kyrie I* are probably in composing score.

BWV 213/11 (P 125). The duet is presumably a parody, since the ritornello is a fair copy and most corrections in the movement occur in the voice parts.[34]

BWV 215/3 (P 139). The movement may be a revision copy, very likely a parody of an earlier composition. The opening ritornello is almost flawless, and the occasional revisions are mostly restricted to the inner parts and to details of declamation and beaming in the tenor part.

[31] It is not at all clear why Bach wrote out the doubling lines. The readings in the instrumental staves—which, incidentally, have no specific designations—are practically identical with the vocal lines, except for the general absence of slurs over neumata sung to one syllable and the occasional appearance of a half-note where the vocal line has repeated quarter-notes to carry the syllables of the text. Perhaps the original instrumental parts from which P 92 was prepared were written for different instruments—in different clefs—from those used in BWV 28/2 and Bach wished simply to facilitate the task of the copyist by preparing the clef transpositions himself. According to BG 5¹ the present instrumentation is as follows:

Soprano: Cornetto, Violin 1, Oboe 1 col Soprano
Alto: Trombone 1, Violino 2, Oboe 2 coll'-Alto
Tenore: Trombone 2, Viola, Taille col Tenore
Basso: Trombone 3 col Basso.

There is no separate staff for a doubling bass instrument in P 92 except for the continuo staff.

[32] The evidence suggesting an instrumental model for Mvt. 1 is presented in NBA I/4, KB, pp. 105–106. Movement 4 illustrates the perils of attempting to reconstruct lost originals from preserved parody movements. Measure 24 of BWV 171/4 is not found in the secular version of the movement, and the appearance of the parody score leaves no clue that this measure is an insertion into the fabric of BWV 205/9. This fact can be ascertained only by comparing the readings of both movements. Hence it would be impossible to guess from examination of the parody movement alone that in the original source for this movement m. 25 (of the parody) follows upon m. 23.

[33] See the facsimile of f. 1r reproduced as Plate VI in Morgan 1970.

[34] See also the literature concerning Sketch No. 142 summarized in NBA I/36, KB, pp. 64–65.

BWV 248 (P 32): All parody movements.[35]

BWV 66/1–3, 5 (P 73)

BWV 100/1 (P 159). The movement is almost identical to BWV 99/1, with occasional changes of detail and text underlay.

BWV 249[2] (P 34): throughout. The score may be a fair copy in Movements 4, 6, 7, 10.[36]

BWV 30/1, 3, 5, 8, 10 (P 44/1)

BWV 197/6 (P 91)

BWV 212/14 (P 167). The movement is presumably a parody.[37]

BWV 191 (P 1145): throughout

Pergolesi-Bach (Mus. ms. 30 199): See the comments above, p. 14.

BWV 232[II-IV] (P 180). All movements except the *Confiteor, Et incarnatus* (composing score), and the fair copy movements mentioned above.

The assertion at the beginning of this chapter that Bach could compose in a calligraphic hand when his invention flowed smoothly and when he so desired, is substantiated by the following movements. The handsome penmanship does not quite manage to conceal the formative nature of many autograph corrections at crucial places in the works.

CALLIGRAPHIC COMPOSING SCORES

BWV 182/2, 6, 8 (P 103)[38]

BWV 152/5 (P 45/3)

BWV 163/6 (P 137). Only the continuo part is notated for this "Choral. in simplice stylo."

BWV 194/6 (P 43/3)

BWV 215/5 (P 139). The ritornello is calligraphic and flawless, but several crucial changes, particularly a concentration of corrections at the close of the B section and the presence of a sketch (No. 146), leave little doubt that the movement is a composing score.

BWV 11/4 (P 44/5). Important changes suggest that this may be a composing score despite the calligraphic script and the lack of corrections in both the opening ritornello and the first vocal passage (mm. 1–15). The movement well

---

[35] See the description in NBA II/6, KB, pp. 167–171.

[36] P 34 is considered non-calligraphic in Dadelsen 1958, p. 71.

[37] See Marshall 1968, p. 574.

[38] See Mendel 1960[1]. The entire score was considered by Spitta to be a fair copy. By analyzing the corrections in the opening chorus, Mendel was able to prove that the movement was a composing score.

illustrates the difficulties of distinguishing revision copies from composing scores.

Credo Intonation in F (Mus. ms 1160): See the comments above, p. 14.
BWV 206/1 (P 42/1)

If the handwriting of a manuscript is not calligraphic, it is particularly difficult—if not impossible—to distinguish a fluent, lightly corrected composing score from a revision copy, since in many composing scores corrections are mainly limited to small details of a grammatical nature such as chord-tone disposition and voice leading, while the more individual details of the work are set down with a sure hand. Thus the essential distinction between revision copy and composing score falls away. Consequently, non-calligraphic scores will be considered composing scores unless they can be shown to be based on earlier sources. Only five movements fulfill this last condition.

NON-CALLIGRAPHIC REVISION COPIES
(known to be, or presumably, based on earlier sources)

BWV 199/8 (P 1162). This is an arrangement of the concluding aria of the cantata omitting the second violin and introducing an obbligato cello.[39]

BWV 194/8 (P 43/3). The cantata is probably a parody of a Cöthen cantata.[40] Movement 8 is non-calligraphic but contains corrections typical of a parody score: changes of text underlaying and beaming (particularly in the tenor) and corrections of the rhythm in the voice parts.

BWV 175/7 (P 75). The movement is based on BWV 59/3. The numerous corrections in the Flute 3 part can be attributed to carelessness. While copying from the alto clef of the viola part in BWV 59/3 to the French violin clef of the Flute 3 part in BWV 175/7, Bach often failed at first to transpose the pitches and entered them one tone too high.

BWV 110/5. See the comments for BWV 110/1, above.

BWV 171/6 (PP). This is a direct transposition of BWV 41/6. The transposition from C to D major resulted in a few corrections. There are some changes of beaming as well.

The following nine scores contain movements with few or no corrections of a formative nature but are written in a non-calligraphic hand. Since no earlier sources for these movements are known to exist, they will be considered composing scores.

BWV 132/2, 3 (P 60). There are no corrections at all in Movement 2. It is

---

[39] See the NBG edition, p. iv.　　[40] See Dürr 1957, p. 62.

conceivable that the third movement, like Movement 1 of the cantata, is a revision copy and that Bach simply failed to maintain the fine penmanship of the first movement throughout the following movements of the work. On the other hand, one frequently observes that the quality of the penmanship in composing scores degenerates in direct relation to the haste, fluency, and certainty with which Bach was able to notate later portions of a movement— those largely based on repeated material. These sections provide a striking visual contrast to the deliberate (if often heavily corrected) script of the opening measures of the piece.

BWV 75/4–6 (P 66). These movements contain very few or no corrections. They should perhaps be considered revision copies in the sense in which this term was used in the discussion of the early cantata manuscripts.

BWV 6/3, 6 (P 44/2). There are perhaps about a half-dozen minor corrections in Movement 3, but they are essentially "formative" and thus suggest that this is a composing score. There are no corrections at all in Movement 6.

BWV 205/5 (P 173). There are no corrections in the ritornello. Most of the corrections later in the movement are concentrated in the tenor part. The aria, therefore, may be a parody.

BWV 35/2 (P 86). This aria may be based on the slow movement of the lost Concerto in D minor, BWV 1059. The present movement is clearly non-calligraphic (the organ figuration, for example, often extends over the bar-lines), and there are fairly numerous redistributions of chord tones in the inner string parts as well as frequent reworkings of the alto and continuo lines. But the opening theme is quite clearly notated and approaches a calligraphic script. The movement may have been recast in a manner similar to the transformation of BWV 1053/2 into the aria "Stirb in mir, Welt," BWV 169/5.

BWV 29/3, 5, 7 (P 166). The existence of a draft for Movement 3 (see Sketch No. 19 and p. 121 below) increases the likelihood that this movement at least is a composing score. Since Movement 7 reworks some of the material of Movement 3, it should perhaps be considered a non-calligraphic revision copy, the earlier source being an earlier movement of the same work. Movement 5 has almost no corrections, but since no earlier source for the movement is known, it belongs by definition in the present category.

BWV 117/3 (PP). The ritornello and vocal entry are almost totally uncorrected. Thereafter there are only scattered corrections, mostly of minor details. The script is clearly non-calligraphic.

BWV 97/8 (NYPL). The comment for BWV 117/3 applies here as well.

BWV 30/6, 11 (P 44/1). There are no corrections visible in Movement 6. Movement 11 is evidently a "clean" composing score. There is some confusion in the placement of the barlines—a frequent trait of the composing scores of recitatives[41]—but the musical text itself contains no corrections.

It has already been mentioned that the opening sinfonia of Cantata 174 is based on the first movement of the third Brandenburg Concerto; the string orchestra of the original has been supplemented with wind parts. A copyist was engaged to enter the string parts into the new score, and Bach limited his role to writing down little more than the newly composed horn and oboe parts.[42] The product of this collaboration was a manuscript that was partly fair copy and partly composing score. Such a coexistence of two autograph or compositional types in a single manuscript is not rare. We have encountered it as well in Bach's arrangement of Caldara's *Suscepit Israel* where Bach himself entered the preexistent lines of Caldara's setting as a fair copy and thereupon composed two new obbligato instrumental lines.

Two compositional procedures are revealed in these manuscripts. Either certain newly composed instrumental or vocal lines, as in BWV 174 (or the Caldara arrangement), were added to a preexistent, self-sufficient whole, or certain *sections* of a movement were newly composed and combined with older sections.

Both of these procedures operate in the score of the chorus "Weinen, Klagen, Sorgen, Zagen," BWV 12/2 (P 44/7). In the A section, the vocal parts are evidently fair or revision copy, but the accompanying string parts appear to be newly composed. In the B section, on the other hand, the vocal parts are heavily corrected and the manuscript here should probably be regarded as a composing score.[43]

The first of the procedures mentioned—the addition of new instrumental parts or voices to a preexistent composition—can be observed in the manuscripts of:

BWV 12	BWV 23	BWV 174	BWV 97
BWV 199	BWV 22	BWV 120a	BWV 100
BWV 132	BWV 169	BWV 29	BWV 197
BWV 155	BWV 207	BWV 243	BWV 191

as well as in the Caldara arrangement.

Newly composed accompanying instrumental parts were apparently added to fair-copy vocal and continuo parts in several early recitatives. The appearance of the autographs in BWV 199/1 (Copenhagen), BWV 132/4 (P 60), BWV 155/1 (P 129), BWV 23/2 (P 69), and BWV 22/3 (P 119) suggests that these movements were worked out at first as secco recitatives and were thereupon copied into the final manuscripts where the accompanying instruments were composed. In any case, the vocal and continuo parts in the surviving manuscripts are

[41] See Chapter V below.
[42] See NBA I/14, KB, pp. 69–71, 95–96.

[43] There are no string parts in the B section although a string accompaniment may have been planned.

considerably cleaner than, and provide a sharp visible contrast to, the sketchy, corrected accompanying parts.

The autograph of Cantata 97/5 (NYPL) presents the same appearance, and it is perhaps significant that this cantata may be a later version—at least in some movements—of a Weimar composition.[44]

The autograph score of the fragmentary "Concerto" in D major, BWV 1045 (P 614),[45] is reminiscent of the manuscript of BWV 174/1: The strings and solo violin parts are fair copies while the vast majority of corrections are concentrated in the trumpet, oboe, and timpani parts. The analogy with the score of BWV 174/1 suggests that this movement, too, had existed as a string concerto.

Bach also added the sonority of filler wind parts to an original orchestration for strings alone when he arranged the first movement of the E major Clavier Concerto, BWV 1053 (or its source),[46] as the opening sinfonia of Cantata 169, *Gott soll allein mein Herze haben* (P 93). The oboe parts of BWV 169/1, like the wind parts of BWV 174/1 and BWV 1045, contain a concentration of corrections and are written in a non-calligraphic hand that contrasts with the remaining parts of the score.

The fifth movement of the same cantata, the aria "Stirb in mir, Welt," is based on the second movement of the E major concerto. Here the alto part was worked into the fabric of the instrumental piece. Bach's procedure was to lead the voice more or less heterophonically with the right hand of the organ part. The appearance of the manuscript confirms that the instrumental parts had previously existed while the voice part had been newly composed. The same technique of "inserting" new lines in preexistent compositions can be observed in the opening chorus of BWV 207 (P 174), "Vereinigte Zwietracht," which is based on the third movement of the Brandenburg Concerto No. 1. In addition to the chorus, the third trumpet and timpani parts are newly composed. Again the genesis of the movement is reflected by the appearance of the autograph.

The soprano aria "Vergnügen und Lust" from Cantata 197, *Gott ist unsre Zuversicht* (P 91), a parody of the bass aria "Ich lasse dich nicht," BWV 197a/6, contains two filler oboe parts that were added to the original orchestration. The parts retained from BWV 197a/6 appear as a non-calligraphic revision copy. A number of corrections in the soprano part were called forth by the new text.

In BWV 100/1 (P 159), "Was Gott tut, das ist wohlgetan," horns and timpani

---

[44] See BG 22, p. xxxiv. It has also been mentioned above that Mvt. 8 of the cantata has very few formative corrections and thus may be a parody movement.

[45] The heading of the manuscript reads *JJ Concerto—à 4 Voci. 3 Trombe, Tamburi, 2 Hautb: Violino*

Conc: 2 Violini, Viola | e Cont. The inclusion of four voices reveals that P 614 contains the opening movement of a planned vocal work.

[46] The actual genealogy of sources will no doubt be investigated in the appropriate critical report of the NBA edition.

were added to the orchestration of BWV 99/1. The new scoring led to one or two changes in the continuo part, but not as many as appear in BWV 174.[47] The remaining parts of the score are written in a calligraphic hand. Horn and timpani parts reappear in the sixth movement, a rearrangement of BWV 75/7. As in Movement 1, these parts are newly conceived, while the rest of the score is basically a fair copy. Along with the addition of horns and timpani, the first measure as well as mm. 32–35 of the movement were (rather cleanly) newly composed in P 159. This score then, like that of BWV 12/2, reflects two additive compositional procedures: the extension of a preexistent source both horizontally and vertically in the new version.

The relationship between BWV 191/3, *Sicut erat in principio,* and the *Cum Sancto Spiritu* chorus of the *B minor Mass,* BWV 232, is similar to that between BWV 100/6 and BWV 75/7. In BWV 191/3, too, the source movement has been expanded by the insertion of extra measures and the addition of obbligato parts: the two flute parts, which in the *Cum Sancto Spiritu* movement are mostly led in unison with the oboes, are here newly composed as independent lines.[48] The characteristic contrast between calligraphic copy and non-calligraphic composing score is particularly clear in the fugal section, mm. 41–67 of BWV 191/3, corresponding to mm. 37–64 in the *Mass.* In the BWV 191/3 version of the fugue, orchestral parts have been added to the continuo accompaniment of the *Mass.* The vocal parts in this section of the parody are essentially clean, while the newly composed instrumental parts contain a heavy concentration of reworking and corrections, the only such concentration in the movement.

It is instructive, finally, to compare the extant fragment of the sinfonia, BWV 120a/4 (P 670), with the autograph of the first movement of Cantata 29 (P 166). Both movements are transcriptions for organ and orchestra of the praeludium from the E major partita for unaccompanied violin (BWV 1006). The accompaniment in BWV 120a/4 is for strings only; in BWV 29/1 three trumpets and timpani are added to this. In the score for BWV 120a/4 the organ part, based on the violin solo part, is clearly a fair copy and the string parts are just as clearly newly composed. Bach later used the score of BWV 120a/4 as the source for both the organ and string parts when he prepared the sinfonia, BWV 29/1. Accordingly, in the score of BWV 29/1 the added parts (three trumpets and timpani) are entered in composing score script above the calligraphic organ and string parts.

---

[47] See NBA I/14, KB, p. 110, for a description of the relationship between the newly added wind parts and consequent revisions in the original continuo line of BWV 174/1.

[48] See the summary of the differences between the source and parody movement in NBA I/2, KB, pp. 162–163. It has already been mentioned that the flute parts in Mvts. 1, 4, 7, and 12 of the D major *Magnificat* (P 39) were newly composed.

IN ADDITION to the autograph of BWV 12/2 discussed above, only the following scores contain movements that are fair copy or revision copy in some sections and composing score in others: BWV 199 (Copenhagen), BWV 119 (P 878), BWV 42 (P 55), BWV 213 (P 125), BWV 215 (P 139), BWV 97 (NYPL), and BWV 66 (P 73). (The composing score *Credo* Intonation in F preceding the (non-autograph) fair copy of Bassani's *Patrem omnipotentem* could also be listed here.)

The appearance of the autograph of BWV 199/2, the aria "Stumme Seufzer, stille Klagen" (written, incidentally, within four weeks after the composition of BWV 12), recalls that of the "Weinen, Klagen" chorus: the A section has far fewer corrections than the B section and is written in the elegant and careful script typical of Bach's Weimar period. It is not at all certain, though, whether the opening section of the movement is a "clean" composing score or a revision copy. The B section, cast in the style of a recitative, presents no such uncertainty. It is definitely a composing score.

The opening chorus of BWV 119 (P 878), a movement in the form of a French overture, is calligraphic throughout, but only the framing *Grave* sections are fair copy. The opening eight measures are perfectly clean and there are only occasional corrections of voice leading or of clef errors in the remainder of the *Grave* sections. The 12/8 allegro section, on the other hand, is quite definitely a composing score, containing numerous crucial formative corrections.

The A section of the aria "Wo zwei und drei versammlet sind," BWV 42/3 (P 55), may be based on the slow movement of a concerto—presumably the same work that served as the source for the first movement. The instrumental lines are written in a calligraphic hand and contain no significant corrections; the alto line, also neatly written, contains a number of changes affecting text underlay and declamation.

These revisions suggest that the alto part is essentially the texted version of the solo part of the concerto, and not—like the alto line in BWV 169/5—a newly invented part that had been worked into the preexistent instrumental fabric. The florid style of the voice part suggests further that the solo instrument in the lost concerto was either a violin or oboe. The middle 12/8 section of the aria is clearly a composing score throughout.

The A section of the chorus "Lust der Völker, Lust der Deinen," BWV 213/13 (P 125), is based on the sixth movement of BWV 184 (or its source) with a pair of horns added to the scoring of the model. The B section of the movement, however, is new and written in composing score. In the autograph score of the chorus "Preise dein Glücke," BWV 215/1 (P 139), the A section again is written as a calligraphic revision copy; the B section is non-calligraphic, more heavily corrected, and presumably newly composed.[49]

The score of the aria "Ich traue seiner Gnaden," BWV 97/4 (NYPL), has fair copy character throughout the A section and the first part of the middle section as well. Only mm. 36–49, the second vocal exposition of the B section, are clearly newly composed, although still written in a firm hand and only lightly corrected. Here it may well have been a matter of a revision of the original (Weimar?) setting rather than the addition or substitution of completely new material.

In the last of the movements that exhibit different autograph types in the different sections, the relationship observed until now is reversed. The fourth movement of Cantata 66 (P 73), *Bei Jesu Leben freudig sein,* is nominally a recitative for alto and tenor, but mm. 22–53 of the 68-measure composition consist of a duet in free canonic style for the two voices. While the framing recitative sections are clearly notated in composing score script, the duet section is essentially fair or revision copy. The surviving score, P 73, dating from 1735, preserves, in fact, a later version of the cantata. The composition was presumably first prepared in Leipzig for Easter Monday, April 10, 1724, from a Cöthen secular source, the birthday cantata *Der Himmel dacht' auf Anhalts Ruhm und Glück.*[50] It is conceivable that in the 1724 version of the fourth movement, Bach parodied the original Cöthen recitative and composed the duet section. The visual appearance of the movement in P 73 suggests that Bach then decided to compose new recitative sections for the 1735 performance, but to retain the middle section that had been composed in 1724.

The coexistence of different handwriting types in the autograph score of Cantata 112 (Morgan), *Der Herr ist mein getreuer Hirt,* also invites chronological speculation. The date for the earliest known performance of the cantata—8 April 1731—has hitherto been established only on the basis of the surviving printed libretto of that year. An examination of the score reveals that the entire manuscript was indeed penned in all probability during the first week of April 1731.[51] But it is evident that the first movement, entered as a fair/revision copy into the extant autograph, must have been composed earlier than the remainder of

---

[49] Werner Neumann has recently demonstrated that the A section of BWV 215/1 is probably based on the lost cantata *Es lebe der König,* BWV Anhang 11, composed for the name day celebration in honor of August II on August 3, 1732. See NBA I/37, KB, pp. 70–72.

[50] See Dürr 1957, p. 68, and NBA I/10, KB, pp. 15, 21–22.

[51] All three sheets of the score contain the same watermark found in the letter of recommendation, dated 4 April 1731, that Bach wrote for Johann Adolph Scheibe. The watermark: a) *"Posthorn an Band, auf Steg,"* b) *"CV oder GV,"* is reproduced as No. 27 in Weiß 1962. In his chronology of the Leipzig vocal works, Alfred Dürr had speculated—without having been able to examine the

the work. The date, April, 1731, represents the time of composition for Movements 2 through 5 only, since only these movements appear in the autograph in Bach's composing hand. Now, Cantata 112 belongs to the second *Jahrgang* of cantatas—the "Chorale-Cantata" *Jahrgang*—which for the most part was composed during 1724–25. It is conceivable that BWV 112/1 was composed at that time—for *Misericordias Domini* Sunday, April 15, 1725—and was to be the opening movement of a typical chorale cantata of that period; that is, it was to be followed by aria and recitative settings of poetic paraphrases of the internal strophes of the chorale. This form, which (with the exception of BWV 107)[52] had been used consistently for the cantatas of the Trinity season of 1724 and for the Christmas, Epiphany, and pre-Lenten seasons of 1725, was discontinued after Easter, 1725, perhaps owing to the indisposition of the librettist (or librettists)[53] responsible for the poetic paraphrases. Bach may, however, have reckoned with a resumption in the delivery of chorale cantata texts by *Misericordias Domini* Sunday and therefore set about the composition of BWV 112/1. Upon learning that the paraphrase verses were not forthcoming—either for this work or for the remaining chorale cantatas presumably planned for the post-Easter season— Bach laid aside the completed movement and composed Cantata 85, *Ich bin ein guter Hirt*. This work, like the preceding post-Easter cantatas (April 2, Easter Monday: Cantata 6, *Bleib' bei uns;* April 8, *Quasimodogeniti* Sunday: Cantata 42, *Am Abend aber desselbigen Sabbats*), returns to a text form already employed in several post-Easter cantatas of the 1723–24 *Jahrgang* utilizing New Testament texts for the opening movements with chorale strophes and freely invented verses for the following movements.[54] He further arranged with the Leipzig poetess Mariane von Ziegler to furnish cantata texts for the nine remaining Sundays of the *Jahrgang*—from Jubilate (April 22) through Trinity Sunday (May 27). When Bach ultimately took up the further composition of BWV 112—in 1731—he had in the meantime essentially abandoned the paraphrase chorale cantata in favor of settings of the literal chorale texts. Accordingly, after copying the first movement from his (lost) 1725 manuscript into the surviving autograph he composed the succeeding movements on the texts of the remaining four strophes of the 16th-century chorale.

---

autograph, but using Spitta's description of the watermark—that the 1731 date for BWV 112 may represent a repeat performance, and that the cantata may actually have first been performed (or composed) c. 1729. Dürr characterized his hypothesis as "unlikely but not completely impossible." (See Dürr 1957, pp. 15f., 52, and 102.) A systematic study of the BWV 112 autograph was not possible before its recent acquisition by the Morgan Library.

[52] See Dürr 1967, especially pp. 112–115.

[53] Dürr 1970 raises as a remote possibility that more than one librettist took part in the preparation of these texts and suggests that—for brief periods at least—the principal pastors of the Nicolai- and Thomaskirchen (Salomon Deyling and Christian Weiß, respectively) may have written them in weekly alternation to coincide with the weekly performances of the cantatas which regularly alternated between the two churches from one Sunday to the next. See Dürr 1970, especially pp. 222–223.

[54] See Scheide 1961, pp. 10f.

FRIEDRICH Blume has suggested in his "Outlines of a New Picture of Bach"[55] that there may be "far more of the rearrangements and parodies [among the early Leipzig church cantatas] than has so far been realized." His suggestion, which was put forth earlier at the 1961 Congress of the International Musicological Society in New York,[56] is based on a consideration of Bach's phenomenal productivity during his first three years in Leipzig and on evidence Blume has found of poor declamation and missed opportunities for word-painting in several arias. His arguments were challenged at once at the New York Congress[57] by Alfred Dürr and Arthur Mendel, and later in answer to his "Outlines" in articles by Friedrich Smend and Dürr,[58] who both conceded that there may still be some undetected parody movements among the early Leipzig sacred works, but that they would hardly be present to the degree envisioned by Blume.

Dürr mentioned at the Congress that the appearance of the autograph score usually provides evidence as to whether or not a movement is a parody composition. The principal clues (not explicitly enumerated by Dürr) would be: a rather clean or calligraphic script, a strikingly small number of formative corrections in the score of the ritornello and in the instrumental parts in general, plus perhaps a concentration of corrections dealing with text underlay and beaming in the vocal parts. The discussion of the manuscript types in the preceding paragraphs of this chapter suggests that in the early Leipzig period of concern to Blume only the following calligraphic fair or revision copies are possibly or probably based on unknown earlier sources:

BWV 42/1	Sinfonia	2nd *Jahrgang*	Apr. 8, 1725
BWV 42/3	Aria	2nd *Jahrgang*	Apr. 8, 1725
BWV 175/6	Aria	2nd *Jahrgang*	May 22, 1725
BWV 28/2	Chorus	3rd *Jahrgang*	Dec. 30, 1725
BWV 35/5	Sinfonia	3rd *Jahrgang*	Sept. 8, 1726
BWV 55/3	Aria	3rd *Jahrgang*	Nov. 17, 1726

Our classification of non-calligraphic revision copies included by definition only movements known to be based on earlier sources and is thus irrelevant to the present discussion. Of the nine manuscripts listed as containing composing scores for movements that are lightly corrected or not corrected at all, and thus possibly providing evidence of parody composition, three manuscripts fall into the main Leipzig period of the three *Jahrgänge*:

BWV 75/4–6	Recit.-Aria-Aria	1st *Jahrgang*	May 30, 1723
BWV 6/3	Chorale Aria	2nd *Jahrgang*	Apr. 2, 1725
BWV 6/6	Chorale	2nd *Jahrgang*	Apr. 2, 1725
BWV 35/2	Aria	3rd *Jahrgang*	Sept. 8, 1726

[55] Blume 1963, pp. 219–220.
[56] See Congress 1961, pp. 128–129.
[57] *Ibid.*, p. 129.
[58] Dürr 1962[2], Smend 1962.

At the most, then, on the basis of the appearance of the autograph, a total of twelve movements would seem to stand a reasonable chance of being parody movements or rearrangements of earlier sources. Of course, several of the remaining movements listed in the tabulations of this chapter may be parody compositions, although they are either secular movements or written too late to be relevant to Blume's argument. The movements concerned are:

BWV 205/5	Aria	Aug. 3, 1725
BWV 171/1	Chorus	Jan. 1, 1729?
BWV 51/1	Aria	Sept. 17, 1730
BWV 29/5	Aria	Aug. 27, 1731
BWV 117/3	Aria	1728/31
BWV 117/6	Aria	1728/31
BWV 232[I]	*Missa*	Apr. 21, 1733?
BWV 213/11	Duet	Sept. 5, 1733
BWV 97/8	Aria	1734
BWV 11/4	Aria	May 19, 1735
BWV 212/14	Aria	Aug. 30, 1742
BWV 30/6	Chorale	1738–42

The number of "newly suspected" parody movements, however, is still not large.[59]

---

[59] It should also be noted that of the five movements mentioned by Blume at the 1961 Congress as possible parodies—BWV 144/2 and 5, BWV 25/5, BWV 2/5, BWV 38/3—three (BWV 144/2 and 5, and BWV 2/5) exist in autograph composing scores that are clearly not parodies. There are no extant autograph scores for BWV 25 and 38.

A comprehensive survey of the extent and nature of Bach's parody process is found in Neumann 1965. The valuable tabulations of bibliographical, textual, and analytical information could have been rendered even more helpful, for our purposes, if they had contained a column with material on the nature of the surviving musical sources—whether they are scores or parts, autographs or copies.

CHAPTER II

The General Nature of
Autograph Sketches and Corrections;
Precompositional Activity:
Manuscript Libretti

THIS ATTEMPT to reconstruct Bach's compositional process will draw on two sources of information provided by the autograph scores: (1) preliminary sketches and drafts, and (2) rejected passages and corrections of detail. It is necessary, though, to describe first the nature of this material and to discuss some of the problems it poses.

Sketches and Drafts: Problems of Identification

Most of the surviving sketches are brief marginal notations found in the autograph scores at the bottom of recto pages. They presumably served as memory aids which were written down while the ink on the page was drying, in order to record the immediate continuation of the music. There are as well a number of tentative marginal sketches for the opening themes of later movements in the score and, more rarely, for works to be composed in the near future. Both types of preliminary sketch usually are similar enough to the final versions to be easily recognized, and hence seldom pose problems of identification. Another group of sketches comprises rejected drafts for the beginnings of movements and for major sections of movements. Since these drafts are separated from the final musical text, they can be regarded as sketches and are therefore included in Volume II along with the marginal sketches. These rejected drafts, like the marginal sketches, are hardly difficult to identify when they are found directly before or above the final version. If the draft began a new sheet, however, Bach often turned the sheet around before writing again, or he temporarily laid it aside. In that event a rejected version for a movement can appear in a later portion of the manuscript[1] or even in the manuscript of another work.[2] In the latter case the draft can usually be identified by an autograph title or the presence of a text.

[1] See for example Sketch No. 88, which appears upside down on the last page of the autograph.

[2] See Sketch No. 41.

Such drafts occasionally provide traces of otherwise lost or presumably lost compositions. It is clear, for example, from the title page above Sketch No. 148 (BWV Anhang 2), located on the last page of the autograph score of BWV 226, the motet *Der Geist hilft unsrer Schwachheit auf* (P 36), that Bach at least planned to write a new cantata for the 19th Sunday after Trinity, 1729.[3] Similarly, by identifying the text in an unfinished draft found in the autograph score of Cantata 120a (P 670), Alfred Dürr was able to demonstrate that Bach probably composed the cantata *Ich bin ein Pilgrim auf der Welt.*[4] The Bach manuscripts, however, have already been finely combed many times, and it is not likely that there will be many more discoveries of this type.[5]

Identification of handwriting in the sketch material, like the identification of a musical passage, creates in general a less troublesome problem than would at first appear. Although many sketches are so short and written so hastily that it is impossible to state with complete certainty whether or not they are autograph, the musical nature of these sketches usually enables a reasonably probable attribution. There is hardly reason to assume that anyone other than Bach would have troubled to write preliminary sketches for later movements or for the following measures in an autograph score, and it is almost exclusively in such cases that there is really any uncertainty about the hand. A small number of sketch-like entries, written to clarify illegible passages, are almost always easily recognizable as non-autograph and often can be positively identified as being in the hand of Friedrich Zelter or Philipp Emanuel Bach. This encourages the assumption that other clarifying sketches of this type, when written in an ambiguous script, are likewise non-autograph.[6]

---

[3] For the dating see Dürr 1957, pp. 98–99.

[4] See Dürr 1958, and the facsimile on the following page (reproduced from NBA I/33, KB, facing p. 58).

[5] Other fragments of lost or planned compositions and movements are transcribed as Sketches Nos. 148–152 in Volume II.

[6] A unique combination of problems concerning the identity of both the handwriting and the musical passage is posed by Sketch No. 150, presumably a fugue subject written in pencil on the back of a cello part which is bound with the autograph score of BWV 49 (P 111). While the cello part is in the hand of Anna Magdalena Bach, the sketch may be autograph. (The handwriting of the cello part is identified in Dadelsen 1957. Kast 1958 attributes the pencil sketch to an unknown copyist. The pencil, incidentally, was invented long before Bach's time.) Positive identification of the hand is not possible, however, since the notation is quite faded. But the general features of the text script and the form of the C-clefs recall J. S. Bach's handwriting even though the pencil and ink script of the same person can vary considerably. The text of the sketch, Psalm 121:2, could not be located among the extant Bach cantatas; thus, if the sketch is autograph, we apparently have a trace of another lost or planned composition. Professor Werner Neumann of the Bach-Archiv, Leipzig, writes in a private correspondence that the psalm was part of the service for the Sunday after New Year in the Leipzig liturgy of Bach's time. Since there are only two extant cantatas (BWV 58 and 153) for this feast instead of the usual three, it is particularly tempting to reckon with a lost cantata for this Sunday. It must be pointed out, however, that the Sunday after New Year did not fall in every liturgical year, so that the two cantatas—together with Part 5 of the *Christmas Oratorio*—may have been adequate for Bach's needs.

I. Fragment of the lost cantata *Ich bin ein Pilgrim auf der Welt*, P 670, f. 6v
(copyist's hand). By courtesy of the Musikabteilung, Staatsbibliothek
(Preußischer Kulturbesitz), Berlin

Corrections: Problems of Identification,
Evaluation, and Classification

The problem of handwriting identification can often be critical when dealing with small corrections: the change of pitch of a note-head, for example, or the beaming and stemming of a short figure. If there are no "controls" there can be no certainty that the corrections are autograph. "Controls" can take the form of later repetitions of the corrected passage in the autograph score which contain only the final reading of the passage in question, or they can take the form of secondary original sources such as the original parts which were prepared under Bach's supervision and presumably used in performances under his direction, and which again present only the final reading. If the ink color of the correction is clearly a different shade from the original reading, the possibility that the correction is non-autograph is increased, although there can still be no certainty, of course, that the correction does not stem from J. S. Bach.

These considerations suggest that one means of classifying corrections would be according to the hypothetical moment at which they were made. Three categories can be introduced from this chronological point of view: "immediate" corrections, subsequent or "delayed" corrections, and what for lack of a better term I will call "chain reaction" corrections.

In an "immediate" correction the new reading is written directly to the right of, or on the staff directly below the original reading. The correction is, ideally speaking, "immediate," since it is clear from its position that no further music was written before the correction was made. Corrections can also be considered "immediate" if all later repetitions of the corrected passage contain the final reading only. It is not possible, of course (nor necessary, for that matter) to know whether Bach in fact entered the final reading in these corrections literally "immediately," i.e., within seconds after writing down the original passage.

Conversely the designation "subsequent" or "delayed" correction indicates that at least one repetition (or copy) of the corrected passage contains the same corrections as does the first statement. The first passage therefore could not have been corrected before its repetition was also set down (unless, perhaps, Bach had forgotten that he had corrected the passage the first time, absent-mindedly entered the original reading, and only later corrected it while proofreading the manuscript).

In a "chain reaction" correction, changes in one part call forth of necessity corrections in another part either because (a) the parts concerned are motivically or thematically related, e.g., through imitation technique,[7] or (b) because the

---

[7] The necessity of correcting an early passage retroactively once its identical repetition had been corrected makes clear that a "delayed" correction is in essence such a "chain reaction" correction.

original sonority or voice-leading relationships established in the first reading but then disturbed in one part made necessary a reorganization of the tones in other parts as well.

It is also possible to categorize corrections according to their musical nature or significance. In this respect it is again possible to introduce three correction types.

The least significant changes are those which were introduced to correct an apparent lapse of attention or slip of the pen. A part may have been entered on the wrong staff, or Bach may have momentarily thought of the passage in the wrong clef (see above p. 21). A moment of inattention may also have caused Bach at first to copy a literal repetition of earlier material incorrectly. Finally, a correction may have been introduced merely to clarify an ambiguous or illegible reading.[8] This category can create numerous difficulties of interpretation. Often what one takes for a deliberate correction may be no more than a slip of the pen or an ink smudge, while what one considers to be a slip of the pen or, say, a momentary clef-confusion may be in fact a change of pitch that reflects a deliberate change of mind.

Of considerably greater significance are the numerous corrections of a "grammatical" nature. An analysis of such corrections reveals that the original readings were grammatically "incorrect." The composer was obliged to reject the first reading in order to remove parallel fifths or octaves or other instances of poor voice leading. Corrections to remove technical impossibilities such as passages that extended beyond the range of a particular instrument or voice may also be included in this category. Grammatical corrections, like slips of the pen, are found in revision and fair copies as well as in composing scores.

While grammatical corrections can be said to represent the obligation of "artistic necessity," compositional corrections reflect the exercise of "artistic freedom." In this third category one grammatically "correct" version replaces another equally "correct" version. In the following chapters we will be primarily concerned with the material of this category. There are two basic types of compositional corrections. The more profound are surely *formative* corrections in which the contour, character, and structure of the musical ideas have been basically altered for purely aesthetic reasons. Just as interesting, though, are *ornamental* corrections in which elaborating notes of diminution have been added to the original reading, or the shapes originally created have been rhythmically dissolved but not basically changed. Corrections of the diminution type reflect a principal characteristic of Bach's composing scores, just as they reflect an essential element of baroque composition in general. The diminution principle

---

[8] For examples of all these instances—and others—in the autograph of the Brandenburg Con- certos see Wackernagel 1955, especially pp. 133–134.

as a principle of elaboration, extension, and enlargement is operative on many levels of the Bach compositional process. For Bach's tendency when changing his original idea was to expand upon it, and add to it rather than to reduce or contract it.[9] This holds true whether it is a question of (1) adding notes to a melody, i.e., diminution in the strictest sense, (2) adding doubling, hetero-phonic, filler, or obbligato parts to the texture, (3) adding measures to the original context, or (4) adding movements to the original composition.

Precompositional Activity: Extant Manuscript Libretti

It seems safe to assume that the first written gestures in a musical autograph were preceded by what may be called a precompositional analysis of the given material. For a vocal work this material is represented primarily by the text, sometimes also by a chorale cantus firmus.

The text must have been considered from two points of view: its structure and its "affect." The general design of the text clearly dictated the general design of the music; the number of movements and their types—recitative, aria, chorus, chorale, and so on. The prosody of the text influenced the composer's choice of meter as well as more specific decisions regarding the rhythm of themes and the placement of tonic accents, i.e., the choice of pitches.

A statement by Bach's pupil Johann Gotthilf Ziegler[10] that Bach taught him how to play chorales according to the affect of the words testifies to Bach's endorsement of the *Affektenlehre*. The composer's understanding of the affect influenced his choice of mode (perhaps of key as well), tempo, orchestration, texture, style, and the employment of rhetorical "figures."[11] External circumstances—the singers and instrumentalists at Bach's disposal (and their abilities)—also played a significant role in his preliminary considerations.

We cannot know with any precision, of course, how extensively Bach engaged in such precompositional activity: how clear a conception he had in advance of, say, specific themes, harmonic designs,[12] overall structural proportions and

---

[9] See also Dadelsen 1961, pp. 11–12, in this regard.

[10] Quoted in Spitta I, 519; translated in David-Mendel 1966, p. 237.

[11] Bach's historical connection with the *Figuren-lehre* and the use of rhetorical figures in his music have been investigated mainly in Schmitz 1950[1] and 1950[2].

[12] Just as there was a corpus of melody types provided by the *Figurenlehre* from which the baroque composer could draw, there was also a number of stereotyped harmonic ground plans for arias and choruses. (See Siegele 1962, pp. 39ff.) The rationalistic mentality of the period, and even more the facts of musical life in the late baroque—the sheer volume of new music continuously expected from a composer—surely led to the development and exploitation of these and other conventions and compositional techniques. (For a general treatment of this *ars inveniendi* see Schering 1925.) Bach was doubtless familiar with—and made use of—practically all of them. That these conventions for the most part served in Bach's case merely to set in motion his seemingly limitless imagination, and that he was able to impress a profound musical individuality upon them need hardly be emphasized here.

dimensions, and instrumentation to be employed in the several movements of a composition. Later chapters of this study will, however, occasionally speculate about the degree to which, and the manner in which, Bach thought out a movement or a passage in advance.

Some limited light on the earliest stages in the genesis of a vocal work is shed by four surviving manuscript libretti, which apparently served as Bach's working copies for the compositions concerned. The four libretti are all for secular cantatas: BWV 208, 216a, 195, and 215.[13]

The sheet containing Salomo Franck's text of the Weimar cantata, *Was mir behagt,* BWV 208, is bound together with the autograph score (P 42/3) and with a later text copy for the parody, BWV 208a.[14] The text of the Weimar version[15] is essentially in a copyist's hand but contains several autograph entries which assign vocal ranges to the characters in the cantata as follows:

> Diana: *Sopr.*   Endymion: *Ten.*
> Pan: *Basso*   Pales: *2 Sopr*

and mention in marginal notations the formal type of the movements: recitative, aria, etc. The movement headings provided by the copyist consist only of the character singing the movement.

The autograph remarks concerning the form of the movements appear as follows. Bach wrote *Recit* or *R.* in the margin before Movements 1, 3, 5, 6, 8, and 10. The concluding section of Movement 5 (in the final version mm. 14ff.) was headed simply *Diana* by the copyist. The poet, therefore, must have conceived this section as a solo number. Bach crossed out the heading and wrote *à 2 Diana R.* | *u. End.* in the left-hand margin, thereby converting the concluding lines of the movement into a duet. The section was ultimately set as an arioso for the two singers.

Movements 2, 4, 7, 9, 13, and 14 were headed *Aria* by Bach. In Movements 4 and 14 he entered fermatas to mark the end of the A sections of these da-capo arias.[16] The copyist wrote out the whole text of the A section once again after the conclusion of the B section in Movements 2, 9, 11, and 12; but in Movements 14 and 15 he entered only the *incipit* of the opening line followed by an abbreviation symbol ⨍, the equivalent of "etc."

An *incipit* of the opening line was also added after the fourth line of the strophe in Movement 13, *Weil die wollenreichen Heerden.* This *incipit* is crossed out—perhaps

---

[13] The manuscript libretto bound with the autograph of BWV 201 (P 175) was prepared for a performance in 1749. (See Spitta II, 740f. and BG 11², p. vii.) A manuscript libretto for BWV 204, again bound with the autograph (P 107), is in the hand of C.P.E. Bach's daughter Anna Carolina Philippina and was surely prepared long after J. S.

Bach's death. See Schulze 1961, p. 87. Cf. also the *Note* to Sketch No. 78 in Vol. II.

[14] See NBA I/37, KB, pp. 91ff.

[15] Reprinted in NBA I/35, KB, pp. 31–35.

[16] Bach also added the indication (*Da Capo*) after the concluding words of the B section in Mvt. 4.

by Bach. In the ultimate setting, the movement is not, in fact, a da-capo aria but rather a one-part quasi-ostinato aria, in which the entire text is set twice, followed by an epilog based on lines 2 and 4 of the strophe.

According to the copyist's heading (simply the word *Diana*), Movement 11 was clearly conceived as a solo (aria). Bach, however, wrote *Aria à 4* in the margin and set the movement in P 42/3 as a free polyphonic chorus.[17]

In Movements 12 and 15 Bach carried out the poet's intentions as revealed by the headings:

> Movement 12. Heading: *Endymion u. Diana zusammen*
>   Bach's notation: *Duetto Aria*
> Movement 15. Heading: *Tutti*
>   Bach's notation: *Chorus*

There is one curious inconsistency between the attributions of the text sheet and the final setting of the cantata. Movements 13 and 14 are assigned in the text sheet to Pan (i.e., Bass) and Pales (i.e., Soprano 2) respectively, and this attribution is not corrected. In the composing score, however, Movement 13 is set for Pales and Movement 14 for Pan. Here, too, there are no corrections regarding the casting of the two movements. Bach, then, either had decided on the change of roles immediately before he began to compose the two arias, or the present setting of the two movements is the result of an oversight.

The autograph text sheet P 613 contains the libretto of the lost cantata *Erwählte Pleißenstadt*, BWV 216a—a parody of *Vergnügte Pleißenstadt*, BWV 216. (The latter work survives only as a fragment.) Several corrections in the text, including the rejection of an entire line, suggest that Bach was the author of the text for BWV 216a and that P 613 represents the original draft of the libretto.[18] Here again, as he had done with the libretto for BWV 208, Bach indicated what voices would be assigned to the characters of the cantata (Apollo: Tenor, Mercurius: Alto), and in the present instance repeated these vocal indications throughout the text together with the name of the character wherever a change of soloist occurred. The arias carry the heading *Aria* and their texts

---

[17] The word *Aria* in a Bach text source did not necessarily prescribe solo performance. See Dürr 1962[1], p. 122.

[18] The text, complete with all corrections, is transcribed in Spitta II, 891–893. A facsimile of the first page is printed in Neumann 1957, p. 191. Zander 1968 (p. 26) suggests that Bach may only have "edited" the text. Bach's role as an editor of the cantata texts he set to music has long been recognized. His adaptations of nine texts by Christiane Mariane von Ziegler in particular reveal the extent and nature of his methods and have been discussed by a number of commentators from Spitta 1892[2] to Tagliavini 1956 and Zander 1968. Zander also regards the large number of unrhymed lines in many of the cantata texts as evidence of Bach's censorial activity: the composer did not refrain from removing lines he considered (musically or theologically) superfluous, even if the result played havoc with the structure and rhyme scheme of the poem. (See Zander 1968, p. 28, also p. 35.)

are indented; the recitative movements have no heading, but since each line begins flush at the left-hand margin of the page, they are clearly set off from the arias. In the framing duet movements of the work, both entitled *Aria à 2tto,* Bach was careful to indicate what lines of the text were to be sung by what character and what lines were to be sung *à 2.*

The poetic structure of *Erwählte Pleißenstadt* is quite straightforward: Movement 1, an opening duet; Movements 2 and 3, a recitative and aria for Apollo praising the wisdom of the city; Movements 4 and 5, a recitative and aria for Mercurius recalling the joy and glory of Leipzig's commerce; Movement 6, a recitative for both singers; Movement 7, the concluding duet. This scheme discloses that the crossed-out letter *M* (Mercurius) in the margin before the heading of Movement 3 represents no more than a momentary lapse of attention on Bach's part, for he could hardly have intended at any time to follow Apollo's recitative with an aria for Mercurius.

The *DC* indication at the end of the opening duet is the only remark in the libretto bearing on musical form. It is hardly remarkable, though, that there are no other indications referring to form in the libretto, since BWV 216a is a parody composition for which, of course, the music already existed. Perhaps the only major change in BWV 216a was the transposition of the soprano part, "Neiße," of BWV 216 to the tenor, "Apollo," in BWV 216a (the second voice is an alto in both works), and this change is indeed carefully noted in P 613.

The last two extant manuscript libretti which served Bach as text sources reveal no evidence of preliminary precompositional activity. Bound together with the late score of BWV 195, *Dem Gerechten muß das Licht* (P 65), is a manuscript text sheet which bears the same watermark as the earliest surviving parts of the cantata.[19] The text sheet,[20] therefore, was Bach's libretto when he prepared the first version of the work. In this case, however, the libretto contains no autograph remarks. The text is laid out as a two-part, eight-movement composition, whereas the extant version is a one-part work in which the three movements of the second part—*Aria., Rec.:, Chor.*—are replaced by a simple chorale with two obbligato horns and timpani. This chorale is written in composing score on f. 2v of the text sheet.[21] The movements of Part I in the text sheet are headed *Chor., Rec.:, Aria., Rec.:, Chor.* The initials *V. A.* are written at the conclusion of Movements 3 and 5 as well as Movement 6 of Part II, and presumably stand for *Vom Anfang* (da capo). The text sheet offers no further information regarding the musical character of the cantata.

[19] See NBA I/33, KB, p. 117.

[20] The handwriting is identified in Schulze 1963, p. 66, as that of Johann Christoph Friedrich Bach.

[21] The second part of the cantata was indeed composed and performed in the original version of the composition. The arias and chorus were probably parodies of movements from Cantata 30a. See NBA I/33, KB, pp. 109–110, 117–118.

For Cantata 215, *Preise dein Glücke,* a copy of the text in the hand of the poet, Johann Christoph Clauder,[22] is bound together with the autograph score (P 139). While Bach himself made no indications in the text sheet, the movements are headed *Aria* or *Recit.*—even the opening and closing choruses of the work are entitled *Aria*[23]—and da-capo indications are provided wherever appropriate.

Bach did not assign vocal types to the movements in the libretti of BWV 195 and 215 as he had done in the libretti of BWV 208 and 216a. In the latter compositions the fact that the voices represented particular characters may have encouraged Bach to determine the voice qualities very early in the conception of these works—in the precompositional stage represented by the proofreading of the libretto. Conversely, the abstract nature of the vocal parts in Cantatas 195 and 215 apparently did not suggest particular voice qualities so "early." Indeed, in twenty movements from other vocal works Bach changed his original intention regarding vocal assignment.[24] And these changes were most often made quite literally at the last moment: the first systems for the movement had already been set down, but Bach had not yet begun to write the music.

A TEXT SOURCE that may prove to be of considerable significance for our knowledge of Bach's precompositional activity is the composer's personal copy of the "Calov Bible," a massive three-volume edition of the Lutheran Bible with commentary by the orthodox theologian Johann Abraham Calov.[25] The numerous autograph entries, marginalia, and (presumably autograph) underlinings throw light mainly on Bach's theological convictions, but they also furnish evidence of precompositional planning of the kind under consideration here. Most pertinent is the following autograph notation:

NB./Erstes Vorspiel,/auf 2 Chören/zur Ehre Gottes/zu musiciren.

(i.e., "*Nota Bene.* First prelude to be performed by 2 choruses to the glory of God") written in the margin alongside Calov's exegesis of Exodus 15:20–21 ("And Miriam . . . took a timbrel in her hand; and all the women went out after her with timbrels and with dances. / And Miriam answered them, Sing ye to the Lord, for he hath triumphed gloriously . . ."). Calov comments (in part):

But Miriam and the other women of Israel did not sing a new [*sic*] song but repeated like an echo what Moses and the Israelite men had sung first . . . and these two choruses must have produced a powerful song and a mighty sound and echo.

[22] See NBA I/37, KB, pp. 60, 67, 69.
[23] See note 17 above.
[24] See Chapter VII.

[25] Although the volumes have been in the library of Concordia Seminary, St. Louis, Missouri, since 1938, their existence has only recently become generally known. See Trautmann 1969.

Christoph Trautmann and Gerhard Herz have both recently suggested[26] that Bach's marginal note must refer to the opening movement of the motet *Singet dem Herrn ein neues Lied* (BWV 225), a double-chorus work based on Psalms 149:1–3 and 150:2, 6. Trautmann speculates further that Bach must first have consulted these Psalm texts in the Calov Bible where the commentary to Psalm 149:3 (viz., "Let them praise his name in the dance: let them sing praises unto him with the timbrel and harp" or "Sie sollen loben seinen Namen mit Reigen: mit Paucken und Harffen sollen sie ihm spielen") refers the reader to the exegesis of Exodus 15:20. The description there of the powerful singing by two choruses inspired Bach with the idea of setting the opening half-verse—*Erstes Vorspiel*—of *Singet dem Herrn* for a "tutti" double chorus, and he recorded that plan in the form of the hasty marginal note quoted above. Trautmann goes on to conjecture that the introduction of antiphonal exchanges between the two choruses in later sections of the first movement, and particularly the verbal direction in the autograph (P 36/2) that the second movement of the work—in which Chorus I sings a choral "aria" and Chorus II a four-part chorale—be repeated with the chorale performed by Chorus I and the "aria" by Chorus II,[27] were suggested by Calov's words: "not a new song . . . but repeated like an echo what the Israelite men had sung first," and his evocation of a "mighty sound and echo" (*mächtiger Schall und Wiederschall*).[28]

---

[26] Trautmann 1970, pp. 238–240; Herz 1970, p. 22.

[27] See the facsimile edition, score page 32: *Der 2. Vers. ist wie d erste, nur daß die Chöre ümwechseln, nur dz. 1ste Chor den Choral, dz 2dre die Aria singe.* Cf. NBA III/1, KB, pp. 29 and 49.

[28] In Trautmann 1970 the author argues that the autograph signature: "JSBach/1733." on the title pages of the three Calov volumes must have been written at the time Bach acquired them, and that the motet accordingly must have been composed after that date. This contradicts the (tentative) dating of c. 1727 suggested in Dürr 1957 and Dadelsen 1958. Gerhard Herz suggests, however (*op.cit.*, p. 23), that Bach may have acquired the volumes long before 1733, and he attempts to connect the 1733 date of the signature with biographical circumstances concerned with Bach's moving to new living quarters in the Thomasschule building in that year.

CHAPTER III

The Preparation, Layout, and Structure of
the Bach Cantata Autographs

IT IS POSSIBLE to trace Bach's composing procedures—or, more modestly put, his music-writing procedures—back to the very beginning: to the *tabula rasa* represented by the totally blank sheet of paper. Since Bach did not often use manuscript paper with printed staves, but ruled the staves himself (or had them ruled) with a five-pronged writing implement known in German as a *Raster* or *Rastral*,[1] the music-writing process can be said to begin with the ruling of the staves on the blank page.[2] It is possible to reconstruct exactly how the staff-ruling process was carried out.

Two general principles apparently governed the ruling of Bach's manuscript paper: the non-calligraphic principle—preparing a large supply of paper in advance, ruling arbitrarily as many staves as could be comfortably fitted on a page, without regard to the musical layout of the score; and, alternatively, the calligraphic principle—ruling exactly as many staves on a page as the music required, often leaving larger spaces between the staves of planned systems than between the staves within a system. These two principles will be considered later in this chapter.

---

[1] For the sake of convenience the German term will be used in this chapter. In recent years considerable attention has been devoted to the nature of the Bach *Rastrale* with a view to deriving from them information bearing on the chronology of manuscripts and compositions. In the critical report to his edition of the *Clavier-Büchlein vor Anna Magdalena Bach . . . 1722*, NBA V/4, KB, p. 9, Georg von Dadelsen reported that at least four different *Rastrale* were employed in the preparation of the manuscript. This marks perhaps the first time that staff widths were taken into account in a description or discussion of a Bach manuscript. Dürr 1957, p. 120, suggests the possibility of obtaining chronological information by measuring the widths of the staves. Such a study has since been carried out by two investigators. Wolff 1963 attempts, in fact, to use the evidence provided by staff-width measurements to invalidate portions of the chronology derived by Dürr and von Dadelsen. The limitations and risks of using the findings of staff measurements for anything but confirming results found by other philological means of dating have been pointed out, however, by Walter Emery in his review of the Wolff article. (See Emery 1964, pp. 168–170.) The Johann-Sebastian-Bach-Institut, Göttingen, in the meantime, has commissioned a complete catalogue of the staff measurements in the Bach manuscripts belonging to the Berlin library complex. The first volume, containing tabulations of these measurements, has been completed: Hans Otto Hiekel, "Katalog der Rastrierungen in den Originalhandschriften J. S. Bachs" (unpublished), but there has not yet been any interpretation or evaluation of this information.

[2] The only Bach autograph written on paper with printed staves is the score of BWV 195 (P 65). It is possible that this exceptional use of printed manuscript paper in a cantata score is connected with the preparation of the printer's copy of *Die Kunst der Fuge*. See NBA I/33, KB, p. 122.

Staff Ruling

THE ORDER OF EVENTS

I will attempt first to show that the steps involved in ruling staves took place in the following sequence. Bach (or whoever ruled the paper for him) first spread out flat the two leaves of the folded sheet; then ruled the two outer leaves from the outer edge of the page to the center fold; then ruled the two inner leaves from the outer edge of the page to the center fold.

Since the staves rarely extend to the outer edge of the page but leave a slight margin, while at the center fold they often overlap onto the opposite side of the fold, the sheet must have been spread out at the time of ruling and ruled from the outer edge of each facing page toward the center fold. There is no evidence that the facing pages of a sheet were ruled together in one stroke from the outer edge of one page to the outer edge of the other.[3] The characteristic margins at the edge of the page and the overlapping of staff-ends at the fold are observable in over 100 manuscripts including every score of the second and third Leipzig *Jahrgänge*.[4] As a rule, wherever single sheets were to be gathered into fascicles, they were completely ruled before the gathering was formed. This is clear again from the overlapping of staff-ends. Only in the score of BWV 119 (P 878), which has the structure III + II, was the gathering set up at least in part before the staves were ruled. Here there is an overlapping of the staff-ends from one leaf onto the leaf of another sheet of the fascicle (f. 1v onto f. 2r).

In a non-calligraphic score the number of staves per page is more or less constant, but rarely thoroughly so throughout. There is usually an agreement in the number of staves on each of the outer pages of a sheet plus an agreement in the slightly different number of staves on the two inner pages, since the ruling of one page served as an optical guide for the ruling of the facing page. Thus there are many such configurations as

BWV 134 (P 44/3)	Sheet 4	25 staves	ff. 7r 8v
		23 staves	ff. 7v–8r
BWV 194 (P 43/3)	Sheet 2	21 staves	ff. 3r 4v
		22 staves	ff. 3v–4r
	Sheet 6	22 staves	ff. 11r 12v
		23 staves	ff. 11v–12r

---

[3] The pages may have been ruled in this way in the manuscripts of BWV 169, 207, and 198. But it is also possible that the staves on the facing pages of several sheets were so carefully aligned with each other that there is no visible crossing of staves or overlapping at the fold.

[4] On f. 4r of P 42/3, the autograph of BWV 208, two unused half-staves on the bottom of the page extend from the outer edge of the page toward the middle of the page and thus provide additional evidence for the argument pursued here.

BWV 86 (P 157)	Sheet 3	21 staves	title page r 5v
		22 staves	title page v-5r
	Sheet 1	22 staves	ff. 1r 2v
		21 staves	ff. 1v–2r
	Sheet 2	21 staves	ff. 3r 4v
		22 staves	ff. 3v–4r

or

BWV 114 (PP)	Sheet 1	23 staves	ff. 1r 2v
		24 staves	ff. 1v–2r
	Sheet 2	24 staves	ff. 3r 4v
		23 staves	ff. 3v–4r
	Sheet 3	23 staves	ff. 5r 6v
		24 staves	ff. 5v–6r

and so on. This material supports my earlier contention that the two outer pages of a sheet were ruled together as were the two inner pages.

There are manuscripts with the same number of staves on every page of some sheets, while on other sheets only adjacent pages have the same number, for example:

BWV 232^{III} (P 13/1)	Sheet 1	23 staves throughout	
	Sheet 2	21 staves	ff. 3r 4v
		22 staves	ff. 3v–4r
	Sheet 3	22 staves	ff. 5r 6v
		23 staves	ff. 5v–6r
	Sheet 4	22 staves	ff. 7r 8v
		21 staves	ff. 7v–8r
	Sheet 5	21 staves throughout	

and on rare occasions one finds a manuscript with the same number of staves on every page.[5] In fact, since one *Rastral* was usually employed for the ruling of an entire manuscript, the variation in the number of staves could never be very great so long as the goal was simply to draw as many staves on a page as possible. It is rather surprising that there are so few manuscripts with the same number of staves on each page.

---

[5] The only manuscripts that have the same number of staves on every page are:
BWV 75: 18 staves   BWV 65: 21 staves   BWV 176: 22 staves   BWV 27: 21 staves
BWV 28: 21 staves   BWV 169: 21 staves
BWV 72: 21 staves   BWV 248^{I}: 22 staves

THE CHOICE OF *Rastral*

In over forty scores the width of the staves changes in the course of the manuscript, an indication that in each case more than one *Rastral* was employed for the ruling. An examination of a few of these changes reveals that after the outer pages of an early sheet in the manuscript were ruled, a new *Rastral* was taken for the inner pages of the sheet and for the subsequent sheets. This sequence supports the succession of steps 2 and 3 in my reconstruction of Bach's staff-ruling procedure. Consider the following examples:

MS	Structure	Staff Width (in mm.)
BWV 36c (P 43/2)	7 × I	c. 10.5: ff. 3r, 4v; 5r, 6v (= outer pages of sheets 2 and 3)
		c. 9.5: remaining pages of the MS
BWV 19 (P 45/8)	5 × I	c. 7.5: ff. 1r, 2v (= outer pages of sheet 1)
		c. 8.5: remaining pages of the MS
BWV 55 (P 105)	2 × I + 1	c. 7: ff. 1r, 2v
		c. 9: remaining pages of the MS
BWV 225 (P 36/2)	5 × I	c. 8.5: ff. 1r, 2v
		c. 8: remaining pages of the MS
BWV 30a (P 43/1)	V + III + 1	c. 10: ff. 2r, 9v (= outer pages of second sheet of first gathering)
		c. 9: remaining pages of the MS
BWV 77 (P 68)	3 × I + 1	c. 10: ff. 1r–2v; 3v–4r; 5v–6r; 7r–7v
		c. 9: ff. 3r, 4v; 5r, 6v (= outer pages of sheets 2 and 3)
BWV 26 (P 47/1)	4 × I	c. 7.5: ff. 1r, 2v; 3r, 4v; 5r, 6v; 7r, 8v (= outer pages of each sheet)
		c. 8.5: the inner pages of each sheet

In the motet *Singet dem Herrn ein neues Lied,* BWV 225, for double chorus, Bach evidently changed the *Rastral* as soon as he realized that he could fit only 21 staves comfortably on the page using the wider *Rastral.* The 21-stave page accommodated only two 8-stave systems while five staves remained unused. With the 8 mm. *Rastral,* the composer was able to rule 24 staves and enter three score systems on each page.

The *Rastral* in the score of BWV 19 was surely not changed for musical reasons. The small width of c. 7.5 mm. allowed 24 staves (two 12-stave systems) to be drawn comfortably on the two outer pages of the first sheet. With the larger

Rastral it was possible to rule only 21 or 22 staves per page, and Bach was obliged either to draw staves freehand or enter more than one real part on a staff. But even 12-stave systems would not have been ideal, since the opening movement of BWV 19 has fourteen independent parts. Therefore (the nearsighted?) Bach may have preferred the larger staff for the sake of legibility.

The two bottom lines of the narrower *Rastral* employed in the score of BWV 77 are very close together. The user apparently noticed this after the outer pages of sheets 2 and 3 were ruled, and thereupon took a larger *Rastral* for the remaining pages of the score. There are usually no clues, though, to the reasons that prompted Bach to change *Rastrale* in the course of preparing a manuscript.

The Score Layout

Non-calligraphic Manuscripts

The differences between the layout of a hastily written composing score and that of a calligraphic fair copy can be dramatically illustrated by comparing the autograph scores of Bach's *Magnificat* in its E♭ version of 1723 (P 38) and in the D major revision written sometime between 1728 and 1731 (P 39). The first pages from both manuscripts are reproduced on the following pages.[6]

The score of the E♭ version reveals a frugality with paper that is characteristic for non-calligraphic scores. Eighteen measures are crowded onto 22 staves that were evidently ruled in advance without consideration of the peculiar musical layout of the first movement of the *Magnificat*. Nine measures are entered on the upper 15-stave system and another nine on the remaining seven staves of the page. The bottom staves could only be utilized by eliminating the resting voice parts and combining Trumpets 2 and 3, Oboes 1 and 2, and Violins 1 and 2 onto one staff for each of the instrumental pairs.

In the D major version six measures are spaced comfortably on one 17-stave system. The seventeen staves were surely ruled with the layout of the movement in mind; the bottom portion of the page was left unruled. On pages of the manuscript comprising several systems, a larger space was left between the staves of adjacent systems than between those of the same system—a clear indication that the ruling of this manuscript was governed by musical considerations.[7]

---

[6] The facsimiles are reproduced from NBA II/3, pp. vi and vii.

[7] The practice of leaving larger spaces between systems is observable in the autographs of the following works: BWV 71, 61, 225, 84, 240, 249, 226, 243, 66 (sheets 5 and 6), 100, 118[1] (sheet 1), 244, 245, 232.

II. Beginning of the *Magnificat*, First Version (in E♭), BWV 243a.
Autograph, P 38, f. 1r. By courtesy of the Deutsche
Staatsbibliothek, Berlin, German Democratic Republic

III. Beginning of the *Magnificat*, Second Version (in D), BWV 243.
Autograph, P 39, f. 2r. By courtesy of the Deutsche
Staatsbibliothek, Berlin, German Democratic Republic

The nature of the staff ruling and consequently of the layout of the E♭ version is typical for the hasty composing scores of the Leipzig period. A supply of paper apparently had been ruled in advance, presumably with no particular work or score in mind. As has been mentioned above, the principle doubtless was simply to rule as many staves on a page as one could without disastrously impairing the legibility. As a consequence, the number of staves is fairly constant from page to page, and this number often provides too many or too few staves for the musical requirements of the score. In the autograph of BWV 243a there are 21, 22, or 23 ruled staves per page.

LAYOUT OF P 38 (BWV 243a)[8]

Leaf	No. of staves	Movement and Layout
f. 1r	22	Mvt. 1 (*Magnificat*): one 15-stave system (= 1 × 15) and one 7-stave system (1 × 7), omitting the resting choral staves and entering the pairs Tpt. 2–3, Ob. 1–2, and Vn. 1–2 on one staff for each pair
f. 1v	22	Mvt. 1: 1 × 10 (omitting the choral staves) and 1 × 12 (Tpt. 2–3, Ob. 1–2, and Vn. 1–2 on one staff for each pair of instruments)
f. 2r	23	Mvt. 1: 1 × 15 Mvt. 2 (*Et exsultavit*): 2 × 4 (Vn. 2, Va. contracted on one staff)
f. 2v	23	Same as f. 2r
f. 3r	22	Mvt. 1: 1 × 15 Mvt. 2: 1 × 4 (Vn. 2, Va. on one staff) and 1 × 3 (Vn. 1, 2, Va. on one staff)
f. 3v	22	same as f. 3r
f. 4r	22	Mvt. 1: 1 × 15 Mvt. 2 (conclusion): 1 × 5, then 2 blank staves
f. 4v	21	Mvt. 1: 1 × 15 Mvt. 3 (*Quia respexit*): 2 × 3

[8] This table and that for BWV 243 (P 39) on pp. 54–55 are abbreviated versions of the descriptions in NBA II/3, KB, pp. 11–15, 18–21. See also the diagrammatic representations of these layouts on p. 10, *ibid.*

LAYOUT OF P 38 (BWV 243a) *(cont'd)*

Leaf	No. of staves	Movement and Layout
f. 5r	21	Mvt. 1 (end): 1 × 10 (no staves for resting chorus) Mvt. 3: 3 × 3, then 2 blank staves with sketch on the upper one
f. 5v	21	Mvt. 4 (*Omnes generationes*): 1 × 11, and 1 × 10 (with Bc. part in tablature)
f. 6r	21	same as f. 5v
f. 6v	21	Mvt. 4 (end): same as f. 5v Mvt. 5 (*Quia fecit*): 5 × 2 (on the bottom 10 staves after Mvt. 4)
f. 7r	22	Mvt. 5 (end): 2 × 2 Mvt. 6 (*Et misericordia*): 3 × 6
f. 7v	21	Mvt. 6: 3 × 6, then 3 unused staves
f. 8r	22	Mvt. 6 (end): 2 × 6 Mvt. 7 (*Fecit potentiam*): 1 × 10 (no Tpt. or Timp. staves, Bc. in tablature)
f. 8v	22	Mvt. 7: 2 × 11. First system as on f. 8r but with the Bc. on a staff; second system: Tpt. 2–3, Ob. 1–2, Vn. 1–2 each pair on one staff
f. 9r	22	Mvt. 7: 1 × 15 Mvt. 8 (*Deposuit*): 2 × 3; the bottom staff unused except for sketch
f. 9v	23	Mvt. 7: 1 × 15; the next 5 staves blank except for a corrected version of m. 25: S2ATB parts on staves 16–19 Mvt. 8: 1 × 3 (staves 21–23)
f. 10r	23	Mvt. 7 (end): 1 × 15 Mvt. 8: 2 × 3; then 2 unused staves
f. 10v	22	Mvt. 8 (end): 4 × 3 Mvt. 9 (*Esurientes*): 2 × 4; then 2 blank staves
f. 11r	22	Mvt. 9 (end): 5 × 4; 1 × 2. On top staff of bottom system: at first, conclusion of alto (no instruments), then both recorders on one staff (mm. 40b–42a not written out)

LAYOUT OF P 38 (BWV 243a) (*cont'd*)

Leaf	No. of staves	Movement and Layout
f. 11v	22	Mvt. 10 (*Suscepit Israel*): 4 × 5; then 2 blank staves
f. 12r	22	Mvt. 11 (*Sicut locutus*): 3 × 6
		Mvt. A (*Vom Himmel hoch*): 1 × 4 (mm. 1–6)
f. 12v	22	Mvt. 11 (end): 1 × 6, 1 × 5 (no doubling Bc.), 1 × 6
		Mvt. 12 (*Gloria Patris*): 1 × 11 (to the right of Mvt. 11 on staves 12–22; the Tpt. and Timp. parts are on staves 18–21 beneath the conclusion of Mvt. 11)
f. 13r	23	Mvt. 12: 1 × 15
		Mvt. A (cont'd.): 2 × 4
f. 13v	22	Mvt. 12: 1 × 15
		Mvt. A: 1 × 4; then 3 unused staves
f. 14r	21	Mvt. 12: 1 × 15
		Mvt. A (end): 1 × 4; then 2 unused staves
f. 14v	23	Mvt. 12: 1 × 15
		Mvt. B (*Freut euch und jubiliert*): 1 × 7 (actually 1 × 5 with 2 staves crossed out); then one unused staff
f. 15r	23	Mvt. 12 (end): 1 × 15
		Mvt. B: 1 × 5; then 3 unused staves
f. 15v	22	Mvt. B (end): 4 × 5
		Mvt. C (*Gloria in excelsis Deo*): 1 × 6 (to the right of Mvt. B on staves 16–21). Staff 22: Vn. 1 part for Mvt. C
f. 16r	22	Mvt. C (end): 4 × 6 (2 freehand half-staves; on right of staves 21–22 plus a third freehand half-staff: continuation of Vn. 1 part of Mvt. C
f. 16v	22	Mvt. D (*Virga Jesse floruit*): 7 × 3; in the bottom system an unused staff between Bass and Bc. staves

There are several pages with unused staves and pages where lack of space necessitated either the doubling of parts on a single staff, the entering of certain parts (usually the continuo) in tablature, or the drawing of freehand staves. A perfect agreement of the number of staves ruled with the number needed for the music is found on only 4 pages of the 32-page score, and there it is most probably a matter of coincidence.

Most or all of the characteristics just mentioned can be found in all the non-calligraphic scores of the post-Weimar period. A vast amount of material could accordingly be produced at this point to illustrate Bach's practice further. A few examples may suffice.

The autograph of BWV 109, *Ich glaube, lieber Herr* (P 112), has either 20 or 21 ruled staves per page, but by coincidence and clever disposition of the parts hardly any are unused.

LAYOUT OF P 112 (BWV 109)

Leaf	No. of staves	Movement and Layout
ff. 1r–4v	20	Mvt. 1: 2 × 10
f. 5r	20	Mvt. 2: 4 × 2
		Mvt. 3: 2 × 5, 1 × 2 (= mm. 8b–10 with no staves for the resting strings)
ff. 5v–6r	20	Mvt. 3: 4 × 5
f. 6v	20	Mvt. 3 (end): 1 × 5
		Mvt. 4: 2 × 2
		Mvt. 5: 2 × 4, 1 × 3 (by combining Ob. 1 and 2 on one staff)
f. 7r	21	Mvt. 5: 5 × 4; one unused staff with sketch
f. 7v	20	Mvt. 5: 5 × 4
f. 8r	20	Mvt. 5 (end): 1 × 4
		Mvt. 6: 1 × 10, 1 × 6 (by omitting the staves for the resting chorus in mm. 7–11)
ff. 8v, 9r, 10v	20	Mvt. 6: 2 × 10
ff. 9v–10r	21	Mvt. 6: 2 × 10; then one unused staff

A 20-stave page was obviously appropriate for the layout of the music; the existence of 21-stave pages reveals that the pages were not ruled with this score in mind.

The composing score of the *Sanctus,* BWV 232[III] (P 13/1), has one 17-stave system per page throughout the manuscript (ff. 1r–10v); but there are 21 to 23 ruled staves per page. The bottom four to six staves occasionally contain sketches but are usually completely blank.

There are 21 staves on every page of the score for BWV 28, *Gottlob! Nun geht das Jahr zu Ende* (P 92). Movements 1 and 2 are each written on two 8-stave systems per page from f. 1v through f. 9r. This means that there are normally five unused staves on the bottom of these pages.[9] Bach, however, entered Movement 3 on the bottom of f. 9v below the conclusion of Movement 2, although with its 2-stave systems the continuo aria could just as well have been entered on the bottom of f. 1r. The scoring of Movement 4 calls for 5-stave systems that could likewise have been written under Movements 1 and 2. This is true also for the 3-stave systems of Movement 5. The economy-minded composer could surely have saved an entire sheet if he had made use of the blank staves on the bottom of the first five sheets of the manuscript. Bach probably did not do this because Movements 1 and 2 are both written on two systems per page. Wherever Bach entered one or more[10] movements in a score on the bottom staves of several consecutive pages below an earlier movement of that work, only one system for any of the movements was written on any page. Otherwise, confusion could easily have arisen as to when the reader or copyist was to read down from one system to the next and when he was supposed to read from one page to the next.

CALLIGRAPHIC MANUSCRIPTS

As a rule, calligraphic scores have just as many staves on a page as the music requires; the number of staves per page varies according to the layout and size of the score system. In the D major version of the *Magnificat* (to return to our original comparison) the number of staves per page varies rationally from fifteen to twenty.[11]

LAYOUT OF P 39 (BWV 243)

Leaf	No. of staves	Movement and Layout
f. 1r	0	Title page
f. 1v	0	Blank
ff. 2r–9r	17	Mvt. 1 (*Magnificat*): 1 × 17 per page

---

[9] Folio 1r has three, and f. 4v has four unused staves.

[10] The autograph of BWV 213 (P 125) has three movements notated one above the other on ff. 3r–6v.

[11] See NBA II/3, KB, pp. 18–21.

LAYOUT OF P 39 (BWV 243) *(cont'd)*

Leaf	No. of staves	Movement and Layout
ff. 9v–10r	20	Mvt. 2 (*Et exsultavit*): 4 × 5
f. 10v	20	Mvt. 2 (end): 3 × 5
		Mvt. 3 (*Quia respexit*): 1 × 2, 1 × 3
f. 11r	18	Mvt. 3: 6 × 3
ff. 11v–13r	17	Mvt. 4 (*Omnes generationes*): 1 × 13
		Mvt. 5 (*Quia fecit*): 2 × 2
ff. 13v–14r	19	Mvt. 4 (end): 1 × 13
		Mvt. 6 (*Et misericordia*): 1 × 6
ff. 14v–15r	18	Mvt. 6 (cont'd): 3 × 6
f. 15v	19	Mvt. 6 (end): 1 × 6
		Mvt. 7 (*Fecit potentiam*): 1 × 13 (= mm. 1–5, without Tpt. and Timp. staves)
ff. 16r–18r	17	Mvt. 7: 1 × 17
f. 18v	17	Mvt. 7 (end): one-half of one 17-stave system; to the right on the lower 15 staves:
		Mvt. 8 (*Deposuit*): 5 × 3
f. 19r	18	Mvt. 8: 6 × 3
f. 19v	16	Mvt. 8 (end): 4 × 3
		Mvt. 9 (*Esurientes*): 1 × 4
f. 20r	20	Mvt. 9 (cont'd.): 5 × 4
f. 20v	20	Mvt. 9 (end): 4 × 4
		Mvt. 10 (*Suscepit Israel*): 1 × 4 (= mm. 1–4, without Ob. staff)
f. 21r	15	Mvt. 10: 3 × 5
f. 21v	17	Mvt. 10 (end): 1 × 5
		Mvt. 11 (*Sicut locutus est*): 2 × 6
f. 22r	18	Mvt. 11: 3 × 6
f. 22v	18	Mvt. 11 (end): 1 × 6
		Mvt. 12 (*Gloria Patris*): 1 × 12 (= mm. 1–5, no Tpt. or Timp. staves; Vn. 1–2 on one staff)
ff. 23r–25v	17	Mvt. 12: 1 × 17 per page
ff. 26r–26v	0	unruled

But even here, Bach did not throw economy to the winds. On ff. 11v to 14r he seems to have first ruled only thirteen staves to accommodate Movement 4, *Omnes generationes*. He then ruled four or six additional staves on these pages in order to enter the following movements of the work (*Quia fecit* and *Et misericordia*) below rather than after (i.e., to the right of) the *Omnes generationes* chorus.

To save more space, Bach omitted staves for the resting trumpet and timpani parts at the beginning of Movement 7, *Fecit potentiam* (f. 15v) and wrote out the opening measures on a 13-stave system rather than on seventeen staves. This enabled him to use the free space below the concluding 6-stave system of Movement 6.[12]

There is even a place in the *Magnificat* score where two real parts are entered on one staff. The beginning of the *Gloria Patri* is entered on f. 22v below the conclusion of the *Sicut locutus est* on a reduced system. There are no staves for the resting trumpet and timpani parts, and Violins 1 and 2 share the same staff.

The principle governing the layout of BWV 243 is nevertheless clear enough: each page was ruled so as to provide each real part of the musical texture with its own staff as long as this led neither to undue wasting of paper nor undue crowding of parts and of notation. No staves are left unused on the bottoms of pages, no extra staves drawn freehand, no parts entered in tablature between or below ruled staves.

There are not many calligraphic manuscripts of the Leipzig period that are ruled with the same forethought as the score of the D major *Magnificat*. Only the following Leipzig manuscripts display a calligraphic score layout:

BWV 243 (P 39), 1728–31
BWV 232 (P 180), 1733, 1746–49
BWV 11 (P 44/5), May 19, 1735
BWV 249 (P 34), 1732–35
BWV 118[1] (PP), 1736/37?
BWV 234 (Darmstadt), 1735–42
BWV 236 (Darmstadt), 1735–42
BWV 30 (P 44/1), 1738–42
BWV 239 (P 13/3), after 1735
BWV 240 (P 13/2), after 1735

[12] On f. 18v Bach ruled seventeen staves for the conclusion of the *Fecit potentiam*. But rather than leave the space to the right of the movement unused, the lower fifteen staves were set up as five half-systems of three staves each for the beginning of the *Deposuit* aria, which then continues on the next page with six 3-stave systems. In this instance, pointing hands were sketched on the right-hand corner of f. 18v and the upper left-hand corner of f. 19r to clarify the sequence of measures, and to insure that the systems would not be read from left to right across both pages. See NBA II/3, KB, p. 20.

BWV 118² (PP), 1740–49
BWV 244 (P 25), c. 1736?
BWV 34 (AMB 39), 1742–45 (mostly calligraphic ruling)
BWV 245 ((P 28)), c. 1742

Although many portions of the *B minor Mass* autograph (P 180) are evidently revision copy or composing score, the manuscript displays a remarkable degree of planning in the layout of the music upon the page. For the most part, each page was ruled according to the "calligraphic principle." Staves for resting parts were occasionally omitted. On page 20 of the manuscript for example, Bach managed to accommodate the conclusion of *Kyrie II* (two 5-stave systems) and the beginning of the *Gloria in excelsis* ($1 \times 10 = $ mm. 1–12) by omitting staves for the resting voices of the *Gloria* ritornello. On page 21, where there was room for only 24 staves, Bach again set up one 10-stave system for mm. 13–24 of the *Gloria* (still preceding the choral entry). But in order to make use of the remaining staves he was obliged to create a 14-stave system by pairing Sopranos I and II on one staff.[13] For the remainder of the movement, Bach ruled fifteen staves per page for the 15-stave systems, leaving the bottom portion of the page unruled; the same layout prevails in the *Gratias agimus* (pp. 50–52), and in the *Cum Sancto spiritu* (pp. 75–92).[14]

There are three important exceptions to the otherwise near-perfect layout of the *B minor Mass* autograph. Together they shed considerable light on Bach's first ideas regarding the dimensions and format of the movements concerned.

The text of the *Et incarnatus* section of the *Credo* did not at first exist as a separate movement but was incorporated in the closing portion of the *Et in unum Dominum* duet. The new choral version was inserted into the autograph on what is now the leaf pages 111–112. This leaf was ruled on both sides in advance with 21 staves, surely to accommodate three 7-stave systems per page. The movement, however, ends on the second system of the second page, a system with eight staves owing to the independent voice leading of the previously unison violins. Since Bach did not need a third system, there are six unused staves on the bottom of page 42, and the page has in respect to layout the typical appearance of a composing score.

The revised version of the voice lines in the *Et in unum Dominum* duet, with

---

[13] On the first page of the score Bach had similarly left only three staves to represent the resting chorus in mm. 6–10 of *Kyrie I*, with a pair of rests each in the soprano and alto staves to represent Sopranos I and II, and Alto and Tenor. As in the D major *Magnificat*, Bach was able to combine a degree of economy in the use of paper with calligraphic neatness and legibility of layout.

[14] A 17-stave system is used on the remaining pages of the *Cum Sancto spiritu*, pp. 93–95, to accommodate the addition of two independent flute parts from mm. 111 to the end of the movement. See NBA I/2, KB, pp. 162–163, in this connection.

the excision of the *Et incarnatus* text, appears on pages 151–152 of P 180, and is a revision copy in regard to beaming and text underlaying. Here again there is no agreement in the number of staves ruled on the page with the number actually needed. There are eight 2-stave systems on page 151 that indeed fill the sixteen ruled staves. On page 152, however, the movement ends after the seventh 2-stave system, and the remaining two staves of the page are unused. An unpaginated leaf following page 152 was presumably intended as well for the revision of the *Et in unum Dominum* voice parts. The recto has fourteen staves which were clearly ruled in seven pairs separated with large spaces; it was not used at all. The verso was left unruled.

For the final movement, the *Dona nobis pacem*, Bach ruled the pages in advance and apparently miscalculated the number of staves required. Although the score for the movement is a fair copy notated on a 14-stave system, the pages on which the chorus appears (pp. 183–188) are all consistently ruled with eighteen staves. This irregularity more likely represents a last-minute change of mind regarding the notation of the movement, rather than a senseless return to the "non-calligraphic" principle of staff ruling. It is conceivable—indeed it seems probable—that Bach had originally planned to write out independently each of the eight voice parts of the double chorus employed in this movement, as he had done in the *Osanna* movement, and had therefore planned an 18-stave system for the *Dona nobis pacem*. Then—probably as soon as he remembered that there was to be no independently led second chorus in this movement as there had been in the *Osanna*—he decided simply to indicate at the beginning of the movement that each voice part was to be doubled as Soprano I and II, Alto I and II, etc.[15]

AT TIMES both principles of staff ruling were used for different sections of a single score. In such instances the earlier portion of the manuscript usually follows the non-calligraphic principle and the latter portion of the manuscript the calligraphic. The explanation in at least some of these cases may be that Bach depleted his original supply of preruled paper while he was at work on the composition and had arrived at a point in the creation of the work from which the layout of the remainder of the piece could be visualized. From then on to the end of the composition Bach ruled the paper as needed.

In the score of BWV 213, *Laßt uns sorgen, laßt uns wachen* (P 125), for example, the first eighteen folios are ruled according to the non-calligraphic principle, but from f. 18v on to the end of the cantata only the twelve staves necessary for

---

[15] A more enticing notion, entertained by Arthur Mendel, is that Bach may have intended some completely different music for the *Dona nobis* before   he hit upon the idea of parodying the music of the *Gratias agimus*.

the 12-stave systems of the concluding chorus "Lust der Völker, Lust der Deinen" were ruled on each page. Similarly, the last page of the score of BWV 84 (P 108) is ruled with only the ten staves necessary for the two 5-stave systems of the concluding chorale. A large space was provided between the two systems.

The manuscript of BWV 66 (P 73) makes use of two types of paper, each ruled with a different *Rastral:*

Sheets 1–4   Watermark: ZVMILIKAV   Staff width: c. 10 mm.
Sheets 5–8   Watermark: IPD + 2-headed eagle   Staff width: c. 7 mm.

The fourth sheet ends in the middle of Movement 1 and Movement 3, which are entered one above the other. The remainder of the cantata is written on sheets 5–8. Since Movements 1 and 3 are interrupted at the end of sheet 4, it is likely that the whole score was written at one time.[16] Sheets 1 through 4 were ruled in advance without regard for the particular layout of the composition and this paper presumably represents the last sheets of a previously ruled supply. When this supply was exhausted, Bach took new paper and ruled it (with the new *Rastral*) more or less appropriately for the layout of the remainder of the cantata.

Other manuscripts that were partially ruled according to the calligraphic principle are:

BWV 30a (P 43/1): ff. 17r–17v (= final leaf of the manuscript)
BWV 57 (P 144): final sheet
BWV 36 (P 45/2): first two sheets
BWV 97 (NYPL): essentially ruled as needed throughout, except for ff. 9r and 10v which contain unused staves
BWV 100 (P 159): sheets 1–3, 5

Bach's concern with calligraphy in the early manuscripts often urged him to rule the barlines in many movements. This was usually so done that all the systems on a page had the same number of measures and that there was a perfect alignment of the barlines of each system with those of the other systems on the page. A majority of pre-Leipzig manuscripts display this feature:

BWV 131 (PP): throughout
BWV 71 (P 45/1): throughout
BWV 208 (P 42/3): Movement 15 only; the barlines are partly ruled simultaneously for two systems, partly for each system independently.
BWV 182 (P 103): Movements 1, 2, 7, 8

---

[16] See NBA I/10, KB, pp. 7–9, for details of the score layout.

BWV 12 (P 44/7): Movements 1, 2
BWV 199 (Copenhagen): Movements 1, 4, 8
BWV 61 (P 45/6): throughout
BWV 163 (P 137): Movements 1, 3
BWV 132 (P 60): Movement 1
BWV 147 (P 102): Movement 1
BWV 22 (P 119): Movement 1
BWV 23 (P 69): Movement 3

This characteristic disappears almost entirely in the Leipzig manuscripts produced after the two audition cantatas (BWV 22 and 23) written for Estomihi, February 7, 1723, as part of Bach's application for the position of Thomas Cantor. Ruled barlines were probably too much of a luxury in the heavily productive years that followed, and they appear in only two isolated later manuscripts: in the first movement of BWV 171 (PP), and on a single page (f. 2v) of the fair copy autograph of BWV 34 (P AMB 39). This page contains mm. 57–72 of Movement 1. For some reason Bach may have decided at first not to fill in these sixteen measures and wished therefore to mark the measures off with a ruler for the moment, continue with the rest of the copying task, and return subsequently to the skipped measures. In the fifth movement of this cantata, Bach in fact made considerable use of the shorthand device of marking off measures in repeated sections and for doubling instruments which could be filled in at leisure or not at all. In the present instance the blank measures were filled in by W. F. Bach.[17]

This shorthand device, like the use of ruled barlines, appears as an anachronism in the autograph of a work as late as BWV 34. All the other surviving manuscripts containing blank measures belong to the pre-Leipzig period:[18]

BWV 199/4 (Copenhagen), mm. 74–90
BWV 182/8 (P 103), mm. 67–90
BWV 12/2 (P 44/7), mm. 49–92[19]
BWV 134a/4 and 8 (Paris)[20]

It has been mentioned several times that the elegant calligraphic script of the Mühlhausen and Weimar autographs makes it unusually difficult to distinguish a fair copy from a revision copy or composing score. The care and planning

[17] See NBA I/13, KB, pp. 113, 115–116.

[18] It is somewhat surprising that Bach did not make more frequent use of some timesaving shorthand device to indicate large-scale repetitions of earlier material, especially in view of the hectic pace at which he composed during the early Leipzig period.

[19] These blank staves suggested to A. Schering that Bach had planned to compose an instrumental accompaniment in the middle section of the movement but never fulfilled this intention. See the Eulenburg edition of the cantata.

[20] See NBA I/35, KB, pp. 65–66.

evident in these manuscripts extend to the ruling of the staves on the page. Almost every page of every pre-Cöthen manuscript was ruled according to the calligraphic principle. The autograph of Cantata 208, *Was mir behagt* (P 42/3), for example, is clearly a composing score; nonetheless the number of staves per page varies as necessary between 18 and 27, and the unused final page is unruled. Only nineteen of the surviving Bach autographs have such a blank final page:

BWV 71 (P 45/1)	BWV 23 (P 69)
BWV 208 (P 42/3)	BWV 48 (P 109)
BWV 182 (P 103)	BWV 113 (PP)
BWV 12 (P 44/7)	BWV 243 (P 39)
BWV 61 (P 45/6)	BWV 66 (P 73)
BWV 152 (P 45/3)	BWV 134 (P 44/3)
BWV 163 (P 137)	BWV 236 (Darmstadt)
BWV 132 (P 60)	BWV 30 (P 44/1)
BWV 147 (P 102)	BWV 244 (P 25)
BWV 173a (P 42/2)	

With one exception these are all pre-Leipzig manuscripts or Leipzig fair copies. The only composing score of the Leipzig period represented in this tabulation is the autograph of BWV 113, *Herr Jesus Christ, du höchstes Gut*. Bach here must have exhausted his original supply of paper with the third sheet of the manuscript, as he had done in BWV 213, 84, and 66, and then ruled only the first page of the last sheet (with sixteen staves clearly spaced into four groups of four staves) for the concluding chorale of the cantata, leaving ff. 7v–8v blank. There are, on the other hand, almost fifty composing scores from the Leipzig period with ruled but unused final pages.

Fascicle Structure

The fascicle structure of the Bach autographs varies according to the compositional type and the period in which the work was written. It seems that Bach's early practice was to organize his music paper into binio gatherings before he began to copy or compose. The manuscripts of BWV 208, 182, 152, 173a, 22, 23, 75, 76, and 24 all have binio structure. It is quite possible, in fact, that several of the manuscripts from the pre-Leipzig period which now have a ternio structure originally consisted of biniones. If the entire final leaf of a manuscript was unused, Bach often folded it around so as to precede the earlier sheets or gatherings. The two leaves of the final sheet could thus serve as a folder for the rest of the score. The structure of such manuscripts is represented with the symbol ". . . in I" in the chronological source list in Chapter I.

In each of the following pre-Leipzig ternio manuscripts the first sheet of the gathering (ff. 1r–1v) is blank except for the title on f. 1r; the musical score begins on f. 2r.

> BWV 71 (P 45/1), Feb. 4, 1708
> BWV 12 (P 44/7), Apr. 22, 1714
> BWV 61 (P 45/6), Dec. 2, 1714
> BWV 163 (P 137), Nov. 24, 1715
> BWV 132 (P 60),   Dec. 22, 1715

If the ternio had been formed in advance and Bach had decided to use f. 1r as a title page, then he would not have left f. 1v unused, and hence wasted, but would have begun to notate the composition on it. (This, anyway, is his procedure in the manuscripts of BWV 147 and 75.) In this group of ternio manuscripts Bach presumably constructed a binio gathering and then discovered that another page or two was necessary for the remainder of the composition. After completing the score, he folded back the final leaf of the new sheet in the fashion described above and used it as a title page.[21] The score of BWV 152 (P 45/3), falling as it does chronologically in the midst of the ternio manuscripts (Dec. 30, 1714), also tends to confirm the conjecture that these scores were originally planned as biniones. P 45/3 consists of a binio followed by a single sheet. The origin of this structure may have resembled that of the terniones, but here the last recto page (f. 6r) was needed for the notation of the composition and could not be folded back to serve as a title page.

It is evident as well in the scores of BWV 173a, 48, 66, and 134 that the title page is actually the unused leaf of the final sheet, but in these manuscripts the original sheet broke apart into two single leaves, most likely as a result of the refolding and the gradual drying out of the paper.

For the most part, Bach abandoned the use of fascicle structure during the main Leipzig period of cantata composition, 1723–27, at least when preparing composing scores.[22] He was perhaps reluctant to commit more than one sheet at a time to a composition whose dimensions were not yet altogether clear, and preferred rather to take a new sheet only after having completely filled the preceding one. The first surviving manuscript consisting exclusively of single sheets is the composing score of the Cöthen New Year's cantata, BWV 134a, *Die*

---

[21] In P 60 (BWV 132) such a refolding is in fact clearly visible in the creases at the fold of the title page.

[22] Bach, in fact, never really returned to the use of fascicle structure in composing scores. The only later examples are the scores of BWV 30a and BWV 248. In the former case, Bach could pre-sumably reckon from the large number of movements in the work that a great deal of paper would be employed and thus decided to set up large gatherings; the latter case, the *Christmas Oratorio,* is not exclusively, or even primarily, a composing score.

Zeit, die Tag und Jahre macht (Paris). But according to the available evidence, Bach did not begin to use single-sheet structure regularly until July 1723, when he began composition of Cantata 105, *Herr, gehe nicht ins Gericht,* presumably in the week preceding Sunday, July 25, 1723. The single-sheet structure was then used almost exclusively throughout the prolific period of the three Leipzig *Jahrgänge.* Beginning with the score of the motet BWV 226, *Der Geist hilft unsrer Schwachheit auf* (P 36/1), Bach reintroduced fascicle structure for the preparation of fair copies and revision copies where the dimensions of the pieces were already known, as was therefore to some degree the amount of paper needed for their transcription.[23]

The presence of a binio at the beginning of the score of BWV 29, *Wir danken dir Gott, wir danken dir* (P 166), is somewhat puzzling. The first leaf of the gathering is completely blank, unruled, and without a title. The opening sinfonia of the cantata—a revision copy—occupies the remainder of the gathering; Movement 2, the chorus "Wir danken dir," begins on a new sheet. The binio presumably was formed in this case, like the Weimar ternio manuscripts, by turning back the blank final page of the second single sheet used for the notation of the sinfonia. It is curious that Bach did not use this sheet for the notation of the next movement of the work, and it therefore appears that the binio that thus evolved may have been formed to isolate the sinfonia from the remainder of the cantata. This suggests either that (1) the sinfonia was set off from the rest of the cantata with a view to separate performances of it, or that (2) the cantata originally began with the opening chorus, the sinfonia being a separate concert piece that was at some time—perhaps still before the first performance of the work—used to introduce the cantata. In any event, the fact that the movement is a revision copy confirms that in the later Leipzig period Bach used fascicle structure only in fair and revision copies.

The Succession of Movements

The typical layout of the Bach cantata autographs, whether or not they are calligraphic, is the product of Bach's well-known parsimony with manuscript paper. We have seen that this frugality is particularly evident in composing scores. As a result of it, each movement of a work usually follows directly after,

---

[23] In many revision and fair copies which were clearly copied from other sources and which were written before the score of BWV 226, i.e., before October 1729, Bach retained the convenience of single-sheet structure. The manuscripts of Cantatas 42, 110, 28, 35, 169, 49, 55, 207, 171, and 174 all consist of single sheets, although it would not have been difficult to determine in advance the exact amount of paper required for at least large portions of these scores. Presumably Bach did not have the time or did not care at this quite hectic period in his career—1725 to June 1729—to plan the layout of *de-tempore* cantata scores with any great care.

i.e., to the right of or immediately below, the conclusion of the preceding movement. This could only mean that Bach as a rule composed the movements of the vocal works in the sequence in which they were to be performed. This rule in fact admits just one unambiguous exception.[24] In the autograph of the E♭ *Magnificat* (P 38) the four German movements were clearly not composed until the entire Latin text had been set.[25] Verbal directions in the score indicate at what points in the work the German pieces are to be performed. But even in this work the rule was not really broken, for the German movements are troping interpolations which were inserted into the main structure of the Latin Magnificat and were later omitted in the D major version. The movements of the *Magnificat* proper were composed in their normal sequence.

In the case of the Advent cantata, *Schwingt freudig euch empor,* BWV 36, the subsequent insertion of three chorale settings took place so late—after the first performance(s) of the work—that the cantata, like the *Magnificat,* exists in two discrete versions: the earlier, one-section "Kirnberger" version (so-called because the principal source for the version, P AMB 106, was penned by Bach's Leipzig pupil, J. P. Kirnberger) in five movements, and the later two-section version (preserved in P 45/2) in eight movements.[26] Since these chorale settings were inserted into the body of the "Kirnberger" version, one could regard BWV 36 as another example—in addition to the E♭ *Magnificat*—in which the movements were not composed in the order in which they were to be performed. But Bach surely would not have regarded the matter in this way. The "Kirnberger" version represented for Bach a self-sufficient, performable work at the time it was created, and not an intermediate, incomplete stage in the genesis of the eight-movement version. It is even conceivable that the shorter version— like the E♭ *Magnificat* itself—was never completely supplanted but existed along with the longer version as a one-section alternative that was more appropriate on certain occasions.

If a new movement begins at the top of a new sheet in a composing score, there is a possibility that it was composed before the preceding movement or movements of the piece. In the 170 extant autographs there are 72 internal movements which begin at the top of a new sheet; but 45 of these follow upon movements which had completely filled the preceding sheet of the manuscript. These movements, too, then, were composed in the sequence determined by the text. In almost all of the remaining cases there would have been room for perhaps a few measures of the new movement in the free space left over after the conclusion of the preceding movement; but this unused space is hardly evidence enough

[24] Perhaps two; see the discussion of BWV 207 below.

[25] See the layout of this score above, as well as NBA II/3, KB, pp. 10, 37–38.

[26] See NBA I/1, KB, pp. 18–37.

to permit the conclusion that the new movement on the new sheet was not written according to the text sequence. It seems more likely that Bach occasionally preferred to begin a new movement on a fresh sheet—especially where a new sheet would be required for the continuation of the movement. In this way, also, he could have given the preceding sheet immediately to a copyist who could then begin writing out the parts of the completed movement, and thus economize on time rather than on space.[27]

In four cantatas, for example, which belong to the same period

BWV 43/6 (P 44/6), May 30, 1726
BWV 88/4 (P 145), July 21, 1726
BWV 187/4 (P 84),   Aug. 4, 1726
BWV 45/4 (P 80),   Aug. 11, 1726

the "Seconda Parte" of the cantata begins on a new sheet of the manuscript. In P 44/6 and P 84 there would have been room for the first few measures of the second section on the bottom staves of a sheet. Here it seems particularly probable that Bach had already given the early sheets of the score to copyists so that they could prepare the parts of the first sections of the works while he composed the remaining movements.

The desire to accelerate the copying task may also explain why Bach entered the entire second movement of Cantata 13 (P 45/4), a secco recitative, on the top six staves of a new sheet in the manuscript rather than on six unused staves below the conclusion of the opening aria on f. 2v. Since the remaining movements of the score were all clearly written in normal succession, one would have to assume (if one wished to maintain that Movement 2 was not written after Movement 1) that the opening aria was the last movement of the work to be composed, and that by coincidence it filled approximately all four pages of one sheet leaving no unused pages between the first two movements when the sheet containing Movement 1 was placed at the beginning of the manuscript.

As we have seen, there is such an unused sheet, folded back to form a cover page, between the first two movements of Cantata 29. In this instance there is therefore some reason to believe—but no irrefutable proof—that the opening sinfonia was not originally conceived as the opening movement of this cantata.

The score for BWV 207, *Vereinigte Zwietracht der wechselnden Saiten* (P 174), presents a problem similar to that presented by Cantata 29. It is not clear from the layout of the autograph whether the chorus "Vereinigte Zwietracht" or the instrumental *Marche* is the first movement of the work. The march is written

---

[27]An attempt to reconstruct this kind of procedure for BWV 174 appears in NBA I/14, KB, pp. 99, 109–115.

on the interior pages, ff. 1v–2r, of the first sheet of the bound manuscript. Folio 1r serves as the title page, while f. 2v is blank except for 22 unused staves. The chorus, complete with the full heading normally found on the first notated page of Bach cantata manuscripts, begins on what is bound as the second sheet (f. 3r). This sheet, however, according to Bach's own pagination, was considered by him to be the first sheet of the score.[28] The BWV follows the format of the BG edition and counts the march as Movement 1 and the chorus as Movement 2. The NBA edition considers the chorus to be the first movement of the cantata and prints the march in an appendix. Musical considerations, of course, as well as the documentary evidence just described (the heading and Bach's pagination) argue that the chorus is the proper first movement of the composition. The fact that f. 2v was not used also suggests that the chorus was not composed directly after the march—assuming that the march is to be considered an integral part of BWV 207 at all. In fact it is not clear what the relationship is between the march and the cantata.[29]

The appearance of the Bach autographs, then, suggests strongly that, with perhaps a few exceptions, Bach began at the beginning—with the notation of the first measures of the first movement—and proceeded to compose the movements of a vocal work in the order in which they were to be performed. This appearance, though, may conceal the actual order in which the movements were composed. Chapter V will show that Bach's normal procedure when composing recitatives was first to lay out the systems for the movement and then write down the complete text underneath the planned vocal staff of the movement. In this fashion he determined the amount of space needed for the entire movement before actually beginning to compose.[30] Therefore it is possible that Bach, like Handel,[31] first wrote down the formal movements—arias and choruses—and only then composed the connecting recitatives. There are, however, no extant incomplete manuscripts of Bach's vocal compositions which would throw light on this matter.[32]

There is evidence, though, that in a substantial number of works the con-

---

[28] For details of the score layout see NBA I/38, KB, pp. 47–49.

[29] Werner Neumann assumes that the movement was written as part of the festivities connected with the open-air performance of the parody version of the cantata, BWV 207a, *Auf, schmetternde Töne der muntern Trompeten.* See NBA I/38, KB, pp. 76–77.

[30] See Sketches Nos. 160 and 165 and the facsimile reproduced on p. 33 above (also published in Dürr 1958, opposite p. 400).

[31] See the facsimile edition of Handel's *Jephtha*

(ed. Chrysander, 1885) and the foreword to that edition, p. iv.

[32] The incomplete autograph of the *Orgelbüchlein* (P 283) reveals that Bach did not compose the chorales in the sequence in which they were to appear. Analogous to Handel's practice with recitative composition, Bach, in P 283, set aside space for chorales which he did not choose to set at the moment. It seems likely that he first established the layout of the entire *Orgelbüchlein* before he had composed any of the chorales.

cluding chorale was not composed together with, i.e., "immediately" after, the preceding movements. This evidence is provided not by the autograph scores themselves but by the manuscript parts written out mainly by copyists and intended for use at the first performance of the composition. Not infrequently, the final chorale was entered into these parts by a new copyist after the bulk of the part had been completed by someone else.

This phenomenon has been repeatedly documented in the critical reports of the *Neue-Bach-Ausgabe*. We learn, for example, in NBA I/4, KB, that a new copyist entered the final chorale in the original parts of Cantata 190.[33] The critical report for NBA I/12 describes the same state of affairs in the original parts of BWV 128 and identifies the new scribe who entered the final chorale into the parts for Cantata 108 as J. S. Bach himself.[34] Alfred Dürr, the editor of NBA I/12, writes as follows regarding the roles of the participating copyists in the preparation of the parts for BWV 108: "But it was Bach himself who entered the final chorale everywhere but in the secondary untransposed continuo part . . . perhaps because [the chorale] was only composed after the principal scribe had completed his copying task."[35]

Werner Neumann begins his summary of the manner in which the parts for Cantata 78 were prepared thus: "Copyist 1 . . . at first copied Movements 1 through 6 in all parts from Bach's score [i.e., the autograph]. This score apparently did not yet contain the concluding chorale (Movement 7) because it was later added in all the parts by another hand (Copyist 2)."[36]

The autograph score, finally, of the motet *Der Geist hilft unsrer Schwachheit auf,* BWV 226 (P 36/1), does not include the final chorale at all. The chorale in fact appears—in a new hand—only in the manuscript vocal parts, and not in the doubling instrumental parts.[37]

The significance of such evidence is most likely, as Dürr and Neumann suggest, that the concluding chorales were frequently written only after the copying task was already underway. This may mean that the chorale with which the new work was to end had indeed not yet been composed. (We shall discover in the next chapter that Bach evidently did not as a rule expend great effort in composing a four-part chorale. Accordingly, he could well have waited until the "last minute" to add it.) But in some cases it may mean simply that the chorale had not yet been selected, that is, Bach—or the preacher—had not

---

[33] NBA I/4, KB, pp. 14–16. It is in this description, incidentally, that Bach's principal Leipzig copyist, long designated in the literature as *Hauptkopist A* or *Anonymous 3,* was identified by name as Johann Andreas Kuhnau (1703–?).

[34] NBA I/12, KB, pp. 174–179 (BWV 128), pp. 35–38 (BWV 108).

[35] NBA I/12, KB, p. 41.

[36] NBA I/21, KB, p. 118.

[37] See the facsimile edition of the autograph score and also NBA III/1, KB, pp. 66–67, 71, 82.

yet determined what chorale or chorale verse would be used in conjunction with the particular cantata.[38] It is quite possible that the chorale setting which ultimately was to form part of a cantata was not specifically composed for that cantata but rather belonged to a preexistent corpus of chorale settings composed by Bach as an independent activity not directly connected with the production of the cantatas.

The extent of this practice of composing (or choosing) the concluding chorale well after the completion of the other movements may even be greater than the manuscript evidence for it suggests; for it is thoroughly conceivable that the chorale was added at a later time to the parts by the same copyist who had prepared all the preceding movements. Finally, though, there is the possibility that in some cases the chorale entered by a new scribe was indeed already present in the autograph score, but Bach had deliberately entrusted the copying of this movement to a new, inexperienced scribe in order to introduce him to copying work with a short and relatively unproblematic task.

---

[38] The autograph scores often contain only the music for the concluding chorale without the text. If the original parts no longer exist, confusion may arise as to what strophe was intended or actually used. (See Werner Neumann's discussion of the proper text strophe for BWV 77/6, in NBA I/21, KB, pp. 11–12.) In this connection mention should be made of the parts for BWV 184 in which Bach himself added only the music for the chorale setting (Movement 5); a copyist then entered the text.

Although Cantata 184 is a parody composition (cf. NBA I/14, KB, p. 164), the chorale does not furnish a simple example of the Bachian parody procedure in which typically a new text was fitted to the revised vocal parts of the model. While the chorale setting may have been preexistent in the manner presently being discussed, there was no chorale setting in the model for BWV 184, a lost Cöthen secular cantata designated BWV 184a in the NBA. (See NBA I/35, KB, p. 138.)

CHAPTER IV

Autograph Scores of the
Four-Part Chorales

IT IS IN the autograph scores of the four-part chorales, which in general contain only a few scattered corrections, that a classification of fair copy, revision copy, or composing score proves particularly elusive. The simple chorale setting seems as a rule to have presented Bach with remarkably few difficulties. This is not surprising, since the idiom is relatively unproblematic: melody, form, texture, and scoring are all for the most part predetermined. The compositional effort accordingly concentrated to a great extent on such problems of musical grammar and technique as voice leading and chord-tone disposition. As a result, the clean appearance of the chorale autographs testifies primarily to the fact that Bach possessed an extraordinary facility and fluency in the purely technical facets of eighteenth-century composition. The consequence of this is that we are left few clues to Bach's procedures in composing these pieces.

The Order of Events

There is, for example, little visual evidence available to indicate whether Bach worked out the full harmonization of a chorale phrase by phrase, or whether he first wrote down the entire melody, then the entire bass line, and only thereafter worked out the inner voices. One assumes the latter approach, and indeed the available evidence seems to support this assumption.[1] The amount of this evidence is so small, however, that we cannot be sure it is representative.

The clearest indication that the entire melody and bass line of a chorale setting were written down before the inner parts of any phrase were worked out is provided by the score of BWV 43/11 (P 44/6). The outer parts for the whole

---

[1] C.P.E. Bach's testimony is revealing in this connection. In a letter to J. N. Forkel of January 13, 1775, he writes:". . . ad 9um: . . . His pupils had to begin their studies by learning pure four-part thorough bass. From this he went to chorales; first he added the basses to them himself, and they had to invent the alto and tenor. Then he taught them to devise the basses themselves . . ." (quoted in David-Mendel 1966, p. 279). Such pedagogical two-part pieces may be preserved in the "sketch-like" versions of the organ chorales "Gelobet seist du, Jesu Christ" BWV 722a, "In dulci jubilo" BWV 729a, "Lobt Gott, ihr Christen, allzugleich" BWV 732a, and "Vom Himmel hoch, da komm ich her" BWV 738a, which consist only of melody and figured bass. They survive in a copy made by Bach's Weimar pupil Johann Tobias Krebs. See NBA IV/3, KB, p. 11 and NBA IV/2, KB, p. 24–25.

chorale were originally written out in basically half-note motion in a 3/2 meter. The meter was then changed to 3/4 and the note-heads filled in from half-notes to quarter-notes. There is no similar correction in the alto and tenor parts.

In BWV 105/6 (P 99) the concluding note of each phrase is corrected from a half-note to a quarter-note (to make room for the instrumental interludes—see below) in the outer parts (soprano, bass, and continuo) throughout the chorale.[2] The inner parts, however, have no such correction in either the *Stollen* or the *Abgesang*, but present only the final—quarter-note—reading. (See the facsimiles on pp. 72 and 73.)

Although it is evident from these scores that Bach, at least occasionally, did not fill in the inner parts of a chorale harmonization until the entire outer-voice framework was completed, it is not clear from them whether Bach composed the bass line phrase for phrase immediately after writing down each phrase in the soprano, or whether he first wrote down the entire melody and then composed the entire bass line. Some evidence can be advanced bearing on this question.

For the concluding chorale of BWV 163 (P 137) Bach wrote out only the figured bass line with the heading "Choral. in simplice stylo," a clear indication that here the entire bass line was written in one uninterrupted gesture. The same conclusion can be drawn, though less convincingly, from Sketch No. 54. After completing the harmonization of the concluding chorale of Cantata 77 (P 68), Bach began to write out an alternative version, but abandoned the draft after having written down the melody for the first phrase and part of the second. Bach, then, did not in this instance write out in alternation one phrase of the melody, then its bass line, then the next phrase of the melody, its bass line, and so forth, but was apparently about to write down the entire chorale melody in one gesture.

But the autograph score of BWV 65/7 (P 147) provides both corroborating and contradictory evidence for the thesis that Bach wrote the entire melody of a chorale and then the entire bass line. In this movement, the soprano part was rebarred in the *Abgesang*.

Original reading

<hr />

[2] The following concluding half-notes in the outer parts were not filled in, presumably as a result of an oversight: soprano, m. 8, note 2; continuo, m. 8, note 3; bass, m. 19, note 4.

Final reading

That is, Bach wrote down the first phrase of the melody of the *Abgesang*, then wrote down the bass line for this phrase, ending likewise on a dotted half-note, and finally wrote out the remainder of the melody (through the beginning of m. 18) in the original barring. In the final reading he corrected the barring and composed the remainder of the bass line. The rebarring assured that the final note of the chorale fell on the third beat of the measure and thus complemented the upbeat at the beginning of the chorale. The implication from this is that Bach used both the "one-phrase-at-a-time" technique and the "entire-melody-at-once" procedure in writing out at least the *Abgesang* of the chorale.

Corrections of the Chorale Melody

The examples already presented make clear that Bach did not copy the chorale melodies mechanically from a preexistent source into the autograph. The rhythmic form of the chorale in particular often underwent changes in the course of composition. Bach's chorale melodies and settings are written essentially in quarter-note motion, but his sources for these melodies were often notated differently.[3] It has been mentioned that Bach first notated the melody of BWV 43/11 in 3/2 meter. In BWV 77/6, too, Bach apparently began to write out the melody in half-note values.[4] On the other hand, a correction of the first note of the melody in BWV 119/9 (P 878) from a quarter-note to a half-note suggests that Bach momentarily considered entering the melody in quarter-notes before deciding on half-note motion. These changes, of course, affect the notation only and can hardly be considered "compositional." At most they may have affected the tempo at which the chorale movements were to be performed, but this is not demonstrable.

It is clear, too, from BWV 65/7 that the barring of the chorale melodies was not preestablished or at any rate inviolable. In the concluding chorale of BWV 105, scored for four-part chorus and obbligato strings, Bach evidently did not conceive the idea of having instrumental interludes between the phrases of the chorale stanza until he had already written out the outer voices of the two *Stollen*,

[3] The *Neu Leipziger Gesangbuch* (Vopelius, 1682), for example, usually notates the melodies in half-note values.

[4] See Sketch No. 54, Final Version.

IV. "Nun ich weiß ," BWV 105, Movement 6, mm. 1-14.
Autograph, P 99, f. 9v. By courtesy of the Deutsche Staatsbibliothek,
Berlin, German Democratic Republic

V. "Nun ich weiß ," BWV 105, Movement 6, mm. 15-24.
Autograph, P 99, f. 10r. By courtesy of the Deutsche Staatsbibliothek,
Berlin, German Democratic Republic

but had not yet written down the melody of the *Abgesang.* To accommodate the interludes, Bach had to rebar the two *Stollen,* adding half-measure rests between the phrases of the melody.

Original barring

Revised barring

The rebarrings in BWV 65/7 and 105/6 reveal further that the barlines in the Bach chorales have little metrical significance but serve mainly for visual orientation. In BWV 105/6, in fact, the two *Stollen* within each version are barred differently and thus would have different metrical structures if the barlines implied accentuation. It seems clear from this example that Bach did not recognize any accentual distinction between the first and third beats or the second and fourth beats in 4/4 meter. But in no instance did he bring about a shift from the odd to the even beats of a measure or vice versa when rebarring a chorale melody in simple setting. The rebarrings suggest also that the fermatas in the Bach chorales do indicate a prolongation of the final tone of each phrase. This would explain how, for example, Bach was able to change the value of the note under the fermata in BWV 65/7 so casually.[5]

[5] The meaning of the fermata in Bach's chorale settings has never been clarified. Arthur Mendel has sketched the problem in the foreword of his vocal score edition of the *St. John Passion* (New York, 1951), pp. xx–xxi. Future attempts to resolve the fermata question should respect such obvious subdivisions within the chorale genre as organ or choral setting, simple four-part harmonization or one with obbligato instruments and interludes. Such studies should also take into account the date of composition, manuscript evidence, and pertinent testimony on contemporary practice.

In BWV 65/7 the notated shortening of m. 13, note 1 was a delayed correction, introduced only after Bach had decided to rebar mm. 13–17. Bach did, however, occasionally make analogous changes at once, again in order to permit the chorale melody to end on the "right" beat of the measure. In BWV 179/6 (P 146), m. 12, note 3, the soprano melody was changed from a half-note to a quarter-note. The chorale, which began with an upbeat, thereby ends properly on the third beat of the measure. The same correction (half-note changed to quarter-note) was made in m. 8, note 3 of BWV 40/3 (P 63). Since all phrases in this chorale begin on the upbeat and end with a quarter-note on the third beat of the measure, it is possible that the writing of a half-note in m. 8 was due to carelessness, perhaps the result of Bach's having momentarily copied literally from his source.

The final three notes of the chorale melody in BWV 59/3 (P 161) were originally notated ♩ ♩ ♩̂ ‖ in the first violin part. This reading was then changed to ♩ ♩ ♩̂. ‖, again perhaps mainly to complement the opening upbeat of the movement. If Bach's intention, however, was merely to have an orthographically "correct" notation for the sake of the upbeat structure, then he could have corrected the final measure to ♩ ♩ ♩̂ ‖. It therefore seems more likely that the correction was compositional in nature, and was introduced to bring about a measured retard in the final measures of the piece.

There are also instances where the rhythmic form of the chorale melody has been more strikingly recast. In BWV 56/5 (P 118),[6] the quarter-rests at the beginning of both phrases of the *Stollen* were crowded into the measures that originally began ♩ ♩ or perhaps ▬ ♩ ♩. The characteristic syncopation of the final reading, which underlines by rhythmic means the text parallelism of the exhortation *Komm* at the beginning of both phrases, was therefore an afterthought.

[6] See the facsimile edition (Drei Masken Verlag, Munich, 1921), final page.

The melodic contour of the chorale melodies was also at times subject to revision. It seems that on two occasions Bach confused the readings of two variant sources for the chorale melody "O Welt ich muß dich lassen." In the concluding chorale of Cantata 44, *So sei nun, Seele, deine* (P 148), the final tone of the identical second and fifth phrases—m. 4, note 2, and m. 10, note 2[7]—was in each case originally c″, before being changed to a′:

In the concluding chorale of Cantata 13 (P 45/4) the identical notes—m. 4.2 and m. 10.2—were corrected. Although in both places in BWV 13/6 it seems that a c″ was crossed out and changed to a′ as in BWV 44/7, a tablature letter *c* (!) was written above m. 4.2, just as a tablature letter *a* was written beneath m. 10.2. Of the ten Bach settings of this chorale melody printed in Terry 1929 (Nos. 300–309) one further setting (No. 303) retains the cadential form of a rising instead of a falling second in the second phrase. The fifth phrase, however, ends with a falling second. The melodic version of No. 303 (=BWV 393), with a dissimilar approach to the cadence in the otherwise identical second and fifth phrases, agrees then with the version of BWV 13/6.

In BWV 48/3 (P 109) the closing measures of the chorale were reworked so that the original cadence pattern:

was altered to

The correction, although similar to that at the end of BWV 59/3, reveals in this case not a decision to write out a retard but rather a desire to extend the

---

[7] From this point on the formulation "m. 4, note 2," etc., will often be given in the abbreviated form

"m. 4.2," etc., i.e., the same formulation used in Volume II.

final cadence on the word *büßen* ("to atone") with descending chromatic melismas in the middle parts. The striking epilog was therefore an afterthought.

BWV 48/3 (P 109), concluding measures

The descending fourth b′♭, a′♭, g′♭, f′ in the alto part made it necessary for Bach to omit the leading tone a′♮ from the first form of the melody. The formulation of the closing tones of this chorale, the melody "Ach Gott und Herr," was in any case apparently not fixed. In Bach's other four-part setting of the chorale (in C major) the final measure of the melody is simply the descent d″, c″.[8]

BWV 255, "Ach Gott und Herr," final measure

[8] See Riemenschneider 1941, No. 40, and Terry 1929, No. 5.

More significant was Bach's decision to disturb the exact identity of the two *Stollen* of BWV 105/6.

BWV 105/6, mm. 1–11, final version[9]

Bach altered the fourth note of the melody from b′♭ to b′♮[10] in order to accommodate the descending chromatic bass line that effects the transition from the conclusion of the preceding aria in B-flat major by way of c and d to the G minor tonality of the chorale. The ascending scalar motion of the bass in the second *Stollen* clearly presents an antithesis to the motion of the first phrase.[11] Here it is not transitional but rather confirms the tonality of G minor; the chromaticism of the first phrase of the chorale is replaced by the primary I, IV, and V harmonies of the Aeolian mode. The straightforward harmonic and tonal context of the second *Stollen* obviously called for the natural minor third, b♮; this new harmonic context, in turn, was presumably called forth by the chorale text: the tormented conscience in *Stollen I:*

> Nun, ich weiß, du wirst mir stillen
> Mein Gewissen, das mich plagt.

[9] The third of the D major chords in m. 2 (fourth quarter) and m. 8 (second quarter) is provided by the obbligato Violin 1 part. The lack of harmonic self-sufficiency of the four vocal parts may explain why this harmonization of the famous "Jesu, der du meine Seele" melody is not included in editions of the "371 four-voice chorales" nor in the eighteenth-century collections published by C.P.E. Bach from which these modern editions are descended.

[10] There was originally a ♮ sign before the corresponding note of the second *Stollen* (m. 7.2) as well, but it was later smudged out.

[11] Note the inflection of the line after reaching the seventh degree of the scale, which corresponds to an inflection in the first phrase.

contrasted with the comfort of *Stollen II:*

> Es wird deine Treu erfüllen,
> Was du selber hast gesagt:

The dotted rhythm of the melody in m. 7 seems also to have been corrected from four equal quarter-notes, which would have agreed with the rhythmic form of the first *Stollen.* The correction converts the b'♭ into a non-harmonic ascending passing tone which continues the rising eighth-note motion of the lower voices in mm. 6 and 7.

BWV 105/6 is the only chorale among the 56 *Barform* chorales preserved in autograph scores in which Bach made a correction to remove the literal melodic identity of the two *Stollen.* In most settings of a *Barform* chorale, in fact, the harmonizations as well as the melodic forms of the two *Stollen* are identical. Bach generally notated therefore only one *Stollen* and indicated the second with a repeat sign. The only two exceptions to this typical format (besides BWV 105/6) are BWV 24/6 (P 44/4), which like BWV 105/6 is scored for four-part chorus with instrumental interludes between each chorale phrase, and BWV 40/6 (P 63).

BWV 40/6, mm. 1–8, final version

Bach originally planned to compose BWV 40/6 in conventional *Barform* and wrote out the movement in the usual manner, with repeat signs after m. 4 in all voices and a double text for the two *Stollen* entered under the soprano part.[12] After completing the piece, or, in any event, after having laid out the systems and written out the entire soprano melody, Bach decided to harmonize the second *Stollen* (mm. 5–8) independently, and added the new measures after the end of the movement. (See the facsimile on the following page.)

This decision affected the structure of the *Bar.* The two *Stollen* now stand in an antithetical relationship. As in BWV 105/6, the harmonization of the second

---

[12] The melody is actually not a *Bar* but an A A B B form. Bach, however, clearly conceived the chorale at first as a *Bar.*

VI. "Schüttle deinen Kopf und sprich," BWV 40, Movement 6.
Autograph, P 63, f. 8r. By courtesy of the Deutsche Staatsbibliothek,
Berlin, German Democratic Republic

Stollen forms a contrast with that of the first. In Cantata 105 the first *Stollen* was set chromatically and the second diatonically; in Cantata 40 this relationship is reversed. Here it was the highly affective text of the second *Stollen—was erneurst du deinen Stich, machst mir angst und bange—*that may have motivated Bach to give these measures an independent harmonization. The first *Stollen* is set diatonically and expresses in the two phrases the descending fourth bass motion from the tonic to the dominant d′, c′, b♭, a in both large-scale terms (mm. 1.1, 2.3, 4.1, 4.2) and in immediate succession (mm. 3–4); the second *Stollen* completes the exposition of the D minor tonality with a chromatic descent through the lower pentachord of the D minor scale (mm. 7–8) (ending on e♭, d, in analogy to the b♭, a ending of the first *Stollen*), after an introductory chromatic ascent from f to a (mm. 5–7.1).

In both the BWV 105/6 and BWV 40/6 settings, then, the decision not to repeat the first *Stollen* had important structural ramifications. On the most immediate level the two *Stollen* are brought into an antithetical relationship manifested in a dramatic contrast of harmonic character. At the same time, however, Bach managed to integrate the two *Stollen* on another level concerned with the exposition and establishment of the tonality.

Corrections of the Bass Line

In drafting the bass line two conflicting criteria had to be fulfilled simultaneously. The bass, as an exposed outer voice, had to satisfy the requirements of good melodic construction and at the same time clarify the harmonic course of the movement. Bach usually struck at once, to his satisfaction, a proper equilibrium of the harmonic and melodic tendencies of the bass. Corrections in the bass line serve as often to strengthen the one as the other.

In BWV 105/6 Bach was concerned primarily with the bass as a melodic line. The continuo and bass parts of the opening measures were reworked as follows in order to achieve the unbroken chromatic descent discussed above.

First version

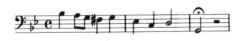

Final version[13]

[13] The elaboration of the cadential ♩|♩ V-I to ♩♩|♩ II⁶-V-I in m. 2 is encountered also in BWV 40/8, m. 4.1.

The continuo line of mm. 9–11 was changed from

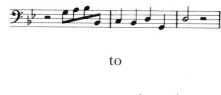

to

again to enhance the linear interest of the part. In mm. 18–19 of the same chorale Bach originally had written a long eighth-note passage in the continuo, rising through the tenth B♭ to d′ and balancing the descent of an eleventh in mm. 15–16:

But this ascent caused parallel octaves with the soprano, and Bach was obliged to change m. 19 to ♩ ♫ ♩ g, f, e♭, d.[14] There are also occasions where Bach replaced a "linearly" conceived bass part, i.e., consisting primarily of stepwise motion, with a more structural version represented by the introduction of larger intervals carrying harmonic significance. In BWV 190/7 (P 127), m. 17, the bass line was changed from a clearly melodic descent to the cadence tone:

to the more harmonic

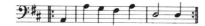

[14] In mm. 9–11, and again in m. 19, the bass has the final reading only, indicating that Bach, in these passages, drafted and corrected the continuo part before the bass. Of the twenty chorales which have an independent staff for the continuo part and in which corrections shed light on the question whether the bass was derived from the continuo or vice versa, seventeen contain evidence that the bass was written first.

In BWV 119/9 (P 878), Bach changed and strengthened the functionality of the bass line of mm. 13–14 from

to

presumably to avoid arriving on a $^6_3$ chord on e at the beginning of m. 15 below the e″ of the cantus firmus:

Such a correction reveals, incidentally, that the reason a particular reading was rejected is at times perhaps not to be found by considering the reading itself but by considering where it was leading. In the passage above, the objectionable note was never written. Conceivably many unexplainable corrections represent the beginning of a train of thought which was rejected before its objectionable features were written down. This is particularly possible in the case of single-note corrections.

Corrections of the Inner Parts

Compositional corrections in the inner voices of simple chorales are mostly restricted to the addition of ornamental tones which add to the melodic interest of the part in which they are inserted, or combine with similar diminution tones in other voices to produce a background rhythmic fabric usually one note-value quicker than the syllable-bearing rhythm of the soprano, or improve the sonority or voice-leading relationships in a passage.

In BWV 119/9 (P 878), the fifth measure of the tenor part was changed from ♩ ♩ a, a to ♪♪♪♪ a, c′, b, a.

BWV 119/9, mm. 4–6

The new reading relieves the otherwise undifferentiated half-note rhythm in the opening measures of the phrase and adds to the harmonic interest of the measure: the simple succession of a D major and a D minor triad is embellished with the addition of a seventh to the first and an accented passing tone to the second chord. At the same time the original lack of melodic and rhythmic motion of the upper parts (soprano: d″, d″; alto: a′, a′; tenor: a, a) has been alleviated.

The characteristically active inner parts of BWV 179/6, "Ich armer Mensch" (P 146),[15] were apparently an afterthought. The reading of the alto, m. 1, at first began simply

This was then reworked into a rather free contrapuntally figured line

introducing an elaborated-suspension technique which is also typical of this chorale setting.

Diminution tones, however, were often added to satisfy grammatical needs rather than to add to the melodic, harmonic, or rhythmic interest of a phrase. The quarter-notes added in both the alto and tenor parts of mm. 14 and 15 of BWV 119/9 serve mostly a grammatical function. Measures 14 and 15 of the chorale originally read

---

[15] See Riemenschneider 1941, No. 339.

and were changed to[16]

The alto part was changed to avoid parallel octaves with the bass and to represent the third of the chord on the fourth beat of the measure. The tenor correction produces better chord-doubling in m. 14.4 (doubled root rather than doubled fifth) and avoids parallel fifths with the bass in the approach to the new reading of m. 15.1. The new tenor reading in m. 15 replaces the empty-sounding tripled root of the first reading, which was combined with the equally unsonorous spacing of an octave between alto and tenor.

Such grammatical corrections—those involving voice leading, the disposition of chord tones and chord-tone doubling—can be studied most appropriately in Bach's simple chorale settings, since it is in the chorales that grammatical problems are encountered in their least disguised form. In the more elaborate movements, arias and choruses, these problems are incidental; in the chorale they represent a predominant part of the compositional task. For, as has been mentioned, melody, form, texture, and scoring are all essentially predetermined. Consequently, the "compositional" problems focus mainly on the invention of an effective and adequate bass line and on the choice of sonorities, while the fixed number of real voices moving in essentially note-against-note style makes the problems of voice leading particularly acute.

It would be possible to present a number of examples similar to that taken from BWV 119/9, mm. 14–15, illustrating Bach's relatively infrequent difficulties with grammar. But such examples taken individually would do no more than demonstrate that Bach did occasionally have such difficulties. The following tabulation, therefore, intends to present in statistical form the results of an analysis of the corrections in 34 four-part chorales to determine the relative frequency of the various types of grammatical corrections (1) in comparison with one another and (2) in comparison with the number of corrections of a more strictly compositional nature. The 34 chorales belong to the early period of Bach's career and represent all the extant chorale autographs of the pre-Leipzig period plus those of the first Leipzig *Jahrgang*. Not only the simple four-part chorale settings are included but also four-part settings with obbligato instruments. But in the latter cases, only corrections in those measures in which the chorus is active

---

[16] The reconstruction of the original reading assumes that Bach did not compose the alto and tenor parts until he had corrected the bass part, as reproduced on p. 83.

have been included in the tabulation, and in the instrumental parts of those measures only corrections of a grammatical nature were taken into account.

The 34 chorales are:

BWV	12/7	179/6	40/6
	*61/6	*77/6	†40/8
	*185/6	119/9	190/7
	*155/5	*138/3	†65/2
	*147/6	138/7	*65/7
	†22/5	†48/3	*81/7
	59/3	*48/7	*144/3
	75/7	*194/6	*144/6
	76/7	*194/12	*67/4
	24/6	*90/5	*67/7
	105/6	*40/3	*86/6
			†44/7

The material at hand eludes statistical manipulation for several reasons. First, it is always possible that a number of corrections were undetected; second, it is often extremely difficult to say what exactly constitutes *one* correction. A corrective gesture may consist of changing a single note (of large or small rhythmic value) or an entire passage, that is, a series of notes regarded either horizontally or vertically. For both these reasons it is not really possible to establish the exact number of corrections in the chorales or in any other genre. Finally, the correction of one note may accomplish more than one purpose and would therefore be counted more than once. In the following tabulation, then, the "counting" of corrections was necessarily inexact, since in every case the writer had to decide anew whether a particular configuration of corrected notes represented one or more corrections, and then whether each of these corrections fulfilled one or more roles. Most characteristic, in fact, of any Bach corrective gesture is its economy. This can be illustrated with the example from BWV 119/9, mm. 14–15 considered above. It is likely that the correction of the three notes in the alto and tenor in these measures was one "chain reaction" correction, i.e., that changing three notes represented for Bach just one corrective gesture. In the tables below, however, these corrections are entered in six categories:

A.1a i: addition of a fifth to achieve full sonority—Tenor, m. 15.1
A.1a ii: addition of a third to achieve full sonority—Alto, m. 14.2
A.3a: avoid parallel octaves—Alto, m. 14.2
A.3b: avoid parallel fifths—Tenor, m. 14.4
A.5a: change of spacing from open to close position—Tenor, m. 15.1
C.1:   addition of diminution tones—Tenor, m. 14.4

Nevertheless, while the tabulation is by no means statistically precise, it does succeed in suggesting the distribution and frequency of the motives leading to corrections in the simple chorales.

Categories of Corrections

Total

A. Chord-Doubling Within the Same Chord
   1. a) To achieve full sonority
        i) add fifth   8
        ii) add other tone   4
     b) Change of chord tone within incomplete sonority
        i) fifth changed to third   3
        ii) other   0
   2. Full sonority sacrificed for sake of line
     a) formative compositional change (rather than grammatical)   5
     b) to avoid parallel fifths or octaves, etc.   2
   3. Voice leading changed, no loss of full sonority
     a) to avoid parallel octaves   20
     b) to avoid parallel fifths   10
     c) formative compositional change   12
   4. To change doublings within full triad or seventh sonority
     a) to achieve doubled root   2
     b) to achieve doubled third   5
     c) to achieve doubled fifth   5
     d) to avoid doubled leading tone   1
   5. Change of Spacing
     a) open to close position   5
     b) close to open position   3
     c) for formative compositional reasons (e.g., *Stimmtausch*)   4

B. Change of Chord
   1. Same root
     a) seventh changed to triad   7
     b) triad changed to seventh   2
     c) major triad changed to minor triad   0
     d) minor triad changed to major triad   2
     e) altered chord changed to diatonic chord   0
     f) diatonic chord changed to altered chord   1
     g) change of position
        i) root changed to $\frac{6}{3}$ 2
        ii) $\frac{6}{3}$ changed to $\frac{5}{3}$ 4

   2. Change of root
      a) root change of third   15
      b) change of fifth or fourth   9
      c) other   1

C. Diminution Tones, Non-harmonic Tones
   1. Added   22
   2. Deleted
      a) to avoid parallels   1
      b) for sake of texture, contour, motive   5
   3. Suspensions
      a) added   4
      b) deleted   3
   4. Non-harmonic tones changed
      a) to avoid harsh dissonances   6
      b) for sake of melodic line or voice leading   8

D. Rhythmic or Motivic Corrections, Compositional Corrections   40

E. Corrections in the Chorale Melody   22

F. Corrections of Notation   2

G. Corrections of Text, Stemming, and Beaming   12
                                                                 ___
                                        Grand Total   257

The tabulation reveals among other things that 1) only about 10 percent of the corrections are concerned with removing parallel octaves or fifths, 2) that about twice as many changes result in fuller sonority (complete representation of all chord tones) than in the sacrifice of full sonority for linear considerations, 3) that most corrections do not affect the original choice of chord, 4) that where there is a change of chord, there is usually a change of root, mostly of a third, 5) that among chordal changes that preserve the original root, Bach is more likely to change a seventh to a triad, and a minor triad to a major triad, than the reverse.

The total of 257 corrections may seem to imply that the 34 chorales contain on the average 7 corrections each. This is deceiving; the chorales are usually not so heavily corrected. Only five chorales contain six, seven, or eight corrections (these chorales are indicated by daggers in the list on p. 86, above), while eighteen, or more than half of the chorales tabulated, contain five corrections or less (each of these chorales is marked by an asterisk in the same list.)[17]

[17] On the other hand, four chorales contain more than twenty corrections, but each of these is a relatively elaborate movement with obbligato instrumental parts:

BWV 59/3: with obbligato strings, 28 mm., 8-stave systems, 28 corrections

BWV 76/7: with trumpet and obbligato strings, 17 mm., 9-stave systems, 30 corrections

BWV 105/6: with obbligato strings, 16mm., 8-stave systems, 39 corrections

BWV 138/7: 2 oboes d'amour, strings, 21 mm., 10-stave systems, 23 corrections

CHAPTER V

Autograph Scores of
the Recitatives

I N NO OTHER form does Bach's music approach the early baroque ideal of treating the text as the "mistress" of the music so closely as in the recitative. While this ideal, which theoretically would involve the suppression of an independent musical logic, is never entirely realized in the Bach recitative (just as it was never realized in the best examples of early baroque music), the musical elements in this form are often so strongly bound to the text that it becomes difficult to discern an autonomous musical organization. In a "textbook" recitative an iambic text would be declaimed syllabically in an undifferentiated succession of eighth-notes. In practice, though, there are always departures from this norm such as sixteenth-note groups, dotted rhythms, and other irregular rhythmic patterns that are suggested by the "affect" and prosody of the text and which are introduced to insure a "natural" declamation. Melodic "invention" for its part consists in the main of perhaps a handful of stereotyped opening and closing formulas variously combined with each other and with patterns of tone repetitions and arpeggio figures.[1]

It is perhaps particularly the syllabic, rhythmic, and melodic styles which reveal most strikingly the primacy of the text in the recitative, but there are other indications as well of the relative lack of musical independence. The repetition of thematic sections according to a preexistent and rational scheme, which plays perhaps the most significant role in the establishment of musical form in the eighteenth century, is notably absent in the "pure," i.e., syllabic recitative style, in which there are no arioso sections and elements. At the same time, owing to the recitative's usual harmonic function as a transition between harmonic areas, traditional tonal design does not seem to be present in the majority of Bach's recitative movements.[2]

---

[1] See Melchert 1958, pp. 24–30, esp. p. 25.

[2] Ibid., p. 88. In the following pages of his study Melchert demonstrates that Bach often employs various schematic methods of organizing the succession of key centers in a recitative, such as a series of falling thirds or fifths or the constructions of tonal *Bogen* forms. But such tonal plans are hardly synonymous with what one could call a classical "tonal" organization.

The Order of Events

In view of the singularly dependent nature of its musical elements, it should not be surprising that Bach eventually adopted the practice, when composing either a secco or accompanied recitative, of writing down the complete text in a naturally spaced, legible hand after he had set up the systems for the movement but before he had composed the first note,[3] a procedure totally different from the one we have already observed in the four-part chorales and from the one we shall observe in the arias and choruses. Bach's mature practice of first writing down the text in a recitative is evident not only from the three drafts mentioned on page 66—in which, of course, the fact is absolutely proven, although strictly speaking only for the three examples concerned—but also from the layouts of the completed recitatives in the Leipzig composing scores. Bach wrote only as many words beneath a staff as could be fitted without crowding the text. No regard was paid at the moment to the future musical rendition of the text. As a result, the music in the completed score just as often breaks off at the end of a system in the middle of a measure—after the first, second, or third beats—as after a full measure.[4]

The beginning of the text, furthermore, was often entered directly to the right of the clef, key, and time signature at the beginning of the first system. Therefore, the initial rest (or rests) typical at the beginning of iambic verse settings was often crowded into the space between the time signature and the first note of the composition, or the first note was displaced by the rest to the right of the corresponding word.[5]

It is often the case that a recitative begins with two rests—a quarter-rest preceding an eighth-rest—and that the first rest is obviously crowded while the second is not. This surely means that the quarter-rest was added as an afterthought, i.e., as a correction; its position cannot be attributed solely to a lack of space.[6] Finally, the disposition of text beneath a long melisma indicates that the text was present before the music was written, and that Bach did not yet have the melisma in mind when he wrote down the text. For the words simply continue beneath the melisma, and, as a result, the notes following it momentarily fall behind, i.e., to the right of the corresponding words.[7]

---

[3] This procedure became the rule only in Leipzig.

[4] For easy reference, see the recitatives in the facsimile editions of BWV 135, BWV 56, the Coffee Cantata, BWV 211, or any of the recitatives in the *Christmas Oratorio.*

[5] See again the recitatives in the facsimiles mentioned above—for example, Movement 3 of the *Christmas Oratorio.*

[6] See Movement 25 of the *Christmas Oratorio*

or Movement 1 of the Coffee Cantata. Decisions regarding the length of the rest with which the voice part is to start often gave rise, in fact, to revisions and corrections which will be discussed presently.

[7] See the melismas on *schnellen,* BWV 135/2, m. 9 (facsimile) and on the word *vieler* in BWV 56/2, m. 20. Other examples, taken at random, are BWV 134a/7, m. 6, on the word *Strom* and BWV 194/7,

These characteristics—with the exception of the divided measure at the end of a system—are most often missing in the pre-Leipzig autographs. The accommodation of melismas by the text[8] is usually accurate, the opening rests are not usually crowded, and there is an irregular spacing of the text—crowded where notes are close together or spread out where there are rests between phrases. Instances where the text falls "behind" the corresponding notes of the score testify further that in the pre-Leipzig recitatives the music was usually written down before the words. In BWV 199/1 (Copenhagen), for example, the text runs on beyond the end of the movement into the free space to the right of the double bar. In BWV 163/2 (P 137) there was no room at the end of the third system, concluding with m. 15 of the movement, for the word *deine* below the last two notes of the measure. The word was therefore written below the previous word, *Herr,* since it would otherwise have run off the edge of the page. In a typical Leipzig recitative where the text was written down first, the word would have been entered at the beginning of the next system.

The manuscript of BWV 163 in general displays ideally the characteristics of a recitative autograph in which the notes were written before the text. Each system of BWV 163/2 ends in fact with a full measure—a feature not at all common even in the pre-Leipzig recitatives—while the text is alternately crowded or well spread out in order to obtain an accurate alignment with the corresponding notes. In BWV 163/4 the words *Fleisch und* in m. 6a, alto, like the word *deine* in BWV 163/2, are written below rather than to the right of the preceding words (*bei mir doch*) at the end of the score system. The opening line of text in the alto, mm. 2–4a, is not even written down except for the *incipit ich,* since the music here is a canonic imitation of the soprano part.

These same "pre-Leipzig" characteristics are occasionally found in Leipzig scores as well. But there they are usually an indication that the autograph is a fair or revision copy. In BWV 147/2 (P 102)[9] the text runs considerably after the final note of the tenor part (in m. 18) just as it runs on in BWV 199/1

---

m. 2, *erfreuet.* In BWV 62/3, mm. 5–6, as usual, no room was left in advance for the melisma on *laufen.* This caused the succeeding notes (m. 6.3–5) to fall behind the corresponding words of the text. In this instance, however, Bach drew oblique guide lines from the notes to the corresponding syllables until the alignment was again normal. On the other hand, it should be mentioned that the melismas on the words *gedenke,* BWV 180/6, mm. 9–11, and *zerstreun,* BWV 10/3, mm. 14–15, are perfectly accommodated. In these instances Bach must have planned the melismas while he wrote down the texts and therefore did not enter the final

syllables of the recitatives until he composed the music. Since *gedenke* and *zerstreun* were the last words of the movements concerned (except for the repetition of the final phrase in each case), Bach was still able, as usual, to enter practically the entire texts in advance, despite the planned melismas.

[8] See, for example, the facsimile of BWV 208/1, m. 5, in NBA I/35, p. vii, and the facsimile of BWV 173a/1, m. 6, in NBA I/14, p. vii.

[9] This movement was not entered into the autograph until Bach's Leipzig period.

and shows in general the irregularities of text spacing found in Weimar autographs. In the fourth movement of the cantata large gaps are left in the spacing of the text for the sixteenth-note passages in the continuo in mm. 4, 6, and 8 as well as for the melisma on *Elenden* in m. 9. Otherwise, as in Movement 2, the text is often closely written or it runs beyond the end of a system.

While the Leipzig recitative autographs reveal unambiguously that Bach began their composition by entering the text for the complete movement below the vocal staff, it is not so clear how he then continued. The evidence suggests that Bach drafted the vocal part before he wrote down the continuo part.

In BWV 40/5 (P 63), m. 9, for example, Bach drew the barline directly after the half-note in the alto part and then wrote the conclusion of the alto part in m. 10. The eighth-notes of the continuo and the sixteenth-notes of the strings in the second half of m. 9 could not be accommodated in the space before this barline and extend over it into m. 10.

The alto part of BWV 90/2 (P 83), m. 14, originally outlined a C minor triad in the second half of the measure:

which was changed to the present reading based on a diminished triad on f♯:

The continuo part, with an uncorrected A, was surely not written until the voice part had already been drafted and corrected.

Similarly, the tenor part of Movement 2 of the *Christmas Oratorio*, mm. 15–16, first read:

(Ma)ri - a   sei-nem vertrauten Weibe,

Bach then decided "immediately" (i.e., before writing down a note for the final syllable of *Weibe*) to postpone the entrance of the f♯ minor cadence for another half-measure in order to include the clause *die war schwanger* as part of the same phrase and corrected the reading to

(Ma)ri - a   sei-nem vertrauten Wei-be die war schwanger

The continuo, however, has an uncorrected E♯ at the beginning of m. 16.

In Movement 22 of the same work Bach had written the bass part to the end of the movement in E minor. He then began to compose the continuo part to this original voice part but abandoned it before writing down the concluding cadential tones and transposed the final phrase up a third to G major. Since the bass part was completed in the original draft while the continuo part was not, it is evident that the former was composed first.[10]

These examples only suggest that the voice part was written before the continuo part for a particular passage; other evidence reveals that Bach composed relatively short passages in the voice part before composing the continuo part. It is significant, for example, that the continuo part as well as the vocal part are entered in Sketch No. 160, and that Bach did not work out the entire vocal line for this short recitative before composing the continuo. In Sketch No. 7 a large space was left between notes 7 and 8 of m. 6 of the voice part to avoid colliding with the continuo part of m. 3, notes 2–3. The continuo of m. 3 clearly must have been written down before Bach composed m. 6 of the voice part.[11] Similarly, in BWV 180/6 (PP) a space was left between notes 1 and 2 of m. 5 of the bass part to accommodate the low E in m. 1 of the continuo in the system above. Examples of this kind are numerous.[12]

Bach, then, composed the vocal and continuo parts in alternation. He may have composed the voice line for one text phrase, then the continuo part for this phrase, thereupon composed the voice part for the following phrase, then the continuo part, and so on until the recitative was completed. The available evidence, however, reveals only that the continuo part of one system had already been entered before the vocal part for the next system was written down.

Accompagnato parts were not composed until the vocal and continuo parts were already worked out. There are a number of passages that have corrections in the voice and continuo parts but none in the accompagnato parts whose readings agree only with the final reading of the former parts. BWV 215/6 (P 139), for example, originally ended in D major in the voice and continuo.[13] The accompagnato flute parts, however, have the final B minor reading only.

The appearance of the autograph of BWV 175/5 (see below, p. 102) suggests that the voice (and continuo?) part for the entire movement may have been written down before any portion of the accompagnato parts had been composed.

[10] For the original reading see NBA II/6, KB, p. 45, and p. 98 below.

[11] See the facsimile included with the sketch in Volume II.

[12] Some further instances are: BWV 194/11 (P 43/3): m. 10.2 of the bass was written after m. 6.2 of the continuo. The bass note is placed to the right of its text word in order to avoid the continuo note. BWV 204/1 (P 107): m. 10.1 of the soprano was placed so as not to get in the way of m. 6.2 of the continuo. BWV 9/4 (LC): m. 9.1 of the bass was placed to avoid colliding with m. 5.2 of the continuo.

[13] See NBA I/37, KB, p. 42, and p. 98 below.

The movement thus presents an instance of successive composition.[14] Whether Bach composed all accompanied recitatives in this manner, or whether BWV 175/5 represents an isolated instance of such procedure, is not clear. But since the accompagnato parts are rarely more than written-out thorough bass realizations, BWV 175/5 is hardly a unique case.

It is clear from correction patterns that the accompagnato parts themselves were filled in from top to bottom. A chord tone originally placed in a Violin 1 part, for example, would be crossed out and placed, as the first and final reading, in the second violin or viola parts, and/or a chord tone originally entered in the second violin part would be crossed out and placed in the viola part. The following corrections appear in the string parts of BWV 48/2 (P 109):

m. 2.1, Vn. 1: g′	corrected to	e′♮; Va.: g,	uncorrected
m. 5.2, Vn. 1: b♭	corrected to	d′♭; Va.: b♭,	uncorrected
m. 10.1, Vn. 1: d′(♯?)	corrected to	f′♯;	
Vn. 2: b	corrected to	d′♯; Va.: b,	uncorrected
m. 11.1, Vn. 1: e′	corrected to	g′♯;	
Vn. 2: b	corrected to	e′; Va.: b,	uncorrected
m. 4.2, Vn. 2: g	corrected to	e′; Va.: g,	uncorrected
m. 13.2, Vn. 2: e′♭	corrected to	c′; Va.: e♭,	uncorrected
m. 14.1, Vn. 2: d′	corrected to	g′; Va.: d′,	uncorrected

The autograph scores of the recitatives reveal, finally, that Bach often thought of the accompanying instruments and hence the basic harmonic rhythm as proceeding essentially in half-note values and consequently composed these parts one half-measure at a time. The original half-note readings were then either subdivided into smaller units—in a manner and for reasons to be discussed below—or tied together to form whole notes or held tones of even greater value.[15]

---

[14] It is just possible, though, that the barlines had been drawn through the voice and continuo staves before the strings were composed and that the continuo was entered still later.

[15] Corrections of this kind are observable in approximately 150 recitative autographs. Within these scores and the remaining ones there are, of course, countless uncorrected whole notes, quarter-notes, and so on. The present paragraph does not intend to suggest that Bach always or even customarily composed the accompanying parts of recitatives in half-measure strokes (there are too many instances where he obviously did not) but simply—as the text states—that he often did so.

For examples of tied half-notes instead of whole notes in published facsimiles of recitative autographs, see the *Christmas Oratorio*, Mvt. 2, mm. 11, 15, 17; Mvt. 30, m. 9; Mvt. 61, Oboe 2, m. 3; the Coffee Cantata, Mvt. 3, mm. 5, 7; Mvt. 5, mm. 2, 6, 10; Mvt. 9, m. 7; BWV 197a/5, mm. 3, 6, 10 (NBA I/2, p. viii); BWV 128/3, m. 69, viola (NBA I/12, p. x); BWV 120a/5, m. 15 (NBA I/33, p. vi); BWV 213/8, mm. 2, 5 (NBA I/36, p. vii); Sketch No. 7, m. 4; Sketch No. 116, final version, m. 4; and the transcription of BWV 174/3, mm. 6, 11, viola; m. 13, continuo (NBA I/14, KB, pp. 77–78).

Harmonic Revisions

It was mentioned during the preceding discussion that Movement 22 of the *Christmas Oratorio* and BWV 215/6 originally concluded in tonalities different from those of the final versions. Similar revisions of the concluding harmonies occur in the autograph scores of eleven recitatives. The following tabulation of these movements reproduces in diagrammatic form the concluding harmony of the movement preceding the recitative, the opening harmony of the recitative, the original reading of the concluding cadence (in parentheses), the final reading, and the opening chord or tonality of the following movement:

1. BWV 76/9 (P 67):	E ‖	F♯ [dom. of Bm]	(Bm) Am	‖ Am
2. BWV 138/2 (P 158):	Bm ‖	Em	(F♯m) Em	‖ Em-Bm
3. BWV 42/5 (P 55):	Bm ‖	D	(Bm) Am	‖ A
4. BWV 36c/4 (P 43/2):	Bm ‖	B [dom. of E]	(A) D	‖ D
5. BWV 205/4 (P 173):	A ‖	G♯ [dom. of C♯m]	(C♯m) Bm	‖ Bm
6. BWV 102/2 (P 97):	Gm ‖	B♭	(F) B♭	‖ B♭
7. BWV 17/6 (P 45/5):	D ‖	F♯ [dom. of Bm]	(A) C♯m	‖ A
8. BWV 213/8 (P 125):	Em ‖	Bm	(G) Am	‖ Am
9. BWV 215/6 (P 139):	A ‖	F♯m	(D) Bm	‖ Bm
10. BWV 248/22 (P 32):	G ‖	G	(Em) G	‖ G
11. BWV 211/5 (P 141):	Bm ‖	E	(D) Bm	‖ Em

As the tabulation reveals, in nine of the eleven movements the final cadence was changed to conclude on the tonic of the following movement.[16] Since this is by far the most frequent relationship between the final chord of a recitative and the tonality of the following movement,[17] these corrections suggest that Bach, unlike Handel (see above p. 66) wrote the recitatives, at least in these instances, before he had composed the succeeding formal movements, or was even certain of their tonality.

The comparative freedom and flexibility governing key succession within the recitative permitted Bach to recast the concluding tonality of the movement with a minimum of revision. The cadences of the eleven pieces are reworked as follows.

---

[16] The revision of BWV 17/6 is therefore particularly puzzling. Bach may have been interested in creating an important pivotal role for the mediant harmony in the tonal plan of the cantata:

MOVEMENT

The symmetries and internal correspondences in this design are both numerous and obvious.

[17] Melchert 1958, p. 86.

BWV 76/9, mm. 8–10

BWV 138/2, mm. 10–11. (The continuo was composed after
the correction was made.)

BWV 42/5, m. 10. (The voice part in m. 10, evidently
leading toward a final cadence in Bm in m. 11, was
corrected before the continuo part was entered.)

BWV 36c/4, mm. 11–12. (The continuo part was composed after
the correction was made.)

BWV 205/4, mm. 4–6, Tenor and Continuo; see NBA I/38, KB, p. 23.

BWV 102/2, mm. 12–13

BWV 17/6, mm. 15–17. (The continuo was composed after
the correction was made.)

BWV 213/8, mm. 8–9

BWV 215/6, mm. 17–18

BWV 248/22, mm. 5–6

BWV 211/5, mm. 20–21

It sufficed merely to change the final few tones of the voice (and continuo)
part—at most the final phrase of the movement—often[18] by simple transposition

---

[18] In BWV 76/9, BWV 102/2, BWV 213/8,
BWV 215/6, BWV 42/5, BWV 17/6, BWV
248/22.

to suggest the new tonality; for a key center in Bach's recitative was in effect "established" simply by placing a dominant function before the chord to be tonicized. Harmonic progression in the recitative consists, in fact, overwhelmingly of the mere succession of dominant harmonies or the alternation of tonics and dominants.[19] The correction of the concluding tonality, as a consequence, rarely had ramifications reaching further back into the movement.

ON AT LEAST four occasions Bach revised the opening tonality of a recitative; twice this correction was immediate. In BWV 175/3 (P 75) only the first tone in both the tenor and continuo was changed:

$$\text{from} \qquad \begin{matrix} e' \\ A\sharp \end{matrix} \qquad \text{to} \qquad \begin{matrix} f'\natural \\ G\sharp \end{matrix} \ .$$

Similarly, in BWV 248/13 the first two repeated notes of the tenor and the whole-note in the continuo were transposed from

$$\begin{matrix} gg \\ B \end{matrix} \qquad \text{to} \qquad \begin{matrix} aa \\ c\sharp \end{matrix} \ .$$

In the two remaining recitatives Bach had more definitely "established" the opening tonality of the movement before he decided to reject it. The first three measures of BWV 208/8 originally began in B♭. Bach then wrote the directions *eine 4te tieffer* and *Quarte tieffer* above the soprano and continuo parts respectively, thereby transposing the beginning of the movement to the key of F.[20] The concluding C major chord of the preceding movement now serves as a dominant to the opening F major of the recitative.[21]

In BWV 33/4 the opening four measures, i.e., the first three phrases, were originally written one tone lower, in G major, then corrected, essentially by transposition, up one tone to A minor.[22] Here again Bach replaced a less frequent tonal relationship between the preceding movement (here in C major) and the beginning of the recitative with a more common one, for the relationship of tonic—relative minor between the two adjacent movements is the most usual one.[23]

The principle of harmonic progression that permitted Bach to change the final harmony of a recitative with so little difficulty also enabled him to change the key of internal cadences. Such corrections are not infrequent. The vocal cadence

[19] Melchert 1958, pp. 91–94.
[20] See NBA I/35, KB, p. 21.
[21] According to Melchert 1958, pp. 85–86, the relationship of a perfect fourth between the conclusion of the preceding movement and the begin-

ning of a recitative is rather frequent, while the relationship of a minor seventh is rare.
[22] See NBA I/21, KB, p. 45.
[23] Melchert 1958, p. 85.

in the twelfth measure of BWV 65/3 (P 147) was deflected with a minimum
of revision from A minor to G major.

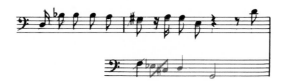

M. 11

The most far-reaching transposition correction of this kind occurs in BWV
204/7 (P 107) in which mm. 3.1–18.5 were originally written one tone higher.

Mm. 2–4

M. 18

Bach changed his mind after having completed the first phrase of the arioso
section of the movement. At this point he evidently realized that the harmonic
plan of the foregoing recitative section had emphasized the sharp keys and led
in fact to an extended arioso beginning in E minor. Bach may have felt that
such a tonal progression was inappropriate in a work which was otherwise cast
in the simple flat keys of F, B♭, and d minor.

Corrections of the harmonic scheme were often made in the service of the
text, to provide a more meaningful connection between phrases. In Movement
2 of the *Christmas Oratorio,* discussed above, the harmonic rhythm of the phrase
was retarded in order to incorporate the parenthetical clause *die war schwanger*
in the foregoing phrase. Similarly, in BWV 134a/7, mm. 7–9, Bach had originally
planned to introduce the B♭ or G minor harmony at the beginning of m. 9,
but then decided to unite the two lines of text "Ja, sei durch mich dem teursten
Leopold | zu vieler tausend Wohl und Lust" by retaining the F–F7 harmony
of m. 8 through m. 9 as well,[24] and postponing the G minor cadence until the
beginning of m. 10.

[24] See NBA I/35, KB, p. 77.

Phrases could be brought into closer relationship also by the selection of the proper type of cadence. Bach had first placed a relatively "closed" cadence of the type

at the end of the line *mit Kälte, Frost und Schnee* in BWV 205/2, mm. 11–12, but changed it to an "open" cadence ending on an F♯ diminished seventh chord in order to propel the musical line forward into the concluding text phrase of the sentence, and to reserve the finality of a full cadence for the end of the sentence in mm. 13–14.[25]

On the other hand, Bach changed a semi-cadence of Phrygian character at the end of the first full sentence of BWV 135/2 (see the facsimile) to a more appropriate full cadence:

Rhythmic Revisions

Since the rhythmic style of the recitative presents for the most part a relatively uninterrupted flow of neutral eighth-notes which faithfully preserves and reflects the irregular verse lengths characteristic of the recitative text, the 4/4 meter in this form is in a sense arbitrary and functions here, as in the chorales, to a large extent solely as a means of external, visual orientation. A number of corrections of rhythm apparently reveal nothing more than Bach's efforts to fit the rhythmic declamation of the text line into this 4/4 framework. Thus the final two notes of m. 12 of BWV 208/5 (P 42/3) were lengthened from eighth-notes to quarter-notes in order to "fill out" the measure. In the following movement of the same work a quarter-rest after the third note of m. 4, which would have created a five-beat measure, was crossed out.

The first movement of the Cöthen cantata BWV 173a, *Durchlauchtster Leopold* (P 42/2), began with the five-beat measure: ♩. Bach evidently never noticed this anomaly until he prepared the parody composition BWV 173, *Erhöhtes Fleisch und Blut,* at least two years later; for the correction of the rhythm of the final two notes of the measure from ♩ ♪ to ♪ ♪ appears in the same

---

[25] See the transcription in NBA I/38, KB, p. 21.

blackish ink that Bach used in Leipzig to enter the parody text in the score of the secular work.[26]

Bach, then, often failed to regard the number of beats in a measure when he was actively engaged in composing the vocal line of a recitative. At times he never became aware of irregular measure lengths at all, and one occasionally finds uncorrected measures in the autograph scores with more or less than four quarters. Two three-and-a-half-beat measures have already been reproduced in the discussion of final cadences. (See m. 9 of BWV 76/9 and m. 16 of BWV 17/6, pp. 97f. above.) Measure 5 of Movement 13 from the *Christmas Oratorio* has the rhythm ♪♪♩ ♩ , ♪♪♪. This five-beat measure was never corrected by Bach and appears in the original parts in exactly this form.[27] Measure 7 of BWV 190/4 (P 127) has an uncorrected total of four and a half beats:

$$| \; ♪ \; ♪♪ \, , \; ♪ \; ♪♪ \, ♪ \, , \, ♪ \; |.[28]$$

Bach, however, usually noticed such irregularities and corrected them.

Bach's confusion about the lengths of measures is revealed further in the autographs of over fifty recitative movements in which barlines were initially placed after the wrong beat. Not all these examples are the result of inattention or absent-mindedness. It is often clear that Bach simply had a false notion of the number of beats in the measure he was composing and drew the barline too hastily. In BWV 35/6 (P 86), for example, Bach mistakenly placed the first barline of the movement after the seventh eighth-note of the opening measure and the second barline four beats later after the seventh eighth-note of m. 2. He then realized his error and corrected the barring.

Barline confusion often arose when a new system of the score began with the second half of a measure. In BWV 56/2[29] the first system of f. 4r ended after the second quarter of m. 14. Bach considered the beginning of the new system to be the beginning of a new measure and drew a barline after the fourth quarter of the new line, i.e., after m. 15a, and consequently barred the remainder of the movement incorrectly as a result of this initial mistake. He presumably realized his error while rereading the movement, crossed out the misplaced barlines, and rebarred the movement from m. 14 on.

The second half of m. 6 in BWV 175/5 (P 75) begins a new page of the autograph (f. 4v). Bach drew barlines after mm. 7a, 8a, 9a, 10a, 11a, 12a, and 13a, but through the bass and continuo staves only. He caught his error when he went back to the top of the page to compose the instrumental parts. Since there are no incorrectly placed barlines in the instrumental parts, it is evident,

---

[26] See the facsimile in NBA I/14, p. vii. The contrast in ink colors is not evident in this plate.

[27] See NBA II/6, KB, p. 246.

[28] Both the BG and NBA have changed this to ♪♪♪,♪♪♪♪,♪. See the facsimile in NBA I/4, p. vii.

[29] See the facsimile edition.

furthermore, from this example that Bach composed the voice part (and perhaps the continuo part as well) from m. 6b to the end of the movement and perhaps for the entire recitative, before he had worked out the accompagnato parts.[30]

It may well have been the barring chaos of Sketch No. 7 (BWV 9/6) that compelled Bach to rewrite the entire movement. He probably did not decide to reject the initial version of the recitative until after he had composed the concluding chorale of the cantata. Again he no doubt discovered that m. 14 of Movement 6 contained only two beats when he reviewed the complete movement. He thereupon decided to rewrite the recitative on a new page after the conclusion of Movement 7 in order to normalize the barring and rework a number of details, particularly in mm. 8–11 of the voice part.

But even while composing the first version, Bach had corrected the barring four times. He had begun to draw a barline after the third beat of m. 6—at the end of a system—but immediately caught this error. He had begun also to draw a barline after the third beat of m. 16 and had mistakenly placed a barline after the "ninth" eighth-note of m. 18. The barring correction of mm. 8–14, however, is more complex and involves a compositional correction: the addition of a half-measure. Only after he had composed and barred these seven measures, i.e., the setting of the second full sentence of the text, did Bach realize he had failed to provide the proper musical punctuation after the first sentence. The rests and full cadence interpolated after the words *diss stärcket unsern Glauben wieder* (m. 8), fulfill this function.[31] The abrupt shift to a $^6_3$ chord on E♯ following the A major cadence prepares the next sentence.

Corrections of barline placement were not always of an orthographical or grammatical nature, but often went hand in hand with rhythmic revisions in the vocal part. In order to understand these changes we would do well to consider again the metrical structure of the recitative.

Though the 4/4 meter in the recitative was to a degree arbitrary, it was nevertheless useful in ordering a regular alternation of accented and unaccented eighth-notes falling on the beginning of the quarter-note beat and on the second half of the beat respectively. This alternation afforded a perfect vehicle for the alternating unaccented and accented syllables of the typical iambic text line.

[30] This paragraph is a paraphrase of the description in NBA I/14, KB, p. 195. There are other instances where the beginning of a new system in the score gave rise to incorrect barring. BWV 75/2, m. 9: Bach evidently thought that the new system began with the second half of a measure rather than a complete measure; BWV 75/13, mm. 3–8: Bach had read mm. 2b–3a at the beginning of the second system of the movement as one measure; BWV 138/4, m. 5: crossed-out barline after the second beat. Bach considered the second half of m. 4, with which a new system begins, and m. 5a as forming one measure; BWV 206/2, m. 3b begins a new system. Bach originally drew barlines after mm. 4a and 5a, then noticed the error.

[31] Since relatively long pauses and full cadences usually appear in recitatives after full sentences (see Melchert 1958, pp. 22 and 27), the revision here, though compositional in nature, can be regarded as the correction of an oversight.

As a rule, too, the baroque composer attempted to have the end of each line of poetry or the caesura in longer lines fall on the accented first or third beats of a measure. The normally iambic scansion determined that the vocal part should begin on the unaccented part of the beat, while the length of the line, and the desire to have the phrase end on an odd beat of the measure, in turn determined whether the voice would enter on the weak part of the first or second beats of the measure.

There were, in fact, in the late baroque, certain rules of thumb which codified the various possible recitative beginnings designed to allow the last "long," i.e., accented, syllable to fall on the first or third quarter. G. H. Stölzel's treatise on the recitative (c. 1740) offers a prescription which can be summarized as follows:

> One- to three-syllable lines can begin on any beat and thus may end also on the second or fourth quarter. But if the accented syllable is to fall on the second or fourth quarter, a tonic accent should be placed on this syllable.
>
> Four- and feminine five-syllable lines can begin on any quarter of the measure.
>
> With a ♪♪♪ opening begin on the first or third quarter; with a ♪♪♪ opening begin on the second or fourth quarter.
>
> Six- or seven-syllable lines: begin only on the second or fourth quarter.
>
> Eight- or nine-syllable lines: like four- and five-syllable lines.
>
> Ten- or eleven-syllable lines: like six- and seven-syllable lines.[32]

While Bach's recitatives for the most part adhere to these principles, the autographs often reveal the composer's uncertainty regarding the length of the initial vocal rest and suggest that Bach was not familiar with rules like Stölzel's, or, in any event, never committed such rules to memory or developed the habit of applying them mechanically.

BWV 9/4 (LC), for example, begins with the eleven-syllable line *Doch mußte das Gesetz erfüllet werden,* which, according to Stölzel's rule should begin after the second quarter of the measure. Although Bach's setting consists of a perfectly regular series of eighth-notes, the autograph score reveals that the opening quarter-rest was crowded into the measure as an afterthought. Bach, therefore, did not count syllables in order to calculate in advance the proper starting point of the recitation, but composed the music first; and only some time after he had written the first few notes did he adjust the opening rest to permit the line to end on the proper beat of the measure.

Movement 2 of the same cantata begins with the six-syllable half-line *Gott gab uns ein Gesetz.* Here, too, the opening quarter-rest may have been added subsequently, but it may have been written above the staff only because the

---

[32] See Steger 1962, p. 124.

text was entered close to the time signature in the manner described above, and Bach wished to place the first note in reasonably good alignment with the first syllable. The opening quarter-rest in BWV 56/2, preceding the six-syllable line *Mein Wandel auf der Welt,* was again apparently entered as an afterthought.

Interpolated quarter-rests often appear at the beginning of internal lines as well as at the beginning of the composition. In BWV 41/3 (P 874) the opening rest of m. 5, before the ten-syllable line *Das Leben trägest du in deiner Hand,* was crowded subsequently into the measure.[33] On the other hand, Bach occasionally entered an initial quarter-rest where it was inappropriate and crossed it out again. Movement 4 of Cantata 56 begins with the eight-syllable line *Ich stehe fertig und bereit.* Since Bach decided to set this line with simple eighth-note motion, the proper beginning was on the second half of the first beat. This is indeed the final reading of the measure, but an initial quarter-rest above the time signature has apparently been crossed out. The second movement of BWV 135 begins with the nine-syllable line *Ach heile mich, du Arzt der Seelen* set essentially in eighth-note motion. Like the eight-syllable line, the nine-syllable line should begin after the first beat. Here again, however, Bach had crowded a quarter-rest into the beginning of the measure and then crossed it out.

Since the spacing of the text often obliged Bach to crowd in the opening quarter-rest before the first note of the movement, it is not possible to determine whether it was in fact a subsequent addition, i.e., written down chronologically after the succeeding notes, wherever it appears to be so. Neumann maintains that the fifth movement of BWV 171 originally began

Und da du Herr ge -sagt

and that the quarter-rest and first barline including the change of meter were part of a correction.[34] This implies that Bach had in fact momentarily considered having the phrase end on the fourth beat of the measure. Such phrase structures do occasionally occur in Bach recitatives, but the composer tried as a rule to avoid them. In BWV 17/4, mm. 5–6, the rhythm of the dactylic line was corrected from

Stim-me   undfiel auf sein An-ge-sicht

(which BG erroneously prints as the final version) to

Stim-me   und fiel auf sein An-ge - sicht

---

[33] See NBA I/4, KB, p. 39.

[34] NBA I/4, KB, p. 96.

The visual appearance of the first two measures of BWV 171/5 is approximately:

There is no visual evidence that the barline and time signature after m. 1 were subsequent additions. Neumann's conjecture rests entirely on the position of the initial rest, which may or may not be an afterthought. If it was inserted, it was evidently still added before the measure was concluded. Bach in this instance apparently never considered having the final word of the opening phrase fall on the fourth beat of the measure, and the decision to set the words of Jesus as an arioso in triple meter belonged, as far as one can tell, to Bach's original conception of the movement.

The composer could assure that a phrase would end on the first or third beat of the measure not only by beginning the phrase after the first or second beat, but by carefully constructing upbeat formulas in a variety of rhythmic patterns. This alternative usually involved the introduction of sixteenth-note declamation which also relieved the monotony of an uninterrupted series of eighth-notes and often served to combine two or more separate phrases into a larger unit. The alteration of an upbeat rhythm often appears together with a barring correction. In BWV 13/4 (P 45/4), m. 7, Bach had written

Der Sorgen Kummer Nacht drückt mein

but changed the rhythm to

Der Sor-gen Kummer Nacht   drückt mein be - klemmtes Herz dar-nie-der

in order to allow the phrase to end on the third beat of the following measure. The three-sixteenth upbeat figure, in fact, is used quite consistently for eight- and nine-syllable lines throughout this movement and takes on a structurally unifying role.[35]

[35] See the phrases beginning in mm. 4, 5, 7, 8, and 10.

The rhythm of BWV 19/6 (P 45/8), m. 2 was changed from

from-men En-gel lie - ben   und sie mit

to

frommen En-gel lie - ben   und sie mit   unsern Sün-den nicht

again for metrical reasons. At the same time the quick upbeat figure prevents a monotonous fourfold repetition of the tone e″ (which resulted from a pitch correction of the figure) in equal eighth-notes, and appropriately gathers together into one beat the three relatively unimportant words *und sie mit.*

In BWV 206/10 (P 42/1), m. 3, the rhythm was corrected from

Trennung bit-ter ein,   doch mei-nes

to

Trennung bit - ter ein,   doch mei-nes   Kö-nigs Wink

making it appear that the correction caused the new phrase to end on the second beat of the measure. The words *doch meines Königs Wink,* however, form only part of the next line which in its entirety reads *doch meines Königs Wink gebietet meinem Willen,* and in Bach's setting ends on the first beat of m. 5.

On at least one occasion Bach altered the rhythmic structure of a phrase in order to have the phrase end on the fourth beat of a measure. Measure 2 of BWV 5/6 (PP) at first read

klein-ste Teil der Welt   und da des Blu - tes

The new phrase, if continued normally in eighth-notes, would have concluded on the third beat of m. 3:

Blu-tes ed - ler Saft

Bach changed the rhythm, however, to

♪ ♪ ♪ ♪ ♪ 𝄾 ♪ | ♪ ♪ ♪ ♪ ♪ ♪ 𝄾 ♪ |

klein-ste Teil der Welt   und   da des Blu-tes ed-ler Saft

reinforcing the irregularity with a syncopated continuo line. The reason for the change was perhaps to provide a contrast to the sturdy, square declamation of the following phrase of the movement:

♪ | ♪ ♪ ♪ ♪ ♪ ♪ ♪ ♪ | ♪

un - end-lich gro-ße Kraft be-währt er - hält.

In the last example an unusual correction had the effect of establishing a contrast relationship between two phrases. Other rhythmic corrections were evidently made to create a structural dependency between adjacent phrases. Such corrections are eminently musical in nature, for they impose a unifying element other than the text onto the composition. By introducing quicker or slower rhythmic groups, Bach often formed balanced musical phrases of equal length in the recitative even though the text phrases were of unequal length.[36]

Bach began, for example, to set the three-foot text phrase *weil ich die ganze Nacht* of BWV 135/4, m. 4,[37] with three sixteenth-notes, then corrected this to eighth-notes, perhaps not only to bring the word *Nacht* on the first beat but also to produce a three-beat phrase that would balance the length of the following phrase. The latter begins with a three-sixteenth upbeat, so that its four metrical feet are declaimed in only three musical beats. At the same time, this rapid upbeat figure serves to connect the two phrases and perhaps to illustrate the words *oft ohne Seelenruh'*.

Again, in BWV 10/3 (LC), m. 3.1–2, Bach had begun to set the new phrase in eighth-notes but changed this to sixteenth-note declamation on the words *Währet immer*. As a result of this correction the tetrameter *und währet immer für und für* ends, properly, on the third beat of the measure, and the musical setting agrees in length and structure with the preceding and following trimeters *wird alle Morgen neu* (m. 2) and *bei denen die allhier* (m. 4). These four-beat phrases are framed by the three-beat settings of the first and fifth lines of the text: *Des Höchsten Güt und Treu* (m. 1) and *auf seine Hülfe schaun* (m. 5). Further symmetry is provided by the use of the same upbeat figure ♪ 𝄾 ♪ between the first and second and between the penultimate and final text line of the opening sentence (mm. 1 and 5), contrasting with the ♩ 𝄾 ♪ figure between lines 2 through 5. The five-beat structure reserved for the sixth line—*in wahrer Furcht vertraun*—breaks

[36] A discussion of the rhythmic-metrical correspondence of phrases in Bach's recitatives appears

in Melchert 1958, pp. 15–19.
[37] See the facsimile edition.

the symmetrical design of the first five lines and, in the manner of a ritardando, brings the sentence to a conclusion. The entire musical structure of mm. 1–6 can be represented as a succession of six phrases with 3, 4, 4, 4, 3, and 5 beats respectively. The structure obviously has its own logic and form—as meaningful as, but independent of, the text structure which consists of two groups, each containing two trimeters followed by a tetrameter.

Corrections of rhythm, of course, did not only serve considerations of relatively large-scale metrical design involving phrase structure, but were often made to assure that a particular word was declaimed with an effective agogic accentuation. The rhythm of the affective word *Sündenbrut* in BWV 199/1 (Copenhagen), m. 3, was changed from the neutral eighth-note declamation ♪ ♪ ♪ to the more emphatic form ♪ ♪♪. In BWV 47/3 (P 163), m. 4, this same literal, agogic rendition ♪ ♪♪ for the word *Teufelsbrut* was found perhaps too obvious and was corrected to the more abrupt, more brutal form ♪♪ ♪ ⁊, with the necessary emphasis of the first syllable provided by dynamic and tonic accentuation. This correction has the additional effect of creating a rhythmic parallelism between the two successive groups.

das vom Ü-ber-mut   als ei-ner Teu-fels-brut

The three-sixteenth upbeat of the second phrase further creates an impression of continuity between the phrases.

Melodic Corrections

Effective text declamation could be achieved as in the last example by melodic as well as by rhythmic means, through the judicious placement of tonic accents. Although there are innumerable pitch corrections in the vocal parts of recitatives in the autograph scores, relatively few of them seem to have been motivated by a desire for more explicit tonic accentuation. For the most part Bach seems to have been satisfied to allow the normal alternation of unaccented and accented eighth-notes, together with occasional agogic accentuation, to guarantee a natural and unobtrusive accentuation of the text. Bach did sometimes introduce tonic accents in order to emphasize particularly expressive words, or in order to illustrate a word pictorially with a rhetorical figure.

The voice part in BWV 56/2, m. 11, originally began with a rising fourth b♭, e′♭ (c′), creating a tonic accent on the first syllable of the word *rufet*. The reading was changed to g, e′♭ (c′). The skip of a sixth or larger interval was the rhetorical figure of the *exclamatio* (in German, *Ausruf*)[38] and was presumably called to the composer's mind here by the text word *rufet*. In m. 16 the phrase *so tret ich aus dem Schiff* seems to have begun with the repeated tones d, d, but was changed to A, d. The verb *treten* is thus illustrated with the decisive melodic gesture of a rising fourth from the dominant to the tonic.[39]

The upward leap of a minor tenth on the words *größte Überfluß* in BWV 75/2 (P 66), m. 3, was similarly an afterthought, corrected in the score as follows:

größ - te Ü - ber - fluß

The great majority of pitch corrections in the vocal parts, however, are devoted to more subtle, often minute, refinements of melodic contour. Occasionally the meaning of such refinements becomes evident when they are considered in context.

The second phrase in m. 2 of BWV 96/4 (P 179) was changed as follows:

Ach füh - re mich, o   Gott, zum rech-ten We - ge

The new reading illustrates the words *rechten Wege* with a stepwise upward motion and resolves the initial g″ of the first phrase in its proper octave. Bach similarly corrected the second phrase of BWV 56/2 so that it could resolve the first phrase more effectively:

Mein Wandel auf der Welt   ist ei - ner Schiffahrt   gleich

The falling third at the beginning of the second phrase now contrasts with the upward fourth at the beginning of the movement, and essentially stepwise motion replaces the arpeggiation of the first phrase. There is also a clear contrast in tessitura between the two phrases: the range of a sixth f to d′ of the first phrase is contrasted with the third e♭ to c in the second phrase, and the unnecessary, indeed disconcerting, tonic accent on *einer* has disappeared.

[38] See Unger 1941, p. 77, and Walther 1732, p. 233.

[39] It is possible, of course, that Bach changed the first d to A before he had written the second tone of the melody. The initial d may thus have been the first tone of an entirely different melodic idea that was rejected before it was ever written down. It is therefore no more than a conjecture that the two observable tones d, d belonged at one time to the same rejected musical idea. The lack of repeated passages in recitatives frequently makes it impossible to determine whether a correction of pitch was immediate or delayed.

The subsequent introduction of arioso elements in recitative autographs is a rather frequent and typical correction, observed in over 60 of the 361 recitatives analyzed in this study. Corrections of this type are by nature "ornamental" corrections. The basic syllabic declamation of the voice part or the held notes in the continuo and accompagnato instruments are embellished with rhythmic-melodic figuration that elaborates the underlying harmonic framework. The newly added arioso elements enhance the musical interest of the movement and frequently serve to illustrate the text with musico-rhetorical "figures."

Although Bach did not usually make allowances for melismas at the time he entered a recitative text below the voice staff, they seem on the whole to have belonged to his original conception of the vocal melody, for in most instances they are uncorrected. On occasion, however, a melisma was an afterthought replacing a syllabic setting of a particular word. The final four-measure melisma on *flehen* at the conclusion of BWV 13/2 (P 45/4), mm. 8–11, was such an afterthought. The original setting was ♪ ♪ 𝄽 a′, g′, after which the movement was presumably to end with the final continuo cadence. In view of the length of this melisma and the eighth-note motion in the continuo, it is perhaps justifiable to regard this correction not only as the introduction of a melisma but as the addition of an entire concluding arioso section, i.e., an element of formal significance.

The melisma on *lebendgen* in BWV 32/4 (P 126), too, was changed from the syllabic reading

freu - et sich in dem le - bendgen Gott

to

freu - et sich in dem le - bend - gen Gott

And in BWV 43/6 (P 44/6), m. 9, the word *Kräfte* was originally set syllabically, as was the word *preisen* in BWV 117/2 (PP), m. 6, and possibly the word *betrübter* in BWV 40/5 (P 63), m. 10.

Like melismas, neumatic formulas were often introduced to emphasize affective text words. The conversion of a simple syllabic declamation with the rhythm ♪♪ to ♫♫ is considerably more common, in fact, than the addition of extended melismas. In such a correction a "harmonic" arpeggio contour was normally softened into a more "melodic" contour by adding stepwise motion, anticipation tones, or small harmonic intervals in place of larger leaps. In BWV 56/2, m. 9, the word *Barmherzigkeit* was originally set

Barmher - zig - keit

and was then changed to

Barm-her - zig - keit

The straightforward syllabic declamation ♪ ♪ d′ a on the words *Gnad und* in BWV 179/4 (P 146), meas. 17 was changed to ♫♫ d′ b a g. The word *Herze* in BWV 39/2 (P 62), meas. 20 was originally set ♪♪ c′ a but changed to ♫♫ c′ b a g♯; and the word *Herzen* in BWV 102/2 (P 97) meas. 6, changed from ♪♪ g e to ♫♫ g f e d. It is needless to multiply the examples.

Arioso elements were usually added in the continuo and accompagnato parts to divide the harmony-bearing held tones into smaller rhythmic values. The sixteenth-note turn figure in the recorder parts of BWV 175/1 (P 75), for example, was an afterthought. Bach had at first written tied whole-notes in these parts in the first two measures of the movement.[40]

The newly added arioso elements often serve in instrumental parts, as in the voice part, to illustrate the meaning of the text. In the first measure of BWV 135/4[41] a whole-note F in the continuo was corrected to a repeated-note figure on the same tone with the rhythm ❜ ♫♩ ❜ ♫♩ illustrating the word *Seufzer*. In order to capture the atmosphere of mystery and fear at the beginning of BWV 42/2 (P 55), "Am Abend aber desselbigen Sabbaths," Bach changed the original half-note B at the beginning of m. 1 to repeated eighth-notes. After continuing this figure at least through the first quarter of m. 3 (but probably through the end of m. 5), he changed the figure to repeated sixteenth-notes—a more graphic suggestion of fear and trembling.

In the opening recitative of the Coffee Cantata[42] the dotted rhythms representing the footsteps of Herr Schlendrian at the words *Da kömmt Herr Schlendrian* (m. 3) were again an afterthought, corrected from a half-note.

The continuo part of BWV 190/4 (P 127),[43] m. 15, read originally ♩♩ B, c. This was changed to the arioso motion ♩ ❜ ♪♫♫ B, B, c, c, d, e—a correc-

---

[40] See the facsimile in NBA I/14, p. xii, and NBA I/14, KB, p. 191.
[41] See the facsimile edition.
[42] See the facsimile edition.
[43] See the facsimile in NBA I/4, p. vii.

tion implying that Bach had only conceived the arioso setting of mm. 15–17 after he had written down m. 15 but before he had composed m. 16 of the continuo line.

On a few occasions Bach immediately struck upon the idea of an arioso accompaniment figure but then decided on a more pictorial form of that figure. In BWV 92/2 (P 873), the continuo originally had a repeated sixteenth-note figure in mm. 17–21. The word *Wellen* in m. 21 then evidently suggested a turn figure to Bach which he introduced in mm. 17ff., where the sea imagery in the text first appears, and continued through m. 23. Similarly, in Movement 18 of the *Christmas Oratorio* Bach had written a sixteenth-note arpeggio figure in the continuo, mm. 5–9, but changed it to sixteenth-triplets to illustrate more vividly the rocking of the cradle.[44]

Arioso elements were often introduced into the accompanying parts of recitatives to provide a form of punctuation of the text at phrase endings where the voice has either a rest or a held note, and to prevent an interruption of rhythmic motion between phrases.

For these reasons, apparently, the sixteenth- and thirty-second-note runs in BWV 92/2 (P 873), mm. 5 and 6 respectively, were added as ornamental corrections of the initial half-notes in the continuo as were the sixteenth-note scales in mm. 37 and 41 of BWV 169/2 (P 93). The continuo part of BWV 5/4 (PP) was changed in mm. 2–3 and 9–10 from basic half-note to quarter-note motion, in both places providing rhythmic activity at the end of a phrase, and in the latter measures introducing a chromatic descending line to illustrate the words *Angst und Pein.*

At the beginning of m. 5 in BWV 103/2 (P 122) Bach had written a half-note B in the continuo, which he immediately changed to a quarter-note. He continued to lead the continuo part in quarter-note motion in the remainder of the measure, filling the rhythmic gap left by the tenor and forming a transition to the active continuo part in the arioso conclusion of the movement.

The revision of the oboe d'amore parts in Movement 3 of the *Christmas Oratorio*[45] replaces the original half-note readings with eighth-note figures at caesuras and cadences and produces together with the alto an almost continuous eighth-note background throughout the movement.

It was not necessary for Bach to add arioso figures in order to form a transition between the phrases of a recitative. It often sufficed simply to subdivide the basic

[44] See NBA II/6, KB, p. 36, and the facsimile edition.

[45] See the facsimile edition and NBA II/6, KB, p. 29.

half-note motion of the accompaniment into two quarter-notes. Measure 5 of
BWV 56/4 was corrected as follows:[46]

(emp)fan - gen,   Wie

In the final reading the first G minor chord completes the phrase ending with
the word *empfangen,* and the immediate restatement of the same chord in a new
position prepares the next phrase in the bass. The resultant quarter-note motion
inevitably fills the lacuna between the phrases.

In the corrections discussed on the preceding pages the original readings in
the continuo or accompagnato instruments invariably consisted of half-notes
which were divided into smaller rhythmic units. They thus provide a further
confirmation of the observation made earlier that Bach frequently composed the
accompanying instrumental parts of recitatives one half-measure at a time.

Changes of Form, Genre, and Instrumentation

While the addition of scattered arioso elements in the recitative is quite
common, the spontaneous introduction of larger arioso sections constituting
complete formal units is rare. Two occasions where concluding arioso sections
were added as part of a correction have been noted already: BWV 190/4 and
BWV 13/2. There are three further instances where Bach decided to provide
a recitative with an instrumental introduction only after he had begun to compose the movement in a more conventional manner. In BWV 92/2 (P 873) Bach
started to write the initial word of the text *Es* at the beginning of the first
measure, but after having written down the *E* decided on starting the movement
with a chorale paraphrase in the continuo. BWV 43/6 (P 44/6) at first began
with what is now m. 2. Then a one-measure rest was crowded in before the
written measure and the string introduction was composed. The conception of
the movement as an accompagnato, however, was certain from the beginning.
In BWV 188/4 (scattered autograph fragments) the string introduction was again

---

[46] See the facsimile edition.

an afterthought. The movement had begun with an eighth-rest in the voice part which was changed to a half-rest.

There are evidently only two instances in the extant autograph scores where the originally planned genre of a movement was rejected entirely and a new genre adopted. Since both instances involve the recitative they may be mentioned here. In the first case the final form is the recitative; in the second the recitative was the original form. It is clear from Sketch No. 116 that Bach first conceived the opening movement of Cantata 183, *Sie werden euch in den Bann tun,* as a bass aria. Judging from the clefs of the draft, Bach planned to score the aria, like the final recitative version, for two oboes d'amore, two oboes da caccia, and continuo. The draft, furthermore, appears in the key of A minor, the same key in which the final version begins.[47]

The third movement of Cantata 28 (P 92) was planned as a secco recitative. Bach wrote the heading *Recit* and the text for the entire movement straight through on the bottom of f. 9v of the autograph without any repetitions of phrases. He did not foresee, for example, the repetition of the words *es soll mir eine Lust sein* in mm. 3–4 and had to crowd in a ⁒ sign after the first statement of the phrase and draw guide lines from the words *daß ich ihnen,* etc. to the appropriate notes; for these words are situated directly under the notes of mm. 3–4. Bach apparently decided on an arioso style as soon as he had begun to compose the movement, and so adjusted the text in mm. 3–4 as just described, crossed out the remainder of the text, and wrote the new text version of mm. 6–10—with repeated phrases—under the continuo part. He then continued the rest of the movement on the top of f. 10r (which had not been used for the initial version of the text), and, as is appropriate in an arioso movement, began writing down the notes before the words.

It seems, too, that Bach was usually quite sure in advance whether a recitative was to be composed secco or accompagnato. At most, 5 of the 101 accompanied recitatives for which the autograph scores survive were planned in secco style.

1. BWV 190/6 (P 127) was originally scored for tenor and continuo. A 2-stave brace with key and time signatures in both staves was entered and then immediately smudged out.

2. In BWV 91/4 (P 869) the decision to set the movement accompagnato was made even sooner than in BWV 190/6. Bach here originally bracketed two

---

[47] The draft is found upside down in the autograph of BWV 79 (P 89, f. 10v). Although the Reformation Cantata was probably written for October 31, 1725, and BWV 183 for Exaudi, May 13, 1725, the key and instrumentation of the draft as well as the watermark of the paper are the same as those found in the original sources for the Exaudi Cantata (see Dürr 1957, pp. 81 and 83), so that it is clear—as Spitta pointed out (II, 831–833)—that the draft indeed belonged to BWV 183 and not to a third setting of this text (besides BWV 183 and 44). (The draft is not mentioned in the critical report for this cantata in NBA I/12, KB, pp. 294–318.)

2-stave systems for the movement. These two brackets were then changed to one 5-stave bracket before any clefs for the secco version had been written down.

3. The uppermost staff of the first system in BWV 187/6 (P 84) originally had a soprano clef which was corrected to a treble clef. This suggests again that Bach only decided at the last moment before beginning actual composition to set this soprano recitative accompagnato.

4. The beginning of BWV 180/4 (PP) appears as follows in the autograph:

The layout suggests strongly that the employment of recorders in the movement was an afterthought.

5. It is possible, but by no means certain, that Bach did not originally plan to set the second half of BWV 10/6 (LC) accompagnato. Measures 1–7 of the movement are entered on two 2-stave systems. Measure 8 begins a new system of five staves with two treble, alto, tenor, and bass clefs. The words (*schwö-*) *ren ist,* however, were entered beneath the uppermost staff of this system but then smudged through. Either Bach began to enter the text in the new system before he had written the clefs (in which case it is conceivable that he still had a 2-stave secco scoring in mind for the succeeding measures), or the clefs were written in before the text, and Bach began to enter the text under the top staff purely by mistake.

On two further occasions Bach revised his original conception of the accompagnato instrumentation. In BWV 119/4 (P 878) he presumably did not at first plan to have a woodwind accompaniment in mm. 6–20 but to limit the participation of instruments to brass fanfares at the beginning and conclusion of the movement. The heading of the movement reads *Recit/Trombe/e/Tamburi/accomp.* and the opening system has seven staves for four trumpets, timpani, bass, and continuo. The viola da gamba parts of BWV 198/4 (P 41/1) were completely revised, apparently to make them more independent of the lutes, thus increasing the sonority of the orchestration.[48]

[48] See NBA I/38, KB, pp. 109f., and the facsimile of the first page of the movement (f. 11r) in NBA I/38, p. x (where it is incorrectly identified as f. 12r).

In at least one case Bach increased the number of instruments in an accompanied recitative at the time the original parts were prepared. The autograph parts for Oboes 2 and 3 of BWV 63 (for which the autograph score is lost) at first had *tacet* indications for Movement 6. These indications were crossed out and music for the movement entered directly on the verso of the page.[49]

Sketch No. 160 represents the only observed occasion on which Bach had originally planned an accompagnato recitative but then decided in favor of a secco. On both ff. 23r and 23v of the *Christmas Oratorio* autograph Bach had set up a 9-stave system for an instrumentation of two oboes d'amore, two oboes da caccia, strings, tenor, and continuo, and even entered the text for the entire movement. Before beginning to compose the movement, Bach decided to set the recitative as a secco for bass. This movement (No. 22) is consequently the only recitative in the *Christmas Oratorio* based on a non-biblical text that is not set accompagnato.[50] The following movement, the concluding chorale of Part 2 of the oratorio, also underwent an orchestration change. Bach had at first set up a 5-stave system for chorus and continuo but decided immediately on a full scoring. It is not inconceivable that the correction of the orchestration of both Movements 22 and 23 belongs to the same corrective gesture: that Bach decided to delete the orchestra in Movement 22 at the same time that he decided to have an obbligato instrumentation in Movement 23. He may not have wished to have three fully scored movements (Mvts. 21–23) in succession.

[49] See NBA I/2, KB, pp. 11, 18, 35.   [50] See NBA II/6, KB, p. 210.

CHAPTER VI

Arias and Choruses:
Melodic Invention and the
Order of Events

THE VARIOUS stages of incompletion represented in the 46 extant drafts and sketches for the beginnings of movements and major sections invite an attempt to reconstruct the sequence of steps in which Bach set down the individual parts in a specific musical context. The 46 sketches are the following:

NINETEEN MONOPHONIC SKETCHES AND DRAFTS

Sketch No.	BWV	Sketch No.	BWV
1	2/3	83	114/4
6	9/3	127	198/10
23	36c/7	130	201/3
30	44/6	132	204/4
40	62/4	139	211/8
42	65/4	142	213/11
67	91/5	150	fugue subject
70	unidentified	153	232^{III}
75	94/2	156	243a/4
80	105/5		

NINE TWO-VOICED SKETCHES AND DRAFTS

Sketch No.	BWV	Sketch No.	BWV
19	29/3	71	91/3
21	30a/9	151	Aria in D
28	43/7	154	232^{III}
36	57/7	162	248/31
45	68/5		

Eighteen Rejected Drafts with More Than Two Parts

Sketch No.	BWV	Sketch No.	BWV
12	20/1	106	149/1
18	27/3	114	179/5
41	65/1	116	183/1
50	76/1	134	205/11
51	76/7	135	206/7
63	88/4	143	214/3
69	91/3?	148	Anh. 2
84	115/1	149	Quasimodogeniti
88	117/1	152	Choral movement

The Opening Theme

The surviving single-voiced sketches for the beginnings of movements indicate that Bach began composition by first writing down a fully formed melodic idea: a motif (Sketches Nos. 23 or 80), a phrase (Sketches Nos. 42 or 70), or a complete ritornello theme (Sketches Nos. 30, 40, or 127).[1] These sketches often reveal traces of Bach's initial understanding of the prosody and affect of the text, so that the sketches and drafts of at least the text-engendered themes (as opposed to those clearly instrumentally conceived) can be regarded as first, rough translations of the text into musical terms which had then to be refined into more idiomatic, convincing musical statements. In comparing a thematic sketch with the final version, it is possible, by observing the elements retained and those reworked or rejected, to determine the constants and the variables in Bach's conception, and in turn to determine what was probably the generating idea of the theme.

Sketch No. 80, a tentative sketch for the opening motif of the aria "Kann ich nur Jesum mir zum Freunde machen," from BWV 105, reveals Bach's interest in designing a ritornello theme that would later bear the first line of the text. A neutral melodic and rhythmic contour (repeated f', repeated eighth-notes) was to prepare an *exclamatio* emphasizing the word *Jesum,* after which the rhythmic and melodic flow would be released. This germinal idea was preserved in the final version but refined in accordance with purely musical considerations. By omitting the fourth beat from the first measure of the original conception the traditionally avoided[2] double skip of a sixth plus a fourth was removed and the

[1] Bach's presumed activity preceding actual composition—the analysis and evaluation of preexistent material—was briefly considered in Chapter II.

[2] It is worth noting that such a double skip is not to be found in any of the themes catalogued in McAll 1962.

melody made more concise (one beat shorter) and tonally focused (the defining seventh f'-e''♭).

Bach's first sketch of the *Pleni* theme for the *Sanctus* of the *B minor Mass* (Sketch No. 153), written on the bottom of the first page of the autograph,[3] indicates that here again the composer's first and primary consideration was to achieve a proper declamation and representation of the text. The words *coeli* and *terra* suggested an upward octave leap followed by a descending seventh; *gloria* called forth a melisma. The dactylic structure of the text was directly translated into triple meter. Bach wrote down the complete subject to the cadence with no apparent concern at the moment about contrapuntal problems or implications. The conception was clearly text engendered and purely melodic. While retaining the essential melodic and rhythmic contour elicited from the text in the first sketch for the *Pleni* theme, Bach turned his attention in a second preliminary draft (Sketch No. 154) to purely musical problems. The text is not only absent here, but was apparently neglected entirely: the beaming of the eighth-note passage in the third measure of the theme overlooks the syllabic requirements of the text. Bach changed the opening interval from an octave to a sixth, perhaps not only to increase the "kinetic energy" of the melody, but for tonal reasons as well. The new tone f'♯ serves a pivotal function in the transition from the end of the *Sanctus* section in F-sharp minor to the D major beginning of the *Pleni*. The first two melodic and harmonic intervals formed by the principal parts: $\frac{a}{F\sharp}$ and $\frac{f'\sharp}{d}$ negotiate between the two tonalities via the ambiguous $\frac{a}{F\sharp}$, while the entire configuration forms a D major chord.[4] This, along with Bach's interest in drafting an obbligato counterfigure, may explain why the continuo part accompanying the fugue subject was entered in this sketch. The final version represents a synthesis of the two tentative sketches: it combines the opening motif of the second sketch with the continuation of the first. After writing down the third measure (or perhaps the fourth) of the *Pleni*, Bach changed the meter from 3/4 to 3/8, probably to clarify the tempo relation between the two sections.[5]

As the preceding examples indicate, the rhythm and meter originally suggested by the text structure were often generating and constant factors in Bach's con-

[3] In several manuscripts thematic sketches for later movements appear on the bottom of the first page of the score (Sketches Nos. 36, 67, 69, 70, 127, 132, and 153), but it would be rash to assume that Bach got the initial idea for the *Pleni* while working on the opening measures of the *Sanctus,* or, in a similar case—Sketch No. 36—that he interrupted his work on the first movement of BWV 57 to jot down the ritornello theme for Movement 7. While these are of course possibilities, it is equally if not more likely that the completed first page lay uppermost on the composer's desk and in his convenient reach.

[4] In the final scoring the orchestra provides the c♯ of the f-sharp minor chord that concludes the *Sanctus* section.

[5] Exactly what this tempo relation is has been a matter of dispute. See the exchange between Bernard Rose and Arthur Mendel in Rose 1959, 1960, and in Mendel 1959, 1960[2].

ception of the theme, but Bach did on occasion recast the musical realization of the text meter. A rejected draft (Sketch No. 19), found upside down on the last page of the autograph score of BWV 29, is presumably the first version of Movement 3, "Halleluia, Stärk' und Macht," which, like the draft, is a tenor aria in A major and begins a new sheet in the manuscript.[6] Apparently Bach at first intended a basically agogic treatment of the trochaic text in triple meter. If the ritornello was conceived as a setting for the first line of the text, the planned underlay may have been:

or

The final allabreve version relies primarily on dynamic and tonic accentuation to insure a convincing musical declamation.

A similar relationship exists between the abandoned draft (Sketch No. 162) and the final version of Movement 31, "Schließe, mein Herze," from the *Christmas Oratorio*. Here, too, the ritornello theme of the draft was probably text engendered and designed to declaim the dactyls in a strict and straightforward syllabic style.

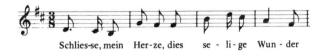

But then Bach decided—perhaps in order to avoid the dance-like quality of the draft—on an agogically emphasized declamation in duple meter:

Some basic elements of the original conception were retained, however: the tonality, voice (alto), and phrase structure (two plus two measures). A number of characteristic melodic formulas are also common to both versions. Compare m. 2 of the first with m. 1 of the final version, m. 1 of the first with m. 2 of the final reading, and mm. 3–4 in both versions.

[6] The draft is catalogued in BWV, p. xiv, as an unidentified sketch, presumably after Schünemann 1935, pp. 25–26.

In the "Halleluia, Stärk' und Macht" and "Schließe, mein Herze" examples, the melody was completely reworked between the sketch and final version, as were meter and rhythm. The same melodic contour, however, is retained in both draft and final version of Sketch No. 23 for the aria "Auch mit gedämpften, schwachen Stimmen" from BWV 36c. Here the change of the meter and rhythm alone was sufficient to transform the character of the ritornello theme. As the transcription reveals, Bach superimposed the new version onto the original reading. The smooth, stepwise melodic motion is now complemented with a gentle rhythmic form more appropriate to the opening words which undoubtedly determined the character of the first section of the movement. This rhythmic revision may also have been made with a view toward creating a dramatic contrast with the middle section of the aria:

In this instance, then, the constant factors were key and melody while the rhythm and meter were recast.

Autograph corrections in several opening ritornello themes of an "instrumental" character make it evident that these themes were vocally conceived, i.e., directly engendered by the prosody of the text. This is quite explicit in the case of the florid ritornello theme for oboe d'amore solo from BWV 124/3 (P 876). The theme began at first with the reading of the tenor entrance in mm. 9–11: a syllabic declamation of the opening line of the text.[7]

BWV 124/3, mm. 1–3, Oboe d'amore

BWV 124/3, mm. 9–11, Tenor

It seems likely as well that Bach at first planned to construct the ritornello theme of BWV 59/4 (P 161) for violin solo with more fidelity to the text prosody. The opening line

Dĭe | Wélt mĭt | állĕn | Kőnĭg-|réichĕn

---

[7] The grace notes reproduced in the BG edition before the first notes in mm. 2 and 3 do not appear in P 876; they are a further embellishment of the theme, added at the time the original parts were written out.

falls naturally into a triple meter; and the time signature in all three staves of the first system of the score originally read 3/4. Even before he had proceeded to set down a 3/4 theme, Bach had decided to cast the movement in duple meter by extending or contracting syllable lengths. This is clearly reflected in the first reading of the opening measure. The reading was finally embellished with the present violinistic figuration, although the rhythm of the rejected instrumental reading is retained in the bass entrance, mm. 8–9.

BWV 59/4, mm. 1–2, Violin

BWV 59/4, mm. 8–10, Bass

"Instrumentally conceived" ritornelli, on the other hand, were occasionally modified at the vocal entrance or even rejected entirely in favor of a more vocal melody. The rejected drafts for the ritornelli of BWV 30a/9 (Sketch No. 21) and BWV 65/4 (Sketch No. 42) were replaced with text-engendered (BWV 65/4) or at least more "singable" (BWV 30a/9) themes.

Similarly, Bach at first intended to retain the highly pictorial—and "instrumental"—ritornello material of the aria "Die schäumenden Wellen," BWV 81/3 (P 120), in the tenor motto, mm. 18–20, but then decided rather (as in BWV 30a/9) on a less demanding formulation.

BWV 81/3, mm. 1–5, Violin 1[8]

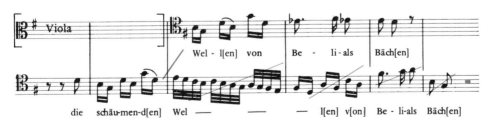

Mm. 16–20, Tenor

[8] The transcription attempts to reproduce the ambiguity of the slur indications in the origi-nal—an ambiguity typical of the Bach autographs.

The new reading results in a reduction of the phrase length from five to four measures.

A comparison of Sketches Nos. 83, 127, and 139 with the final versions provides further evidence that Bach at times rejected his initial choice of meter—or recast the internal metrical structure of thematic ideas—while retaining in essence the original melodic contour. More significantly, the comparison furnishes considerable insight into the nature of meter and phrase structure in Bach's melody.

In Sketch No. 127 Bach notated almost the complete ritornello theme of BWV 198/10, the concluding chorus "Doch, Königin! du stirbest nicht," from the *Trauer-Ode*. The principal distinction between the sketch and the final version is that in the latter the entire melody has been shifted one half-measure "to the left." The successive melodic motives of the opening measures now begin on the upbeats to the first beats of the measures, with the result that the cadence tone of each phrase, including the final cadence of the ritornello in m. 12, falls in the middle of a bar. By thus removing the cadence tones from the downbeats and placing them on secondary accents, Bach perhaps intended to "mute" the melody—to have the metrical structure contribute, along with the predominant triplet and stepwise motion of the melody, to its gentle and flowing character.[9]

The continuo ritornello for the chorale aria "Kein Frucht das Weizenkörnlein bringt," BWV 114/4 (Sketch No. 83), was originally drafted as an eight-measure theme in triple meter. The insertion of eighth-rests at the beginning and end of each of the original two-measure motives expanded the ritornello in length from 24 to 32 eighth-note units while it "reduced" the theme from eight measures of 3/8 to four measures of common time. The rests were no doubt added in order to represent the scattering of seeds suggested by the chorale text by dividing the more or less continuous theme of the sketch into four separate—and separated—motivic particles. The rests also serve to displace by one half-beat the

---

[9]There are, too, a number of melodic variants between the two versions. Most prominent is the change of the opening interval from a minor third to a minor sixth, again introducing the *exclamatio* figure—this time to declaim the words *Doch, Königin!* at the entrance of the chorus in m. 13. Measures 1–4 are otherwise identical in the sketch and final version. In the following *Fortspinnung* of mm. 5–9a the exclusively stepwise motion of the sketch is replaced in the final reading by a combination of scalar and arpeggio figures. A more substantial discrepancy in the readings of the following measures has the result that the final reading in mm. 9–10 is one-and-a-half instead of only one-half measure "behind" the sketch reading. (The second half of m. 9 was not worked out in the sketch.)

But in the last measures of the two versions the distance is reduced again to a half-measure. The sketch version, accordingly, if it had been completed, presumably would have cadenced on the first beat of m. 13, perhaps as follows:

instead of, as in the final version, in the middle of m. 12. The corrections in m. 11 of the final version produce a melodic climax on the tone b″ and thus avoid the redundant repetition of g″ which, before the correction, had served five times as a climax tone in the second half of the theme alone.

original accents of the melody, since the theme now begins after, instead of on, the downbeat. There is, then, a significant transformation of the metrical structure of the theme both in the large (triple to duple meter) and in the small (originally accented notes now placed on unaccented parts of the measure). This is quite different from the examples of rebarring observed earlier in chorale melodies and recitatives which involved no real changes in metrical structure.

The relationship between sketch and final version in the BWV 114/4 ritornello vividly confirms the common observation that the eighteenth-century Classic conception of phrase structure is not often applicable to Bach's melodic style (except in dances and dance-like movements). It indicates further the less familiar fact that even the notion of an "organic" theme is essentially irrelevant in a discussion of Bachian melody.[10] The ritornello of BWV 114/4 did not represent for Bach an eight- (3/8) or four- (4/4) measure "theme" but rather a chain of motives that, like molecules, could be joined together or detached as the composer saw fit. It was this flexibility—and from a later standpoint, arbitrariness—in regard to meter and phrase structure (reflecting perhaps a survival to some extent of the organization of mensural music) which permitted Bach to insert extra rests or additional measures into his themes and phrases. Conversely, rests, motives, or measures could be recombined into new configurations or omitted altogether.

The differences between the sketch and final version of the ritornello theme from the aria "Heute noch," BWV 211/8 (Sketch No. 139), are both numerous and obvious: the sketch is in A major, the final version is in G;[11] the original version begins on the downbeat, while in the final version the theme begins on the upbeat (providing another instance where the original metrical accents

---

[10] Werner Neumann first called attention to the "non-organic" nature of Bach's melodic idiom in his study of the choral fugues (see Neumann 1938). Later studies by Alfred Dürr (of the arias, in Dürr 1951) and by Emil Platen (of the chorale fantasias for chorus, in Platen 1959) have confirmed Neumann's observations.

[11] The tonal plan of the cantata is:

Mvt.	1	2	3		4	5	6	7		8	9	10
	G–D	D	e–f♯		b	A–e	e	C–D		G	e–e	G
or	I	V			III	II		VI	IV–V	I		I

i.e.,

in the theme have been completely redistributed). The final version presents a more refined text underlay. The straightforward

Heu - te noch

declamation is replaced with the restless, impatient

Heu-te   noch

figure, known at the time as the *anticipatione della syllaba*.[12] Finally, the opening phrase has been increased from three to four measures. This demonstrates clearly that for Bach the four-measure phrase structure was by no means a self-evident norm or natural preexistent framework, as it was, say, for Beethoven;[13] rather it testifies that Bach most likely conceived of melody as the sum of a variable number of smaller motives.

The genesis of the opening ritornello of BWV 43/7 (Sketch No. 28) reveals Bach's remarkable ability to reinterpret and redefine the function of the various melodic components in a thematic complex. It is apparent from the clefs in both systems of the draft that Bach originally conceived the movement as a continuo aria. He had initially written bass clefs on the upper staves of the two systems for the voice part. The continuo part of the ritornello could easily serve as an ostinato theme and presumably was conceived and written down as such before Bach decided to add the trumpet part: what is now an accompanimental part was at first an independent melodic part. It is clear, furthermore, that the opening measure of the final reading—the assertive descending C major scale—was an afterthought, and that the original first measure became the second measure, i.e., what was the beginning of a melodic phrase became the continuation of one. Measure 1 was thus the last measure of the theme to be invented. It was presumably added to the melody to establish more firmly the key of C

---

[12] See Walther 1708, p. 153. Compare also the related correction introducing an anticipation to represent Lieschen's impatience in Movement 4 of the cantata, described on p. 181, below.

[13] Otto Neumerkel in his little-known but highly enlightening study of Beethoven's sketches points out that Beethoven's "'first ideas' (*Einfälle*) are, with few exceptions, strict four- or eight-measure structures. This four- or eight-measure form is, to be sure, at first external, only a dead shell into which the musical content is poured, and which is either too narrow or too wide. What is and remains essential is that Beethoven bestows this form even on the first jottings of his 'ideas.' . . . The four-measure formal scheme therefore is not a goal, not an ultimate objective, but only a means, the preliminary support of the budding musical thought." Neumerkel 1935, pp. 55–56.

major before introducing the flatted seventh and perhaps to present in concentrated form the basic melodic course of the entire ritornello:[14]

The example thus illustrates the interchangeability of the function of melodic elements in Bach's style: the interchangeability of melody and accompaniment and of beginning and continuation.[15]

THE EXTANT autograph material for choral fugues reveals that Bach on several occasions drafted a subject consisting essentially of a repeated-note motif. He then made this motif more "melodic." The first version of the fugue subject from BWV 65/1 (Sketch No. 41) read:

Sie wer-d[en] aus Sa - ba al - le ko - - - (mmen)

and was entered in this form in all four voices before it was changed to the intermediate stage:

Sie wer-d[en] aus Sa - ba al - le ko - - -

---

[14] The rapid scalar descent through the octave at the beginning is balanced by the arpeggiated descent at the close of the theme. The arpeggio exposes the interval c'''-g'' which terminates the secondary descent within the melody:

It is also possible that the c''', b'' of mm. 3–4 arrived at in sequence to the bb'', a'' of mm. 2–3 is to be interpreted as a cancellation of the c''', bb''.

[15] Cf. Sketch No. 75. Does the sketch here represent Bach's original conception of the opening measures of the theme before which two measures were then prefixed (i.e., the "beginning" changed to a "continuation"), or was the sketch from the first a tentative notation of mm. 3–4, entered on f. 2v of the autograph before being written on f. 3r after mm. 1–2?

a reading which already presents the final form of the opening four notes. The purpose of this alteration may have been to obtain a closer melodic relationship with the opening theme of the movement.[16]

Sie werd[en] aus Sa - ba al - le kom[en] aus

M. 9–10

The countersubject of the fugue beginning in m. 33 of BWV 67/1 (P 95) was changed "immediately" as follows.

der auf - er - stan - - - - (den)

Mm. 33–35

And the subject of the *Pleni* section of BWV 238 (P 13/5) was changed (again "immediately") thus.

(Saba) oth ple - ni sunt coe - li et ter - - - ra

M. 26

A similar revision was made in the *Sicut locutus* chorus of BWV 243a (P 38).

Si - cut lo - cu - - - tus

M. 1–2

Perhaps the "immediate" correction of the subject of BWV 105/1 (P 99) should also be mentioned here

deñ vor dir wird k[ein] Le - ben - - - (diger)

Mm. 47–48

as should the alteration of the octave leap in the *Pleni* subject of the *B minor Mass Sanctus* described above. Both are surely indicative of the same tendency.

---

[16] A detailed discussion of the genesis of this fugal exposition appears below.

Since there are repeated-note (or repeated-note-plus-an-octave-leap) fugal subjects that were never altered,[17] it is not necessary to presume that the original versions of the fugue subjects just discussed were in actuality consciously tentative gestures written by Bach in order to fix only the declamation or opening pitches of the fugal entrances; nor did he look upon them as schematic outlines rather than as real melodies. The surviving autograph material testifies, not only here but throughout, that Bach's initial melodic ideas as a rule were completely formed by the time he set them to paper, although he often corrected them and on occasion rejected them. There is little evidence that Bach ever deliberately wrote down abstract contrapuntal, melodic, or numerical schemes which were to be elaborated afterwards.[18]

BACH's practice of beginning composition with the melody may afford one explanation of his well-known rejection of Jean Philippe Rameau's theories.[19] We know from the obituary written by Philipp Emanuel Bach and J. F. Agricola that " . . . Bach did not . . . occupy himself with deep theoretical speculations on music . . . ,"[20] and since there was no German translation of Rameau's theoretical writings during Bach's lifetime it is improbable that he was familiar at first hand with the details of Rameau's doctrines. It is quite conceivable, however, that Bach had heard Rameau's tenet, "it is harmony that is generated first"[21] and that he shared Mattheson's opinion that "We consider the melody as the basis of the entire art of composition and cannot understand it . . . when it is maintained counter to all reason that the melody is derived from the harmony[+] . . . . [+]See *Traité de l'Harmonie* par M. *Rameau,* L. II Ch. 19, p. 139, Ch. 21, p. 147. Most astonishing, it is maintained that the harmony is engendered first. I admit: what is engendered must have parents."[22]

Curiously, the issue of the priority of melody or harmony was anticipated by J. G. Walther in his *Praecepta der musicalischen Composition.*[23] In the chapter entitled "Of the Parts and in Particular the Principal Parts," Walther presents the following cogent and pragmatic evaluation of the arguments for beginning composition with the melody as well as those for beginning with the bass:

§9. It is easy to calculate what part is to be written down first. Since the

---

[17] See, for example, Sketch No. 156 and the subjects of BWV 75/1 (p. 139f. below), BWV 76/1 (p. 205 below), BWV 187/1, mm. 66ff., and BWV 19/1, mm. 1ff.

[18] Sketch No. 101 for BWV 135/1 presents only the principal voice-leading motion of the three upper voices, without regard for text declamation or even the precise melodic shape of the first beat of m. 20. It may therefore be an example of Bach

having composed schematically—in outline— rather than in detail.

[19] See David-Mendel 1966, p. 450.

[20] See the reprint in Richter 1920, pp. 25–26, and the English translation in David-Mendel 1966, p. 224.

[21] Translated in Strunk 1950, p. 571.

[22] Mattheson 1739, p. 133.

[23] Walther 1708, p. 104.

discant and bass, as the two extreme voices are heard more clearly than the others, one of these must necessarily be written first. It is most advantageous if the discant, which as the highest part is the most easily perceived by the ears, is invented first. One can give it any melody one pleases and is not bound to anything. If, on the contrary, the bass is written down first, one can no longer give the discant so lovely and pleasant a form as one would wish. In the event that no "inventions" occur to one, however, the latter procedure serves well. One should simply write down a bass and construct the other parts above it. A melody will then appear which was not and could not possibly have been invented. Once the melody has been brought forth in this way, as it were automatically, the composer can subsequently refine it as he wishes.

§10. It is also the most concise and easiest way of composing, when the other parts are constructed over the fundamental bass. If one were to begin with the upper parts and lay the foundation under them afterwards (in the manner of some curious architects) the musical structure would be more shapely (as was explained in the preceding §) but this would be much more tedious and difficult, especially for the beginner.[24]

The significance of Bach's preferred practice, described on the preceding pages, in the light of Walther's precepts is all too evident—and hardly surprising.

The Homophonic Ritornello

The sketch evidence available for a reconstruction of the sequence of steps following the drafting of the opening melodic idea,[25] while admittedly sparse, is sufficient to indicate that even within one musical style Bach composed in different ways on different occasions. One is tempted to maintain from one chain of evidence that Bach composed homophonic ritornelli as follows:

1. wrote down the melody for the first phrase (Sketches Nos. 42, 70, or 80);
2. composed the continuo part for this phrase (Sketches Nos. 19, 21, 36);
3. filled in the inner parts for the first phrase (Sketch No. 148);
4. drafted the melody for the following phrase (Sketch No. 116);
5. wrote the continuo for the second phrase (Sketch No. 88), and so on until the ritornello was completed.

This hypothesis, considered from the point of view of musical logic, is quite appealing. But as early as the second stage it rests on an assumption—derived from the fact that there are no extant single-voiced opening sketches of accom-

---

[24] Similar discussions appear no doubt in earlier writings, too. The citation from Walther seems particularly relevant, though, in view of the close personal relationship between him and Bach.

[25] The 27 multi-voiced sketches mentioned at the beginning of this chapter.

panimental continuo parts above which the upper melodic part was later composed—that the melody in two-voiced melody-continuo sketches was written
before the accompanying continuo part. But this was surely not the case, as we
have seen, in Sketch No. 28, discussed above.[26] By the third stage the number
of different possibilities has further increased, for it is now also possible that Bach
composed the continuo in Sketch No. 148, for example, after having written
down all the upper parts. Indeed, there are sketches that show that Bach did
occasionally write down the middle parts of a homophonic texture before the
continuo, suggesting that in these instances his interest in textural detail took
precedence over the establishment of the outer-voice framework. Consider
Sketches Nos. 71 and 151, where the continuo line does not appear at all.[27] Here
it is quite possible, however, that the fact of the continuo's staying on the tonic
throughout the measure or measures was taken for granted, i.e., that the outer-
voice harmonic structure of the passage was in a sense conceived first, and that
the persistence of the continuo on the tonic was actually the first element to
be conceived—so much so, in fact, as perhaps not to have received any conscious
attention. But Bach had surely not yet conceived the specific formulation of the
continuo line at the time these sketches were written down, i.e., the rhythmic,
melodic, and/or motivic form of the part—a held-note, repeated-note, or arpeggio
pattern, etc. At this point speculation encroaches on the "unknowable biographical factors" mentioned on the first page of this study, this time raising the
question whether one can assume that the first part to be written down was
always the first part to be conceived, or its converse: what Bach had not yet
written down he had not yet thought of.[28]

By the fourth stage we must also reckon with the possibility that Bach first

---

[26] It should be stressed, though, that the continuo
part in Sketch No. 28 was probably conceived as
an ostinato *theme,* and was thus not strictly accompanimental, as, say, the continuo part in Sketch
No. 148.

[27] For a fuller discussion of Sketch No. 71, and
its relationship to Sketch No. 69, see the discussion
of "Changes in Textural Style," Chapter VII below.

[28] Riemann 1909 deals rather extensively with
the entire complex of such questions involved with
the analysis of sketches as clues to the "creative
process." Riemann's main thesis can perhaps be
summarized as follows: composing is done only in
the mind, not on paper. Only the imagination
creates; reason criticizes this creation, but the
correction is again a product of imagination alone.
Therefore even sketches teach nothing about the
process of composition, since this process is internal.
Particularly relevant to the present question is the

following remark: "The composer must first conceive that which later . . . becomes the written
composition. What he conceives are not notes . . .
but . . . real, sounding tones, and not single tones,
but tones incorporated into large complexes. . . .
Sketches are indications of a principal voice in a
many-voiced, variously shaded complex whole,
understandable only to the composer himself, in
whom this whole was immediately called to memory when he saw the sketch. Anyone else, however,
who is not at least familiar with the final product,
can not possibly have an adequate notion of what
the composer heard when he jotted the sketch for
himself" (pp. 37–38). These remarks were made in
specific reference to the Beethoven sketches. To
what degree they are valid for Bach's compositional
procedure should become clear in the course of this
study.

wrote down two or more melodic phrases of the ritornello before returning to the beginning to compose the continuo—or the inner parts—for the first phrase. The following diagram attempts to illustrate a few of the various possible combinations of stages.

SOME OF THE POSSIBLE ORDERS IN WHICH BACH
CONSTRUCTED HOMOPHONIC ARIA RITORNELLI

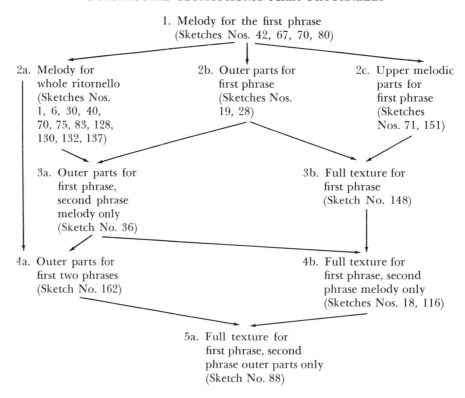

A careful examination of the manuscripts may help at times to eliminate some of these possibilities. One can regard the position of the barlines: (a) what part or parts are most naturally accommodated by the barline, (b) what part or parts are obviously crowded into the available space or even go over the barline, (c) what parts have "too much" room.[29] It is also possible to examine the vertical alignment of the parts: (a) the alignment of notes to be sounded together within the bar, (b) the evidence of notes placed to avoid colliding with a previously written part. A high note on a leger line, for example, may have been set to avoid colliding with a low note on the staff above.[30] An analysis, finally, of any corrections present may yield valuable clues concerning the order in which the

---

[29] See, for example, m. 4 in the facsimile of Sketch No. 148 provided in Volume II.

[30] See the facsimile of Sketch No. 88. The position of m. 9.6 of the flute part in relation to m.

2.1 of the continuo indicates that the continuo for the first phrase was composed before the melody of the second phrase. See also Chapter V, p. 94, above.

parts were composed. Such material will be evaluated later in this chapter.

Several sketches shed light on Bach's procedures when composing basically homophonic ritornelli with polyphonic elements. Sketches Nos. 84 and 114 suggest that Bach first sketched in the opening imitative entrances. As soon as the point of imitation was completed and the texture became homophonic, he continued the principal melodic part to the cadence. In the two present sketches, Bach thereupon drafted (and in Sketch No. 84 completed) the outer-voice framework to the next full cadence. Here, too, some supposition is involved: it is also possible—and there is no unambiguous visible evidence to the contrary—that Bach first wrote down the outer-voice framework and only then entered the points of imitation in the middle voices.

In Sketch No. 106, Bach worked out the outer-voice framework for the entire ritornello and entered the independently led oboe parts in mm. 4–14 to form a melodic and rhythmic web with the trumpet and continuo parts. The exact sequence of these steps cannot be reconstructed.

The chronology of events in Sketch No. 134 is similar to that of Sketches Nos. 84 and 114. Again Bach seems first to have written out all the parts in the opening measures—in order to establish the texture, sonority, and "idea" of the ritornello—and then to have spun out the principal melodic part to the next important cadence. That part in the present case is the continuo. Through a series of falling fifths it outlines an harmonic progression to the dominant: d, g, c♯, f♯, b, e, a, d, g, A, whereupon the main melodic material returns in the trumpets and horns in mm. 19–22.[31]

Choral Fugues

The surviving sketches and drafts for choral fugues, as well as the evidence of the composing scores, hardly allow a more certain reconstruction of the compositional stages than was possible for homophonic ritornelli. It seems that Bach's usual, but not exclusive, procedure when drafting a fugue subject was as follows. After fashioning a satisfactory subject from an idea suggested by the text,[32] Bach would write in the statements of answers and subjects in the remaining voices, thereby establishing the order of successive voice entries as well as the pitch and time intervals between them. He next drafted the shape of the countersubject in the first voice and entered it consequently in the other parts,

[31] The transcription of this sketch in Schünemann 1935, p. 20, gives the impression that the notations in the bass and continuo staves in mm. 5–10 represent two independent lines that should be played simultaneously. Undoubtedly, Bach first wrote the continuo part on the proper staff, corrected it, and then wrote a third version of the part on the bass staff above.

[32] See Sketches Nos. 45, 150, 153, and 156.

and so on. There is no evidence that he in reality composed choral fugue expositions in homophonic "blocks" to work out the details of the invertible counterpoint in advance as seems to be implied by Neumann.[33] Bach's procedures after
inventing the subject accord rather with traditional notions of how one goes
about writing a fugue. This traditional method of fugal composition, moreover,
satisfied more objectives simultaneously than the preliminary construction of
vertical *Stimmtausch* blocks would have done. When the third counterpoint (the
fourth *Stimmtausch* element) of a four-voice permutation fugue exposition was
finally added in the first voice, sounding together with the fourth statement of
the subject and the statements of the two remaining counterpoints, the complete
Stimmtausch block arose, as it were, by itself, and Bach could then check the voices
and correct errors of voice leading and adjust the parts to permit permutation
of the counterpoints.[34] Composing in the traditional manner had also fixed the
order of voice entries, and the time and pitch intervals between these entries;
and it enabled the composer to judge immediately the effectiveness of the horizontal sequence of subject, first, second, and third counterpoints in a single voice.
The first steps of Bach's fugue-writing procedure are visible in Sketch No. 45,
in which he drafted a fugue subject based on the opening line of text, then wrote
down the answer in the next entering voice, and finally began to draft the first
countersubject in the first voice.

The genesis of a Bach choral fugue composition can best be illustrated with
the drafts and final version of mm. 19–22 from the chorus "Sie werden aus Saba
alle kommen," BWV 65/1, transcribed as Sketch No. 41 in Volume II.[35] It is
possible, by separating the individual layers of corrections, to distinguish ten
stages in the evolution of this fugue exposition.

1. The original one-measure subject or the beginning of it was written down
in all voices before the countersubject was entered in any part. This is evident

---

[33] Neumann 1938, pp. 14–52. He does not ex-
pressly suggest that Bach composed homophonic
Stimmtausch blocks of invertible counterpoints as the
starting point of his compositional activity, but the
reader is likely to have this impression from the
manner of Neumann's presentation.

[34] A modification of this procedure is evident in
the composing score of BWV 182/2. See Mendel
1960[1], pp. 292–293, and below.

[35] The fact that the drafts are found in the
autograph of BWV 81 (P 120), below the concluding chorale of that cantata (see the facsimile in
Volume II), leads one to suppose at first that Bach
wrote the draft of the middle section of the
Epiphany Cantata, BWV 65 (first performed
January 6, 1724), after he had completed the

cantata for the fourth Sunday after Epiphany,
BWV 81 (first performed January 30, 1724). This
would clearly have wide-ranging consequences for
our notions of Bach's work rhythm in the first
Leipzig years. A closer examination of both manuscripts reveals at once, however, that Movement
1, m. 19 of BWV 65 begins a new sheet in the
autograph (P 147, f. 3r). Bach, then, had taken a
new sheet, left the upper nine staves free for the
instrumental parts and had begun to draft the
fugue exposition on staves 10-14. After discarding
the draft, he laid the sheet aside until he composed
BWV 81. The case is completely analogous to those
discussed earlier (see pp. 31f. and 121), except that
this time Bach did not turn the sheet upside down
before reusing it.

from the vertical alignment of the voices in mm. 2–3 and from the low swing
of the abbreviation hook of *werden* in m. 4 (see the facsimile):[36]

2. Bach next wrote in the first version of the countersubject in the bass and
tenor lines:

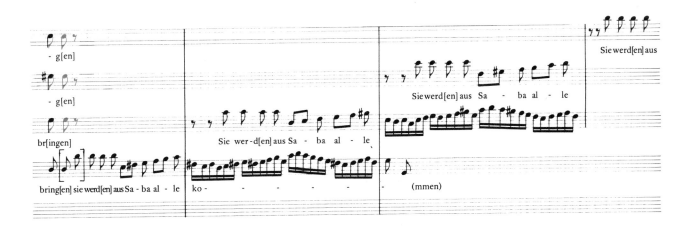

3. The opening motif of the subject was now altered to the intermediate
reading (as discussed above) in all four voices. Perhaps simultaneously Bach
revised the countersubject—before the original reading had been entered in the
alto—apparently to shift the tonal orientation of the exposition from G to C

[36] Bach may have written in the first few notes
of the original countersubject in the bass and tenor
parts at this stage, but then it would be curious
why he did not do the same in the alto part. See
the next two stages.

major. At this point, too, Bach entered the continuo part in the first measure of the draft:

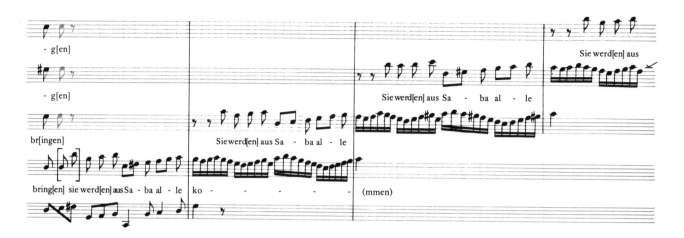

That the continuo part was not added before this stage is evident from the final tone of the part—g—which is possible only with the revised version of the countersubject. Also the fact that the second beat of the first measure of the continuo part moves in parallel tenths with the revised reading of the subject supports this assumption.

4–6. Bach decided now to increase the length of the subject from one to two measures, and this obliged him to begin a new system. This fundamental change had a twofold purpose: to offer a contrast to the stretto-like entrances of the first theme (m. 9 of the score), and to lend a formal symmetry to the movement, which in its final reading has the following proportions:

$$
\begin{array}{cccc}
& A & B & A' \\
\text{Mm.} & \text{1-18(19)} & \text{19-45} & \text{45-53 or} \\
& 18 & +\quad 27\quad + & 9\quad \text{measures} \\
& & \underline{\qquad 27 \qquad} &
\end{array}
$$

The next three strata of corrections are devoted to refining the opening measure of the subject:[37]

4.

5.

6.

after which (7) Bach entered the answer in the tenor and (8) drafted the new countersubject:[38]

9. Now that Bach had found what he believed to be the final version of the opening subject and countersubject, he took a new sheet of paper (P 147) and copied the last reading anew, at the same time changing the reading of the second measure of the countersubject:[39]

10. Finally, the form of the second measure of the subject was revised:

[38] The space left in m. 3 of the bass part to insure proper alignment between tenor and bass illustrates quite clearly that the answer was written down before the countersubject was composed (compare the remarks concerning stage 1 above).

[39] The correction of the beaming in the first measure was doubtless made necessary by a lapse of attention.

presumably in order to add metrical emphasis to the structural tones of the line:

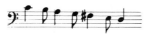

The revision also avoids the monotonous tone repetitions on every strong beat within every sequential unit and relieves the unbroken stepwise motion of the original figure.

It is not clear at what stage the continuo part was added to the draft. If it was added at the penultimate stage before the revision of the sixteenth-note figure of the subject, then this revision could be understood as a grammatical correction: the B of the continuo in the second measure clashed with the c′ of the bass and the e of the continuo with the f♯ of the bass; and in the fourth measure the e of the continuo clashed with the f of the tenor and the A with the b of the tenor. Also, the octave a-A on the sixth eighth-beat of the second measure was approached by similar motion. It is also possible, however, that the continuo was not added until after the sixteenth-note figure was corrected, and that these grammatical considerations did not motivate the change.

WHEN COMPOSING choral fugue expositions, Bach did not always follow the procedure evident in the draft of BWV 65/1, just as he apparently composed homophonic ritornelli in more than one way. In his analysis of the autograph of BWV 182/2, "Himmelskönig, sei willkommen," Arthur Mendel writes that "Bach starts out as follows, writing in the first brace the whole four measures of the soprano"—i.e., the subject and counterpoints 1, 2, and 3—and only then wrote "the rests plus three measures of the alto, then the rests plus two measures of the tenor and finally the rests plus the subject in the bass."[40] Such a procedure would contradict the interpretation of Bach's fugue-writing practice discussed in general above and just illustrated with the drafts for BWV 65/1. In the case of BWV 182/2, too, I prefer to think that Bach first wrote the subject in all four voices, then entered counterpoint 1 in the upper three voices, then counterpoint 2 in the upper two voices, and only then invented counterpoint 3 in the soprano and encountered the voice-leading difficulties described on p. 293 of the Mendel article.

The autograph[41] offers no conclusive visual evidence for either hypothesis. But it does *seem* that the word *sey* in m. 2 of the soprano part (and, as a consequence, presumably the notes of the soprano part as well) was written down before the entrance of the subject in the alto where there is a large space between the

---

[40] Mendel 1960[1], pp. 292–293.

[41] See the facsimile (Plate 2) after p. 294 in Mendel 1960[1].

seventh and eighth notes to accommodate the word. This tends to support Mendel's assumption. At least Bach may have written two measures of the soprano part before entering the alto part.[42] On the whole, all parts of the exposition are equally well accommodated by the barlines, so that the latter shed no light on the problem.

The evidence of barline placement in the autograph scores of choral fugue expositions tends to indicate, when it is at all revealing, that Bach usually, but not always, proceeded in the manner observed in the drafts of BWV 65/1. The autographs of choral fugues in cantatas of the first Leipzig *Jahrgang* offer the following material bearing on the matter.

In BWV 40/1 (P 63) Bach had at first written the soprano entrance of the fugal exposition in m. 33, two measures after the bass entrance—just as the bass entered two measures after the initial statement of the subject in the tenor—and drawn the barlines through all four vocal staves. But then he decided on a three-measure interval between the bass and soprano entrances. He therefore placed a one-measure rest between the barline and the quarter-rest at the beginning of the soprano measure and proceeded to compose the counterpoints in the tenor and bass parts, crowding the notes into the available space (f. 3v):

The subject was clearly entered in the soprano part before the counterpoints in the remaining parts were invented.

In the fugal exposition of BWV 105/1 (P 99) the second and third counterpoints in mm. 63–65 go over the barlines in the bass and tenor parts respectively, while the subject and the first counterpoint (which moves in half-notes) are accommodated within the barlines. The first counterpoint in the bass of BWV 119/7 (P 878), m. 19, goes over the barline. As in BWV 105/1, the subject—this time in the tenor—was written down first.

On the other hand, the autograph score of the fugue "Euer Herz soll ewiglich leben," BWV 75/1 (P 66), mm., 68ff., reveals quite consistently that Bach wrote

---

[42] See also the discussion of BWV 75/1 below.

in the first counterpoint in each voice before he had entered the subject in the new voice, thus according to a degree with the manner of procedure described by Mendel in his analysis of the "Himmelskönig" fugue. Since the subject of the "Euer Herz" exposition moves in slower note-values

than the first counterpoint

it is likely that the sixteenth-note figure probably would have gone over the barline or been crowded into the available space if the subject had been written down first in mm. 70–71, 73, 75–76. It is perfectly clear from the autograph, however, that the barlines were drawn to accommodate the sixteenth-note figure. Moreover, in P 66 the vertical alignment of the parts sounding the subject and first counterpoint in the measures just cited is excellent. This would not be the case if Bach had not written down the first counterpoint first. In this exposition, then, Bach wrote the subject and first counterpoint in each voice before he wrote the subject (and first counterpoint) in the next entering voice—schematically, thus:

(3) Subject   +   Counterpoint 1
(4) Subject   +   Counterpoint 1
(1) Subject + Counterpoint 1
(2) Subject   +   Counterpoint 1

It is also clear from the relationship of the parts to the barlines that counterpoint 1 in the bass was entered before counterpoint 2 in the tenor, and counterpoint 1 in the soprano before counterpoint 2 in the bass and counterpoint 3 in the tenor. Bach did not, then, first write out subject, counterpoint 1, counterpoint 2, and counterpoint 3 in the tenor before composing the bass, and the subject, counterpoint 1, counterpoint 2 in the bass before composing the soprano, and so on, according to Mendel's assumption for BWV 182/2.

The autograph of BWV 144/1 (P 134) [43] offers mutually contradictory barline

[43] See the facsimile in NBA I/7, p. vii.

evidence which in fact points up the futility of attempting a reconstruction of the steps of Bach's procedures based too exclusively on such material. In m. 4, counterpoint 1, a figure with the rhythm ♩ ♪♪♩ ♪♪ is well accommodated by the barlines and was therefore presumably written down before the subject in the bass. But in m. 10 the subject in the soprano was evidently written down before the counterpoints in the tenor and bass, since both go over the barlines. More paradoxically, the appearance of m. 12 suggests that the subject in the alto was written down before counterpoint 1 in the soprano, which goes over the barlines, while in m. 13 the spacing and alignment of the two parts suggest that counterpoint 1 in the soprano was written down before the subject in the alto.

Bach, then, did not compose fugal expositions according to a mechanical, predictable routine any more than he drafted homophonic ritornelli in accordance with an invariable scheme. Our attempt to codify the steps of Bach's composing process has proven just as futile in the one genre as in the other, and it is necessary to repeat that even within the same musical style, Bach composed in different ways on different occasions.

Continuation Sketches

It was mentioned earlier that most Bach sketches are found on recto pages in the autograph scores and record the continuation of the music that was to be written on the following verso once the ink had dried. One can consider such sketches—which are usually found on the bottom of the page on any spare staff or staves—to be essentially extended *custodes*.[44] If no staves were available, the sketches were written below the score in tablature.

Reaching the end of a recto page probably caused a considerable interruption in the compositional act. The composer had not only to wait until the ink dried, but also to write down the brackets, clefs, signatures, and perhaps even rule the staves[45] on the new page before he was able to resume composing.

---

[44] Sketches Nos. 89 and 161, in fact, actually employ the *custos*.

[45] As was pointed out in Chapter III, Bach ruled the staves for an entire sheet (four pages) in advance, before beginning to write on it. Therefore the need to rule staves in the middle of work on a composition occurred only when Bach completed one sheet and took a new one—assuming he had not ruled enough paper beforehand for the whole composition. Usually, though, he must have had an adequate supply of ruled sheets on hand, for continuation sketches on the last page (verso) of a sheet are exceedingly rare. The second sketch (Sketch No. 154) for the *Pleni* theme of the *B minor Mass* discussed above is one such sketch. Of course Bach may have temporarily interrupted his work on a composition—and thus felt the need to write a continuation sketch—for any number of reasons besides that of having to rule more paper.

The continuation sketches contained in the extant autographs of the vocal works are:

Sketch No.	Sketch No.	Sketch No.	Sketch No.
2	44	89	121
3	46	90	122
4	48	91	123
5	49	92	124
8	52	93	125
9	53	94	126
10	55	95	129
11	56	97	131
13	57	98	133
14	58	99	136
15	59	100	137
16	60	101	138
17	61	102	140
20	62	103	141
22	64	104	144
24	65	105	145
25	66	107	146
26	68	108	147
27	72	109	154
29	73	110	155
31	74	111	157
32	76	112	158
33	77	113	159
34	81	115	161
35	82	117	163
37	85	118	164
38	86	119	
39	87	120	

Since there are only 110 continuation sketches, they are obviously not found on every recto page of every composing score. Such sketches, in fact, were necessary only when the page turn interrupted the free invention of new musical material. Therefore, they do not appear in recitatives or in simple four-part chorales (which in any event rarely go over the page) where the melodic material, rhythm, and texture were predetermined. The absence of continuation sketches in the recitatives[46] suggests that they were not thought out at all in any detail in advance but were conceived in very small melodic units—often as small as half-measures, perhaps governed by the affective and prosodic character of the text.[47]

But in the freer forms, the choruses and arias, there are also relatively few continuation sketches. If a page turn occurred while Bach was writing out a major repetition of an earlier passage (usually a quotation of ritornello material), continuation sketches were rarely necessary, for such a passage normally involved literal copying or perhaps mechanical transposition of "preexistent," i.e., earlier, material. Similarly, the tight organization of choral fugues—based largely on the permutation and combination of a limited number of musical elements—reduces the role of "free invention" here even more than in the arias and homophonic choruses based on a ritornello, and explains the rarity of continuation sketches in these movements.[48]

The continuation sketches that are present, though, reveal not only what part (or parts) in a particular musical genre and situation was conceived, or rather written down, first, but also how far in advance this part was thought out. With few exceptions, these marginal notations lead the new melodic idea that had been interrupted at a page turn to the next significant cadence or caesura. Accordingly, they vary greatly in length—from two notes (Sketch No. 38) to fourteen measures (Sketch No. 147). Bach rarely sketched the beginning of a completely new passage when the end of the page coincided with a major articulation,[49] which suggests that he normally thought in complete melodic phrases but usually not more than one at a time. This is not to say that Bach as a rule had no idea what he would write after he completed the phrase on which he was at work at the moment, but that he normally conceived in detail only one phrase at a time, just as a writer of prose may have in mind a general idea

---

[46] The only extant continuation sketch in a recitative is Sketch No. 87 from BWV 116/5 (Paris). Sketch No. 100, from BWV 134/3 (P 1138) is not a continuation sketch but part of a copy. With the exception of the autograph sketch P 1138 is a fair copy in a copyist's hand. The manuscript, consisting of one four-page sheet, preserves in part the first version of the cantata *Ein Herz, das seinen Jesum lebend weiß*, BWV 134, a parody of the secular Cöthen cantata, *Die Zeit, die Tag und Jahre macht*, BWV 134a. P 1138 was evidently prepared as a substitute for the (missing or unusable) first four pages of the Cöthen score fragment (Paris MS 2) which served otherwise as the score for the first parody version (see NBA I/10, KB, pp. 77–87).

Since the first $26\frac{1}{2}$ measures of Mvt. 3 were missing in the Cöthen score, it was necessary that they be included in P 1138. Because of a lack of space, mm. 25–26a had to be entered in a sketch-like manner in tablature.

[47] See Chapter V, particularly the opening and concluding remarks in the discussion of "The Order of Events."

[48] See the analyses of Bach's compositional techniques in Dürr 1951, pp. 104–151 (the arias) and in Neumann 1938 (the choral fugues), *passim*.

[49] Sketch No. 157 is such a rare example. In Sketch No. 31 Bach recorded his intention to repeat the text line *nämlich: Gottes Wort halten*, etc., in the next passage of the chorus.

of the content of an entire paragraph but knows the specific wording of only one sentence—or one phrase—at a time.[50]

As one would conclude from the preceding remarks, the continuation sketches occur predominantly for the leading instrumental part of opening ritornelli or for the voice part of later freely composed passages, i.e., sections essentially independent of major quotations of earlier material. They thus confirm the impression received from the opening drafts that Bach usually wrote down the principal melodic part first in a given context. Vocal sketches usually include the text, and otherwise carefully notate the beaming—testimony once more to Bach's meticulous concern with problems of declamation and to the text-engendered character of his melodic invention. Sketch No. 25 may serve as a typical example. The sketch concludes the final vocal episode of the movement before the closing ritornello.[51] Occasionally Bach did not complete the melodic phrase entirely but sketched only the essential contour, the conclusion presumably being regarded then as inevitable. There are numerous sketches in which the sketched phrase is complete except for the last few cadential tones.[52]

Several continuation sketches reveal that Bach at times first drafted the harmonic progression represented by the continuo part. In such passages the upper parts embellish the harmonic framework defined by the continuo rather than develop an individual melodic character. This technique is especially typical of Bach's homophonic choruses and elaborately orchestrated movements, in which the upper parts can often be regarded as written-out thorough bass realizations, characterized by scale and arpeggio figures, broken chords, and similar rhythmic and melodic diminutions of the fundamental chord tones. Sketch No. 154 for the concluding measures of the *Sanctus* section of the *B minor Mass* that precede the *Pleni* section illustrates this technique. One could perhaps maintain that the continuo (and bass) line here was sketched as the principal bearer of the melody, developing the dominant triplet motif of the movement. But its primary function is clearly to spin out via this motif the harmonic sequence of fifths initiated in

---

[50] In a private communication Alfred Dürr envisioned this aspect of Bach's creative process as follows: ". . . Bach had an approximate idea of the entire cantata, a somewhat more precise idea of the movement on which he was working, a still more precise idea of the section of the movement on which he was working, and so on. That he only sketched a single phrase in advance need not imply that he did not have an *almost* precise idea of the next phrase."

[51] The placement of the syllable *-fer* at the beginning of m. 59 in the sketch suggests that in this instance the text was written down before the music. The beaming makes the underlay unambiguous.

[52] See Sketches Nos. 2, 11, 22, 27, 32, 46, 65, 66, 68, 95, 108, 111, 112, 113, 115, 117, 122, 133, 146, 147, and 164. Sketch No. 146 breaks off after a *custos* on the note a♯, which suggests that the cadential tone b was to follow "inevitably" in m. 136. As the final version reveals, however, Bach then decided to extend the phrase to m. 137 by repeating the basso part of m. 135 in m. 136. This decision was no doubt made necessary in order to accommodate all the words of the text line.

m. 41 in B minor to the final F-sharp minor cadence. The violins move essentially in parallel motion with the continuo while the upper voices of the chorus and the doubling instrumental parts provide a realization of the thorough bass, rhythmicized to accommodate the syllables of the text. Other continuation sketches for homophonic choruses are Sketches Nos. 24, 46, 94, 133, 155, and 161.

In arias, on the other hand, the principal melodic parts were only rarely written down after the continuo part. The three extant marginal sketches for the continuo line in aria movements (Sketches Nos. 90, 109, and 125) are confined to passages based on ritornello material. Sketches Nos. 90 and 125 indicate the modifications of the harmonic structure of the ritornello necessary for the immediate tonal development of the music. Bach wrote Sketch No. 125 apparently to remind himself that m. 30a of the instrumental interlude was to have the same harmonic and melodic function as the original statement in m. 5 (transposed down a fourth) in contrast to m. 21 where the harmonic rhythm had been retarded:

Here again, as in Sketch No. 154, the continuo part is also melodically the most significant, for the two gambas have held chord tones.

Sketch No. 90 fixes the continuo part in the middle of the basso ostinato period that extends from mm. 55–63. This period is a varied version of the continuo line in mm. 1–9. The page turn occurred at the critical moment in the progress of the period where the theme modulates from B minor to F-sharp minor. This turning point is marked by the entrance of the oboe with the ritornello melody in the tonic. The continuo line of mm. 55–63 differs from that of mm. 1–9 from the moment of modulation on by omitting the motion to the subdominant characteristic of mm. 5–7 (in which key, of course, the former period began) and replacing this motion with an insistence upon the dominant.

Mm. 1–9

Mm. 55–63

Sketch No. 109, on the other hand, was apparently written to record a formal nuance: the quotation (in transposition) at the conclusion of the B section of the same continuo figure that had appeared at the conclusion of the opening ritornello (m. 7) and at the end of the A section (m. 32).

On occasion Bach sketched the continuation of a purely melodic part within a literal repetition of earlier material, a repetition which entailed, properly speaking, no "free" invention. Here, too, it is usually possible to reconstruct his deliberations. As Emil Platen[53] has demonstrated, the instrumental interludes of Bach's chorale fantasias for chorus and orchestra consist almost exclusively of elements extracted literally from the opening orchestral ritornello, but shortened and spliced into new configurations as well as transposed, if necessary, to prepare the entrance of the next line of the chorale strophe. Sketch No. 98 presumably notes the continuation of the Violin 1 part in m. 52 of BWV 133/1. The final reading, however, is written directly on the new page without any traces of corrections and bears no resemblance to the sketch.

Measure 52 belongs to the fourth interlude of the movement. This interlude is constructed from the following measures of the ritornello:[54]

Fourth interlude:	m.	47b	48	49	50	51	52	53	54	55	56	57
= Opening ritornello:	m.		0^{-3}	1^{-3}	2^{-3}	3^{-3}	4^{-3}	5^{-3}	6^{-3}	9	10	11	12
							(or	6	7)			

The tonal function of the interlude is to form a transition from the B minor cadence in m. 47 to the entrance of the fifth line of the chorale in A major. The sketch suggests that Bach initially planned to continue the interlude after m. 51 by joining mm. 15–17 of the opening ritornello, rather than mm. 5–6 (or 6–7) plus 9–12, onto the first four transposed measures of the ritornello. The original combination would have effected the desired harmonic progression via E to A major more quickly than the final version.

BWV 133/1, Violin 1, m. 48ff., original plan

BWV 133/1, Violin 1, mm. 51–57, final version

[53] Platen 1959, pp. 164–204.
[54] The exponent $^{-3}$ refers to the interval of transposition: down a minor third. The absence of an exponent indicates a non-transposed repetition of the corresponding measures of the ritornello.

But it would not have permitted a natural *Einbau* of the chorale into the subsequent measures of the ritornello theme: note the parallel octaves in the hypothetical mm. 54–55 between the chorale melody and the obbligato Violin 1 line.

Sketch No. 118 occurs also within what is in a sense a literal repetition of earlier material. It records Bach's original intention to have the soprano part—the last part to enter in the choral fugue exposition beginning in m. 66—conclude the fugal melody with the same cadential figure he had given to the bass (m. 75), tenor (m. 78), and alto (m. 79).

(-sät-) - - - ti-get

M. 75, Bass

Bach may have decided to disregard the original pattern and to extend the soprano phrase to the beginning of m. 82 in order to emphasize the arrival on B♭ with a perfect authentic cadence. This cadence not only marks the conclusion of the first exposition of the fugue but forms one of the principal structural points in the movement; the basic tonal outline of the chorus is:

	gm	D	B♭	gm
= mm.	1–28	49–66	82	98

The final version of the soprano in m. 82 reads accordingly:

(ge-)sät - - - ti - get

The Composing Scores

One major conclusion drawn from the survey of continuation sketches was that Bach generally first wrote down the principal melodic part in a given context. This was (1) the leading instrumental part in the opening ritornello, (2) the vocal part in freely composed passages where there is no ritornello or cantus firmus material in any instrumental part, or (3) the continuo part in certain homophonic choruses featuring no characteristic melodic material in the upper parts. This conclusion is corroborated by other evidence found in the composing scores. The relevant material is quite extensive but falls into three general categories familiar to the reader from previous discussions in this chapter:

(1) deleted passages, in which one or more parts or measures were crossed out before the passages were completed, (2) evidence pertaining to the position of various parts within a measure in relation to the barline, and (3) corrections of detail.

DELETED PASSAGES

A draft for the concluding measures of the B section of BWV 96/5 (P 179), the aria "Bald zur Rechten, bald zur Linken," reveals—not unexpectedly—that Bach at first led the bass part to the final cadence before he composed the accompanying continuo part.

BWV 96/5, mm. 62ff. (P 179, f. 9v)

Bach's decision to add a melisma on the word *Pforte*, and thus lengthen the phrase one measure, obliged him to abandon the draft.[55] Similarly in BWV 206/3 (P 42/1), "Schleuß des Janustempels Thüren," Bach drafted the bass part from m. 45 to m. 62, i.e., for the conclusion of the vocal portion of the A section,

[55] It is worth noting that the clefs were not written down in advance for the new system. As the example shows, Bach originally counted the staves incorrectly, placing the bass clef for the voice part on the fifth staff instead of the sixth; he then changed the bass clef to an alto clef for the violin line. Bach was also careless in setting up the system for the final version; the system has six staves instead of seven, although a seventh staff was available on the bottom of the page.

before any other part had been composed. This initial draft was crossed out and the new version of the passage written on the blank staff above.[56]

The composing score of BWV 110/6 (P 153), "Wacht auf, wacht auf," reveals again that Bach drafted the leading melodic part (the trumpet) in mm. 6–9 of the opening ritornello to a cadence before he had entered any other part. Measures 6–9 begin a new page of the manuscript (f. 18r). Bach wrote down the trumpet part for four measures in advance on the uppermost staff of the new page (again before he had written the clefs for the remainder of the system). The draft was crossed out and the new version of the trumpet part written on the second staff.[57]

Rejected passages indicate as well that Bach first wrote down the preexistent material in vocal sections where the instrumental parts are based on ritornello material into which the vocal part was fitted (*eingebaut*). The following draft for mm. 20–24 of BWV 10/2 (LC), "Herr, der du stark und mächtig bist," written on the bottom three staves of f. 5r of the autograph, was probably rejected simply because there was no room for the notation of the second violin and viola parts on the reduced system:

The draft indicates clearly that the instrumental parts based on the opening ritornello (mm. 21–24 are a repetition of mm. 7–10, transposed up a fifth) were written down first with the intent, as the final version shows, of working the vocal part into this context. In the first (freely composed) measure of the draft the soprano as the leading melodic part was doubtless notated before the clearly accompanimental instrumental parts.

[56] For the original reading see NBA I/36, KB, p. 129. In P 42/1, Mvt. 3 is written below Mvt. 1 on the bottom five staves of the page. Movement 1 occupies staves 1–14; staff 15 is as a rule blank, and Mvt. 3 is written on staves 16–20. But since Bach used what is normally the viola staff on ff. 5v-6r for the new version of the bass part, the string parts were entered on staves 15–17 instead of staves 16–18. The bracket at the beginning of the system embraces, as usual, staves 16–20, but the clefs are not changed. As in BWV 96/5, Bach did not enter the clefs for the system until he had first written down and corrected the bass part.

[57] Actually the revision of the passage extends back to m. 5 at the end of f. 17v. See the original reading of the passage, transcribed in NBA I/2, KB, p. 109.

In the autograph of BWV 48/1 (P 109), "Ich elender Mensch," the trumpet and oboes which sound the cantus firmus in canon were first entered and corrected as follows

M. 126ff.

before the free string and choral parts were composed.[58] Here again, then, as in the preceding example, the preexistent material of a passage was written down before the free parts were composed.

BARLINE EVIDENCE

The conclusions thus far drawn regarding the order of events can be further corroborated by observing the position of the individual parts in relation to the barline. The assumption underlying the evaluation of this evidence is that Bach drew the barline after he had written the first part in a measure, and that the remaining parts had to be disposed therefore in the space already measured off. If a secondary part then was notated in smaller rhythmic values than the first part, and thus had more notes to the measure, some of the notes in the part would go over the previously drawn barline or the part would obviously be crowded into the available space.

Since the evidence of barline placement in the composing scores of the choral fugues has already been presented, the following remarks will be confined to homophonic movements. First it must be mentioned that Bach did not always draw the barline through all the staves of a system. Often he first drew short barlines for the principal part only and did not extend them through the remaining staves until he began to compose the secondary parts. This is evident in Sketches Nos. 42 and 142.[59] In both instances Bach drew a brace on the

[58] To be more precise: Bach revised the passage in the trumpet and oboe lines only after he had entered a quarter-note f' in the alto and a quarter-note G in the continuo lines on the first beat of the crossed-out measure, but before he had proceeded further with the composition of the free parts.

[59] The presence of Sketch No. 142—recognizable as the theme of *Et in unum Dominum* from the *B minor Mass*—in the autograph of BWV 213 has given rise to considerable discussion in the Bach literature. This literature is summarized in NBA I/36, KB, pp. 64–65. I agree with the assumption

in NBA I/36 that the sketch was copied from a source and does not represent a new melodic invention. In the latter case Bach would surely have composed the two canonic parts simultaneously and would not have written out one part through to the cadence, leaving the imitation to be worked into the pauses and held notes of the *dux*. When Bach copied from a source, however, he first wrote in the top part for a whole line before writing the other parts. See NBA I/10, KB, p. 29, for a description of a relevant copying error in the autograph (P 73) of BWV 66/3, mm. 139–149.

left-hand side of the page, thereby joining the staves into a system, and then wrote down the principal melodic part to the first cadence, drawing the barlines through the staff of this part only. This practice thus often helps one to recognize what part was written down first. In BWV 175/2 (P 75), "Komm, leite mich," mm. 3–6, the Recorder 1 part has separate barlines and was doubtless written to the cadence in m. 6 before the inner parts were filled in. Again, in the autograph of BWV 32/5 (P 126), "Nun verschwinden alle Plagen," the solo oboe part in the opening ritornello has separate barlines and was therefore presumably written down before Bach composed the Violin 1 figuration of the same melody. This reveals, furthermore, that Bach composed heterophonically related parts, too, in different ways on different occasions: in the present case the simple oboe melody was subsequently elaborated in another part; in the autograph of BWV 105/5 (P 99), "Kann ich nur Jesum mir zum Freunde machen," on the other hand, the horn part was clearly derived from the more elaborate Violin 1 part. Both parts are written on the same staff throughout the movement with stems for the horn part added to the Violin 1 part (see the final version of Sketch No. 80 in Volume II).

In the autograph of BWV 57/3 (P 144), "Ich wünschte mir den Tod," the barlines for the Violin 1 part in mm. 25–32 are disconnected from the rest of the system. One concludes again that the ritornello quotation in the violin part was written down before the soprano part, and that the soprano reading had been worked into the ritornello material here as it had been in BWV 10/2.

Other barline evidence confirms that Bach first wrote down the preexistent material in a given passage before composing the free parts. The voice line of BWV 180/5 (PP), "Lebens Sonne, Licht der Sinnen," was clearly crowded into the available space in mm. 16–17 and thus written after the ritornello quotation in the orchestra. In Movement 3 of the same cantata, the barline evidence is somewhat contradictory. The cello part in m. 9 goes over the barline and was therefore written down after the chorale cantus firmus in the soprano, and in mm. 18–19 the cello part was crowded into the available space between the barlines. In m. 35, however, the alignment of the two parts indicates that the cello was written down before the voice part. A space was left between the second and third beats of the voice part to avoid colliding with the low sixteenth-note beam of the cello part.

The chorale cantus firmus in the soprano part of BWV 49/6 (P 111) was again written down before the bass and obbligato parts: the latter parts consistently go over the barline in mm. 34–41.

Barline placement in continuo arias based on a quasi-basso ostinato reveals that the "thematic" ostinato period in the continuo was written down before the freely composed voice part. In BWV 62/4 (P 877), "Streite, siege, starker

Held," the ostinato sequence in mm. 30–32 was evidently written before the voice part, since the last notes of the bass in m. 32 go over the barline. There are numerous places in the autograph of BWV 42/4 (P 55), "Verzage nicht," where the vocal parts go over the barline or are crowded and therefore were not written until the ostinato continuo phrases had been written. And, in the autograph of BWV 10/4 (LC), "Gewaltige stößt Gott vom Stuhl," the last four notes of the voice are crowded in m. 14 above the ostinato. The autograph score of BWV 130/1 (PP), "Herr Gott dich loben alle wir," suggests—as we have already seen in other homophonic choruses—that the continuo part was written down first: in mm. 1–3 and 7–8, the string parts go over the barline.[60]

EVIDENCE OF CORRECTIONS

Corrections of detail frequently shed light on the order in which the parts were composed. A comparison of the original and final readings of a correction often makes it evident that a particular part was written down and revised before the remaining parts were entered, since the reading of the secondary parts would not have been possible with the original reading of the corrected part. It was clear in the discussion of BWV 65/1 that the continuo in the first draft was not entered until the countersubject was revised. Similarly, the soprano in mm. 25–26 of BWV 208/2 (P 42/3), "Jagen ist die Lust der Götter," originally cadenced on c″ before it was changed to g′. The continuo part, although corrected, too, was conceived from the first to form the g cadence with the soprano and was thus not written until the soprano part was worked out.[61]

The continuo part in mm. 16.2–17.1 in the ritornello of BWV 5/1 (PP), "Wo soll ich fliehen hin," was originally written one tone lower than the present reading. Since the remaining parts agree with the final version, it is evident once again that the continuo was the first part to be composed in the homophonic ritornello of a choral movement.

In the opening chorus of BWV 9 (LC), "Es ist das Heil uns kommen her," on the other hand, Bach first drafted the leading melodic flute part in mm. 11–16 one tone below the final version. The remaining parts underwent no similar transposition and consequently must have been entered only after the flute part had been revised.

The continuo part in mm. 23–24 of BWV 10/5 (LC), "Er denket der Barmherzigkeit," was changed thus:

a correction that in essence amounts to a transposition of a fourth. While the

---

[60] See also Sketch No. 94.

[61] The original reading of these measures cannot   be completely reconstructed. See NBA I/35, KB, p. 16.

continuo part here in both readings is consonant with the chorale cantus firmus in the unison instrumental part (which was probably the first part to be set down) the voice parts could not have been written until the continuo was corrected.

It is clear as well from corrections in the autographs of choral movements that Bach normally first wrote down the vocal parts before the doubling instrumental parts. The revealing corrections are of three types: either (1) the choral part has a correction while the unison instrument has the final reading only, or (2) the vocal reading was at first copied mechanically into the doubling instrumental staff with no regard for the difference of clef, or (3) Bach at first literally copied or transposed the reading of the vocal part into the doubling instrumental staff but then elaborated the passage with additional heterophonic embellishment. A few examples will suffice to illustrate these three correction types.

Type 1. In BWV 208/11 (P 42/3), the chorus "Lebe, Sonne dieser Erden," m. 2.7 of the Soprano 1 part was changed from f″ to d″—perhaps to avoid parallel fourths with the second soprano in the two-part texture. The doubling Violin 1/Oboe 1 line has the final reading only.

The soprano part in BWV 75/1 (P 66), m. 98, was changed as follows:

fis e d cis d h cis d

There is no such correction in the unison oboe parts but only the final reading.[62]

Type 2. The tenor reading in mm. 83–84 of BWV 22/1 (P 119), "Jesus nahm zu sich die Zwölfe," was copied exactly onto the viola staff with no regard for the difference of clef, thus making the notes—read in alto clef—a third too high. The reading was then transposed and changed to the present reading which presents a diminution of the vocal part (as in correction type 3).

The Violin 1 part in BWV 182/7 (P 103), "Jesu, deine Passion," at first had individually stemmed eighth-notes (as in the alto part) in m. 13 (first two notes), mm. 50–51 (m. 50.2–51.4), m. 53 (notes 3–5); these were then changed to eighth-note beams. In mm. 49–53, in fact, Bach absent-mindedly wrote the alto text beneath the Viola 1 part. The first two notes of the Viola 2 part in m. 21 were similarly changed from stemmed to beamed eighth-notes, betraying the derivation of the part from the tenor line.

Type 3. Bach had originally written a half-note g′ in both the Violin 2 and

---

[62] The Violin 1 part is not written out in this measure but has the indication *avec Sopr.*

Oboe 2 staves of m. 107 from BWV 6/1 (P 44/2), "Bleib bei uns, denn es will Abend werden," a reading literally extracted from the alto part. He then elaborated the ♩ to ♫♫ g', f', e'♮, g'.

In BWV 24/3 (P 44/4), the chorus "Alles nun, das ihr wollet," the Violin 1 part in mm. 17 and 62–66 originally doubled the soprano part in unison; in mm. 74–77 the second violin and viola readings originally agreed with the alto and tenor readings respectively; and the continuo part in m. 86 at first had the same reading as the bass part.

Both the Oboe 3 and Violin 2 parts were changed in m. 50 of BWV 119/1 (P 878), "Preise, Jerusalem, den Herrn," as follows:

that is, from an abstraction to an elaboration of the first beat of the alto part.

It is hardly necessary to demonstrate further that in choral movements Bach generally derived the doubling instrumental lines from the vocal parts. But even in this regard Bach's practice was not thoroughly consistent. There are several occasions where he seems to have written down the instrumental part before the unison or heterophonic voice part.

The opening chorus of BWV 171 (PP), "Gott, wie dein Name, so ist auch dein Ruhm," is presumably based on an instrumental piece, and several corrections in the autograph indicate that the vocal parts were derived from the doubling instrumental parts.[63] But since this movement is a parody piece and not an original composition, it cannot be taken as representative of Bach's *compositional* procedures.

A correction in the autograph score of BWV 9/1 (LC) seems to suggest that the continuo part was composed before the bass part. In mm. 28–30 the bass originally agreed with the reading of the continuo but was then elaborated:

This, then, is apparently a variation of correction type 3. It is conceivable, however, that Bach first wrote the original reading in the bass part, copied it into the continuo part, and only then revised the bass line.

Less ambiguous in their significance are the following corrections in the score of BWV 67/1 (P 95), the chorus "Halt im Gedächtnis Jesum Christ." In both the Oboe 1 and Violin 1 staves the second note of m. 102 was changed from g'♯ to e'; the unison soprano has the final reading only. In m. 103 the final note

---

[63] See the summary in NBA I/4, KB, p. 105.

in the Oboe 2 and Violin 2 staves was originally b′, then corrected to g′♯; there is no such correction in the alto part, only an unchanged g♯. These corrections indicate that—in these measures at least—the instrumental parts were composed and corrected before the vocal parts were set down.

FINALLY, it is necessary to mention that the notes in an individual part were not always written down in the sequence in which they appear. That is, the second note of a measure, say, may have been written down before the first note. Bach proceeded in this manner on a few occasions when composing transitional passages. After writing down the completion of one phrase he wrote out the next phrase and only then composed the bridge passage between the two phrases.

It is clear, for example, from the autograph of BWV 13/3 (P 45/4), the chorale aria "Der Gott, der mir hat versprochen," that Bach wrote down the second eighth-beat of m. 11 in the two violin parts, marking the reentrance of the first measure of the ritornello theme, before he had entered the transitional notes at the beginning of the measure:

And, in the autograph of the opening chorus of BWV 94 (P 47/2), "Was frag ich nach der Welt," Bach wrote down the second half of m. 20 in the Violin 1 part—a repetition of the violin figure of mm. 2–3—before he had composed the beginning of the measure:

Similarly, Bach had written the continuo part in m. 16 of BWV 243a/4 (P 38), the chorus *Omnes generationes,* before composing the second half of m. 15. He had originally written the continuo of m. 16 an octave higher than the present reading, then transposed it into the lower octave, and only then composed the transitional tones at the end of the preceding measure:[64]

The genesis of the Violin 2 part in mm. 17–18 of BWV 171/2 (PP), the aria

---

[64] See also the description in NBA II/3, KB, p. 60.

"Herr, so weit die Wolken gehen," may serve as a final example of this practice. In the present passage Bach composed the Violin 2 part in a sense backwards in three stages from the second beat of m. 18 to the second beat of m. 17. He first wrote down

then added the upbeat to m. 18

and finally filled in the second through fourth beats of m. 17

CHAPTER VII

Arias and Choruses: Corrections
of Detail

P AUL MIES has pointed out in his study, *Die Bedeutung der Skizzen Beethovens zur Erkenntnis seines Stiles,* that "the course of a correction calls one's attention to details [of style] which seemed the best to Beethoven's musical intelligence."[1] No doubt the working scores, drafts, and sketches for a composition make one aware of details and refinements of the work which one may have taken for granted or even overlooked, but which are the results of a highly conscious process of revision and self-criticism. Nevertheless, it would be extremely difficult, if not impossible, to uncover the stylistic principles of a composer's music by studying such autograph material alone. The nature of the difficulty was illustrated in the preceding chapter with the discussion of the original versions of several fugue subjects. It was mentioned that on five or six occasions Bach originally drafted a fugue subject based essentially on a repeated-note figure. This figure was then refashioned into a more "melodic"—as opposed to purely "declamatory"—contour. But it was not possible to derive either a general working principle or a stylistic principle from this evidence. For while Bach drafted and kept a repeated-note subject for the *Omnes generationes* chorus of the E♭ *Magnificat* written for Christmas Day 1723 (Sketch No. 156), he rejected the original repeated-note form of the fugue subject for the *Pleni* section of the Sanctus in D, BWV 238, presumably written for the same day.

The corrections, then, were apparently not made in conformity with any general attitude on Bach's part concerning repeated-note subjects, but rather with regard to specific relationships being established in the particular work of which these fugal subjects were a part. In the case of the fugue subject from BWV 65/1, for example, it was suggested that Bach revised the subject to relate it melodically to the opening theme of the movement and thus to provide the chorus with a degree of motivic unity.

The evidence provided by the autograph corrections of details thus poses an enormous task for the prospective investigator. A particular correction has first to be analyzed in terms of the specific context in which it occurs, i.e., in terms of the immediate passage to which it belongs, and then in terms of the entire movement of which the passage is a part. Thus each correction properly should

[1] Mies 1925, p. 3.

call forth a careful stylistic and structural analysis of the movement in which it was made. If several corrections of the same type are found in various works, it will be necessary further to determine whether they represent no more than a collection of similar but isolated instances, each a response to a specific and unique compositional situation, or whether they indeed testify to a general principle of style. To determine this it would be necessary to know whether Bach ever wrote and retained passages of the kind that were rejected in the corrections at hand. If there are such passages—just as there are repeated-note fugue subjects—one would have to speculate whether Bach simply failed to correct them owing to a momentary lack of vigilance—they being consequently simply not as "successful" as the corrected passages—or whether these passages are rather the result of a different set of structural and stylistic criteria in reference to which they are just as successful as are the corrected passages in their contexts.

The program just outlined is clearly gigantic and not only would explode the limitations of the present study but is surely of great enough magnitude to occupy several future generations of Bach scholars. For it involves complete analyses of all the movements of the vocal works, analyses that ideally would explain and evaluate the relevance and appropriateness of every single note or rest in its context. It also involves a complete cataloguing of every melodic, rhythmic, harmonic, and orchestral configuration to determine its degree of frequency or rarity in the Bach canon so that statements regarding its "typicalness" for the Bach style can be safely made. Such a task is surely only possible, if at all, with the aid of modern computer techniques. Finally, the program involves the most highly developed critical insight imaginable on the part of the investigator, an insight that would enable him to declare in every musical situation that the given configuration of notes from every point of view is or is not the best solution of the specific compositional problem presented.

In the light of these remarks it would appear futile to proceed with any discussion of the formative corrections observed in the Bach autographs. The following sections in fact attempt no more than to survey the wealth of material provided by corrections of detail in the autograph scores of the arias and choruses. As a matter of convenience, the presentation will take the form of separate discussions of melody, rhythm, harmony, form, and orchestration and texture, insofar as such an isolated treatment of each of the musical parameters is at all possible. There will be no hesitation to consider the rhythmic ramifications of a melodic correction and vice versa, while cross references between sections will be inevitable and frequent.

Since I am well aware of the difficulties involved in trying to make "significant" statements about such material, it will often be presented essentially in outline form, with "explanatory" remarks kept to a minimum. Detailed explanations and interpretations will have to be left to future Bach scholarship, which will first have carried out the necessary preliminaries suggested in the preceding paragraphs.

Formative Corrections of Melody

CORRECTIONS TO AVOID LITERAL MELODIC REPETITIONS AND SEQUENCES

Many[2] corrections were evidently made to embellish or remove an immediate literal repetition or sequence. By the simple correction of one tone, for example, Bach changed the static repetition of a melodic figure in the horn parts of m. 3 of BWV 65/1 (P 147) into an antecedent-consequent relationship. In the final version the upward skip to the dominant in the first group is balanced by a stepwise descent to the tonic in the second group:

Similarly, in BWV 51/1 (P 104), m. 4.5 of the trumpet part was changed from e″ to c″ so that m. 4a now complements rather than mechanically repeats m. 3b, and at the same time produces a climactic leap to the f″:

Measures 3–4 of the oboe part in BWV 214/5 (P 41/2) originally presented a varied repetition of mm. 1–2. The reading was changed from

to

resulting again—as in BWV 65/1—in an antecedent-consequent relationship: the answer of the fifth degree of the key with the tonic.

On two known occasions Bach added diminution tones to the sequential repetition of a motif, producing thereby an increase in rhythmic activity in the

---

[2] I am aware of over 30, but there may well be more.

second member of the sequence and thus introducing a sense of growth and development into the phrase. Both examples occur in the opening measures of a ritornello theme.

BWV 135/3 (Leipzig), m. 3, Oboe 1

BWV 33/3 (PP), m. 1, Violin 1

A correction in the opening theme of BWV 168/5 (P 152) achieves this sense of development by introducing an apparent foreshortening of the original motif. The sequential repetition of a one-measure unit in mm. 1 and 2 is followed in the final reading by a sequence of half-measure units in the third measure:

The final form of the third measure, while contrasting rhythmically and melodically with the first two measures, retains the basic structure of the original one-measure motif (itself a varied sequence of half-measure units) and thus provides a logical continuation of the preceding figure:

In BWV 105/3 (P 99), mm. 74–78, Bach again had apparently begun to write a literal three-member melodic sequence but then varied the third member.

Mm. 75f., Oboe

The replacement of the ♪♫ ♪♫ pattern of mm. 75–76 with continuous sixteenth-note motion in m. 77, together with the shortening of the climax tone of m. 77 from a quarter- to a sixteenth-note, achieve the same effects of foreshortening and of increase in rhythmic momentum at the approach to the cadence that were observable in BWV 168/5.

Bach once more made use of this principle of written-out rhythmic stringendo,[3]

[3] The written-out stringendo will be considered further below.

in BWV 90/3 (P 83), mm. 3–4, in order, presumably, to relieve a monotonous sequence. His original idea was to have a sequence of three half-measure members in the trumpet:

This was then changed to a two-member sequence of one-measure units, each of which is composed of three groups (the first two in the trumpet, the third in the first violin) arranged as a steady increase in rhythmic activity:

In this example, then, a threefold presentation of a half-measure unit was replaced by a single sequential repetition of a one-measure unit. Such a corrective gesture, replacing relatively many repetitions of a small unit with fewer statements of a larger unit, is evident elsewhere as well. In BWV 124/1 (P 876) the continuo part in mm. 11–14 was changed from a triple repetition of a one-measure group to a single repetition of a two-measure group:

The correction in the continuo part of BWV 176/5 (P 81), mm. 5–7, is essentially the same:

In BWV 134a/8 (Paris), mm. 235–237 of the alto part comprised at first basically a fourfold sequence of a one-measure unit:

which was changed, as in the preceding examples, to a single sequential repetition of a two-measure unit:

A modification of this principle was applied in mm. 63–66 of BWV 14/2 (P 879). The soprano melisma originally read:

This 4 × 1—or, more precisely 2 × (2 × 1)—structure was then changed to the following 2 × 2 structure:

but the original reading of the soprano part in mm. 64 and 66 was placed in the Violin 1 part so that the original sequential design was still retained but converted from a monotonous sequential chain in one part into a two-part imitative passage. The correction thus entailed primarily a change of orchestration and texture, while the change of melodic structure is more apparent than real. Similar corrections involving the subsequent "polyphonization" of an originally single-line melody will be discussed below.

The pitch corrections in the first four measures of the ritornello theme from BWV 28/5 (P 92):

serve once more to avoid literal and sequential repetition. The correction of m. 3 (which, unlike the immediate correction in m. 2, is a delayed correction, appearing again in mm. 13, 19, and 25) again has the effect of creating one large melodic entity—articulated through the motion f′, e′, d′, c′—from two smaller units.[4]

On two occasions, both found in the autograph score of BWV 51 (P 104), Bach began to design a melody based on sequential repetition but then abandoned the sequential structure altogether or effectively concealed it in favor of a freely spun-out organic phrase. This was accomplished in Movement 3 by changing one note.

Höch-ster   Höch-ster ma - che dei - ne Gü - te fer - ner al - le Mor - g[en] neu

---

[4] The change from 6/4 to 6/8 meter was made after the seventh measure of the movement was written; for the alto part in m. 7 was originally written as six single quarter-notes which were changed to stemmed eighth-notes. In m. 8 the eighth-notes are uncorrected.

In Movement 4, a complete recasting of the second measure of the theme was necessary.

Original version

Final version

These two examples from BWV 51 illustrate the same tendency toward the creation of larger melodic units that was observed on the immediately preceding pages—and will be encountered again.[5]

CORRECTIONS TO RELIEVE STEPWISE MOTION

A number of corrections were introduced apparently to interrupt an unbroken stepwise motion. The motivations prompting such corrections can no doubt be reduced to a desire simply to avoid melodic contours or progressions that in a particular context would have been too "obvious," "mechanical," or "predictable."[6]

In four instances known to the present writer the correction consisted in suppressing an obvious and "inevitable" scalewise step of a second and replacing it with a leap of a seventh.

BWV 40/4 (P 63), m. 88, Bass

BWV 116/2 (Paris), m. 51, Oboe[7]

---

[5] See below pp. 164–165.

[6] Corrections in the "opposite direction"—the addition of passing tones to the original form of a melody—are, if anything, at least as numerous.

Such changes will be discussed in the section below on ornamental corrections.

[7] The ✕ is Bach's usual notation of the double-sharp.

BWV 243a/5 (P 38), m. 24, Bass[8]

BWV 163/3 (P 137), m. 53, Violoncello 2

In BWV 243a/5 Bach replaced a simple turn formula with a more expressive arpeggiated figure. The *Fortspinnung* of the countertheme in the bass in m. 10 was corrected (immediately, as the sequential repetition in the next measure makes clear) as follows:

The following correction in BWV 114/5 (PP), m. 44, illustrates that the *exclamatio* and the convoluted melodic contour of the voice part was an afterthought. The original version was a simple upbeat figure in the form of a written-out inverted mordent:

In the opening measures of BWV 175/2 (P 75) the recorder parts were revised to introduce skips and changes of direction, thereby relieving the simple stepwise progression of the original idea:

At the same time the pitch repetition between the fourth and fifth notes of the first measure, which had the effect of dividing the phrase into separate triplet groups, was changed to a second, thus joining the two groups into a larger unit.[9]

---

[8] See the comment regarding this correction in NBA II/3, KB, pp. 61–62.

[9] Cf. above. Compare, however, the opening horn melody of BWV 65/1 which, also in 12/8 meter, is clearly divided by repeated notes into separate triplet groups.

Similar to the examples just mentioned are several corrections in which a small interval—not necessarily a second—was replaced with a larger interval, apparently to add a degree of "kinetic" energy or thrust to the melodic line. In BWV 71/4 (P 45/1), m. 38, the beginning of the melisma sequence was changed:

and in BWV 133/2 (P 1215) the opening measure of the ritornello and the vocal entrance in m. 10 were corrected thus:[10]

CORRECTIONS TO INTRODUCE MOTIVIC REFERENCES

About twenty[11] melodic corrections introduce into freely composed passages references to, or literal quotations of, important motivic or thematic material. The following examples should serve to illustrate the principle.

In the opening ritornello of BWV 134a/4 (Paris) Bach had initially written a half-note c in the continuo part at the beginning of m. 5, no doubt as part of a plan to continue the ♩ ⅋ ♫♩ pattern of the first four measures. But he then

---

[10] It is interesting to compare with BWV 133/2 the opening motif of BWV 208/7, "Ein Fürst ist seines Landes Pan" (P 42/3). In m. 58 of this movement, in fact, it seems that Bach momentarily forgot the contour of the opening measure of the ritornello, for the oboe part here appears as follows:

At first glance the change appears to be almost an exact reversal of the corrective gesture in BWV

133/2. The nature of both themes, however, is quite different. The theme of BWV 133/2 is essentially chordal, and this is emphatically reinforced in the final reading. The theme of BWV 208/7, on the other hand, is clearly scalar, the sixteenth-note upbeats serving a purely rhythmic function.

[11] The number of corrections here is deliberately imprecise. This is true as well for many other numerical statements in this chapter. These statements are intended only to give the reader a notion of the approximate frequency of a particular corrective gesture since the possibility is so great that a number of instances have been overlooked.

hit upon the idea of quoting a variant of the opening motif as a counterpoint to the sequential *Fortspinnung* of the first violin.

M. 1, Violin 1

M. 5, Bc.

In m. 23 of the same movement, part of a repetition of the opening ritornello, Bach apparently intended at first to have a freely composed vocal *Einbau*

before he decided to incorporate the characteristic mordent figure and the ♩♫ rhythm of the opening motif:[12]

Again, in BWV 138/1 (P 158), m. 5, Bach began to compose the tenor prologue preceding the chorale entry as a non-thematic passage.

This reading was then smudged away and the present phrase, beginning with a quotation of the first eight notes of the opening oboe theme, was entered in m. 6.

Similarly, in BWV 110/2 (P 153), m. 9, a reminiscence of the ritornello theme was worked into the originally free *Fortspinnung* figure of the continuo part.

Original version

Final version

[12] For the complete genesis of this measure see NBA I/35, KB, p. 69. The change in beaming described there argues that the similar beaming change in mm. 17–18 was a delayed correction.

Also the first four notes of the continuo part in BWV 105/5 (P 99), m. 17, were changed as follows:

perhaps to recall the first four notes of the Violin 1 figuration in mm. 6 and 14 and mm. 19, 22, and 37:[13]

In BWV 175/2 (P 75), mm. 6–7, the continuo part originally ended with a simple cadential formula. Bach then decided to repeat the opening continuo passage of m. 1, thus rounding off the ritornello symmetrically and introducing the vocal entrance in m. 7 with the same figure that introduced the flutes in m. 1:

Miscellaneous Melodic Corrections

Bach occasionally introduced corrections to prevent a melodic contour from centering statically on a single note or interval, or moving too exclusively in one direction. Such corrections are clearly motivated by the same critical impulse that frequently prompted the removal of literal and sequential repetitions of phrases and motifs: the desire to provide melodic variety and a sense of development. Thus Bach changed the original reading of the alto and tenor parts in m. 17 of BWV 134a/4 (Paris)[14] from

to

---

[13] The placement of the slurs here reflects the (careless) placement in the autograph.

[14] Concerning the beaming change, no doubt introduced to replace the natural agogic disposition ♪♪♪ strei - ten ♪ with a less obvious underlay, see p. 166 above.

The opening measures of BWV 176/3 (P 81) were corrected as follows:

The frequent changes of melodic direction in the final version produce a sharper contour within the original structure. The correction also clearly involves the familiar elimination of literal sequences and the addition of ornamental diminution tones.

In the ritornello theme of BWV 163/1 (P 137) Bach avoided redundancy and at the same time refined the structure of the melody by changing a single tone. The passage reads in the autograph:

The correction avoids a repetition of the b′ as the last sixteenth-note of two successive beats and breaks up three successive rising upbeat figures b′-e″, b′-c″♯, a′-d″. The primary purpose of the change, however, was presumably to introduce the d″ as a pivotal tone signaling the turn of the melody toward D major. In the final reading the figure f″♯, d″, c″♯, b′ which clearly defines b minor is answered by d″, c″♯, b′, a′ which just as clearly belongs to D major (see the bracketed notes).

It may be mentioned here that the subject of the c minor two-part invention in the *Clavier-Büchlein vor Wilhelm Friedemann Bach*[15] originally began with a static insistence on the tone c″ followed in the opening measures by an immediate repetition of the general contour of the second beat on the third beat. This was all relieved once again with the correction of one note:

The new reading not only presents a constant variety of melodic contours but also contains a rising background melodic line (indicated by asterisks) that imparts to the melody a compelling sense of structure and direction.

THE CANTATA AUTOGRAPHS indicate that the choice between chromatic and diatonic melody was normally made before Bach set the melody to paper. Bach, therefore, evidently did not look upon chromaticism as an ornamental addition

---

[15] See the facsimile edition, p. 102.

or refinement of a basically diatonic melody, that is, in a sense as an aspect of the baroque diminution technique, but rather as belonging to the essential character and structure of the melodic idea.

On several occasions, though, chromatic tones were added to diatonically conceived passages. The alto line in BWV 22/2 (P 119), m. 70, which is part of the extended melisma on the word *leiden* concluding the B section of the aria, originally had a held tone ♩.♩ f′(♮). The affective chromatic inflection ♩.♩ f′♯ f′♮ in the final reading of the measure was therefore an afterthought.

A comparison of Sketch No. 120 for the concluding measures of the ritornello theme of BWV 197/3 (P 91) with the final version reveals that Bach at first planned a straightforward diatonic reading for the melody. The refinements of these measures—chromaticism, syncopation, and rhythmic stringendi (half-notes, followed by quarter-notes, then eighth-notes and dotted rhythm)—were added subsequently, presumably as an illustration of the affect suggested by the word *Sorgenkummer* (see the alto part in mm. 48–50).[16]

Chromatic tones were also added subsequently in the opening measures of two continuo ritornello themes. Both movements, by coincidence, are duets and chorale arrangements. The opening theme of BWV 10/5 (LC) was corrected[17]

so that the melody now consists of two descending chromatic lines interwoven into a latent polyphony: d′, c′♯, c′♮, b♮, b♭, and a in the upper tones answered by g, f♯, f♮, e, and d at the fifth below.

The first three measures of BWV 42/4 (P 55) were changed thus:

Along with the introduction of chromatic tones, the change introduces a subtle conflict of accentuation into the melody. The pitch structure of each measure divides naturally into 2 × 3 tones which opposes the 3 × 2 division of the 3/4 meter.

Numerous pitch corrections were made in the vocal parts of arias and choruses in the service of effective text declamation or illustration rather than purely musical factors. They are of the same nature as many corrections observed in the autograph scores of recitatives. The critical augmented fourth in the vocal

---

[16] P 91 has *Sorgen Kummer.* This is modernized in Neumann 1956, p. 390, and in NBA I/33 to *Sorgenkummer.*

[17] The same correction appears in the repetitions of the motif in the tenor, mm. 5–6, and alto, mm. 6–7.

motto at the beginning of the B section of BWV 33/3 (PP) was perhaps introduced to emphasize—and illustrate—the word *Sünden*.

mich drü - kt[en]   Sün - d[en]La - st[en] nie-der

BWV 33/3, mm. 39–41, Alto

And the following correction in the tenor part of BWV 62/2 (P 877), mm. 90–96,
is meaningful only in terms of declamation and text illustration:

Weltd[er] höchste Be- herr -   -   -   -   - [scher]

The principle hardly needs to be demonstrated with further examples. Other
improvements in text declamation, achieved mainly by adding diminution tones,
will be discussed in the next section of this chapter.

This section on formative melodic corrections can be concluded by returning
once more to the matter of repeated-note imitation subjects. Bach originally
drafted the theme of the B section of the duet "Entziehe dich eilends, mein
Herze," BWV 124/5 (P 876), as an essentially monotonic subject which he
thereupon gave a more melodic contour, in the fashion familiar from the discussion above.[18]

Weñ künf-tig dein   Au-ge den   Heyland

Weñ künftigdein   Au-ge den Heyland er -blickt dein Au -   -   -   - (ge)

BWV 124/5 (P 876), mm. 82–89

But the imitation subject begun in mm. 54–55 of BWV 42/4 (P 55), the duet
"Verzage nicht, o Häuflein klein," was changed from a "melodic" form to a
pure repeated-note declamation:

es wird [nicht] lan-ge   wäh-r[en]

(wäh)-r[en] es wird [nicht] lange   wäh - r[en]

[18] Measure 88.3, Soprano: thus in P 876, but the
f′♯ in the BG edition—based on the original parts
—is obviously a preferable reading.

We are thus confronted again with the problems posed at the beginning of this chapter: when did Bach prefer repeated-note themes and when not; is a correction always an improvement?

Ornamental Corrections

In contrast to the last section, which was concerned with formative corrections of melody, the present section will consider ornamental corrections. Such revisions, although still "compositional" in nature,[19] do not entail fundamental changes in the structure of the musical material but, it will be recalled, simply embellish and elaborate the original ideas, leaving them essentially unaltered in basic character and contour.

While ornamental corrections reflect on several levels the pervasive diminution principle of baroque composition (see pp. 35f. above), we are concerned here with diminution in its most restricted sense: the embellishment of a melody by the addition of tones and the subdivision of a long note into a number of shorter notes of various pitches.

An ornamental correction frequently consists of the simple addition of a written-out ornament—for example, a mordent, slide, or turn. The thirty-second-note mordent figures in the recorder parts of BWV 65/6 (P 147), "Nimm mich dir zu eigen hin," mm. 5–8, were such an afterthought as were the thirty-second-note couplets throughout the opening ritornello of BWV 86/5 (P 157), the aria "Gott hilft gewiß." (They do not appear unchanged until m. 12.) The same thirty-second-note ornament found in the ritornello of BWV 86/5 appears in the final version of the violin part in BWV 182/4, "Starkes Lieben." Here the figure was never added at all in the original score (P 103) but appears as a correction only in the original violin part (St 47).[20]

The subsequent addition of ornamental figures is particularly evident at the end of phrases—the usual position in baroque music for the employment of ornaments. In BWV 199/2 (Copenhagen), "Stumme Seufzer, stille Klagen," ornamental thirty-second-notes were added to the third beat of m. 4 in the oboe part directly before the cadence:[21]

[19] See the terminology developed in Chapter II.
[20] See the discussion in BG 37, pp. xviii–xix.

[21] The NBG edition has an even more elaborate version which represents a further revision of the passage in the original parts, St 459.

Similarly, the alto part in m. 22 of the *Esurientes* aria from the D major *Magnificat*, BWV 243/9 (P 39), originally read:

thus agreeing with the version of this measure in the E♭ *Magnificat*, BWV 243a. The passage in BWV 243 was corrected, however, to:

again an embellishment of the approach to the cadence which at the same time provides a varied repetition of the cadence figure of m. 9.

Ornamental or diminution corrections by nature are, of course, just as much corrections of rhythm as of melody. This is especially clear in cases where figuration was added to subdivide long notes (half-notes or longer) into values two or more degrees shorter (i.e., the relationship between a half-note and an eighthnote). The oboe part in mm. 6 and 8 of BWV 72/4[22] (P 54), "Mein Jesus will es thun" was apparently changed thus:

Similarly, Bach at first sketched in the oboe part of BWV 23/3 (P 69), mm. 140–143, in dotted half-notes which he then elaborated:

In the chorus "Jesu, deine Passion," BWV 182/7 (P 103), the penultimate tone of the cantus firmus was changed from a whole note a′ to the figure:

The correction represents at the same time another instance in which Bach decorated the conclusion of a phrase with an ornamental figure.

Sketch No. 166, an abandoned two-measure draft for an organ chorale prelude in the *Orgelbüchlein* manuscript (P 283), demonstrates once more (as does the correction in BWV 182/7) not only the subsequent rhythmic subdivision of a

---

[22] For the number of movements in this cantata see the note to Sketches Nos. 47 and 48 in Volume II.

long-note cantus firmus, but also the ornamental character of these additions, in this instance *Nachschläge* and trills.[23]

Clearly related to Bach's practice of dissolving long tones into basically ornamental figures is his tendency, observed primarily (but not exclusively) in the composing scores of movements in motet style, to write out a passage at first in half-notes and then subdivide it into smaller values, usually quarter-notes or combinations of quarter- and eighth-notes. These changes are apparently not motivated only or even primarily by a desire to decorate the long notes, as in the examples just cited, but rather to insure rhythmic continuity and to fulfill text-underlay requirements.

Thus in the autograph of BWV 179/1 (P 146), "Siehe zu, daß deine Gottesfurcht," there are numerous instances of half-notes corrected to quarter-notes. These corrections fall into three categories according to their apparent purposes, which are to maintain a continuous quarter-note background motion (m. 7.1, continuo: ♩ g changed to ♩ ♩ g, a); or to provide enough notes to bear the syllables of the text (m. 22.3, bass [and continuo]: ♩ g changed to ♩ ♩ g, G for the word *falschem*; m. 89.2, soprano: ♩ d″ changed to ♩ ♩ d″, d″ for the word *diene*); or to add ornamental diminution tones (m. 74.1, soprano: ♩ e″ changed to ♩ ♫ e″, d″, c″♯).

Other corrections of half-notes to quarter-notes in this manuscript are not really "compositional" corrections at all but reveal simply that Bach often mechanically wrote the final tone of a phrase in such allabreve movements as a half-note which he then had to change to a quarter-note if the next phrase was to begin with, say, a ♩ ♩ ♩ upbeat pattern. In the present movement the following corrections—all of a half-note changed to a quarter-note—are of this nature:

m. 13.1, bass	m. 68.1, tenor
m. 19.1, tenor	m. 76.1, bass (and Bc.)
m. 25.1, soprano	m. 84.1, tenor
m. 31.1, soprano	m. 88.1, soprano

These corrections indicate only that Bach was not always immediately certain about whether or in what voice he would enter the *und diene Gott* motif.

---

[23] It is interesting to note that Bach did not prepare this draft by, say, first writing out the entire cantus firmus for the first chorale line, but by writing down only the first three notes of the cantus, and then establishing the texture and thematic content of the lower voices. Having thus determined the character and treatment of the chorale, he apparently felt free to leave the further composition of the piece for a future date. Exactly this procedure is evident in Sketch No. 167. Whereas the sketch was probably written in 1723, Bach did not complete the movement before the middle of 1724 (see Dadelsen 1958, pp. 99–101). The nature of this draft—full-voiced texture in the opening measures followed by the continuation of the melody part alone—is reminiscent of Sketches Nos. 18, 84, 114, and 134.

The composing scores of the following motet-style movements contain diminution corrections of the types evident in the autograph of BWV 179/1: BWV 86/1 (P 157), BWV 144/1 (P 134), BWV 2/1 (PP), BWV 28/2 (P 92),[24] BWV 118[1] (PP).

The belated addition of diminution tones to produce a continuous rhythmic background is also observable in the autograph scores of other types of movements.[25] The second violin and viola parts at the beginning of BWV 134a/8 (Paris), "Ergetzet auf Erden," were changed as follows:

thus complementing the sixteenth-note rhythm of the first violin and oboe parts in m. 2 and creating a typically Bachian background motor rhythm. At the same time, the correction transforms the lower string parts, momentarily at least, from mere chordal filler parts into independent countervoices.

The correction of the continuo part in BWV 132/5 (P 60), m. 26, second beat, from ♪♪ e, d to ♪♪♪♪ e, f♯, e, d, while doubtless introduced primarily to break up parallel fifths between the continuo and the alto part, serves further to catch the rhythmic activity of the Violin 1 part at the beginning of the measure and to mediate between that ♪♪♪♪ rhythmic figure and the ♪♪ rhythm on the third beat of the measure.

Diminution tones, however, were added most usually in the vocal parts of arias and choruses and introduce neumatic formulas or melismas into originally syllabic settings. The motivations for such subsequent elaboration of the vocal part were no doubt precisely the same here as they were in the recitatives, and the reasons offered in the discussion of the recitative corrections are applicable here: the enhancement of the melodic line—"harmonic" arpeggio contours replaced by "melodic" stepwise motion; and illustration and emphasis of particular words.

A few selected examples should suffice to illustrate this already familiar corrective gesture.

The addition of neumatic formulas to fill in a triadically and syllabically

---

[24] It was mentioned in Chapter I that the autograph of BWV 28/2 was probably prepared from a set of parts. It is likely, furthermore, that the movement is a parody, for there are practically no corrections in the score except for several half-notes changed to quarter-notes, in order to accommo-date the (extra?) syllables of the new text. For example, m. 10, tenor, was changed from ♩♩ c', e' to ♩♩♩ c', d', e'; and m. 12, alto, from ♩♩ b', a' to ♩♩♩ b', e', a'.

[25] See also the discussion of the four-part chorales in Chapter IV.

conceived vocal theme is clearly demonstrated by the correction of the tenor entrance in BWV 108/2 (P 82), mm. 12–13:

mich kañ ke[in] Zwei - (fel)

whereas the short melismas introduced in m. 42 of the tenor aria "Wohl dir, du Volk der Linden," BWV 119/3 (P 878), were no doubt introduced to illustrate the word *überschwenglich:*

(ge-) le - g[en] die ü - ber-schwengl[ich] thut

The bass melismas on the word *verscherze* in m. 24 and again in m. 26 of the aria "Jesu, beuge doch mein Herze," BWV 47/4 (P 163), were similarly later additions:

Heyl verscher-ze⸺⸺ zeme[in] Heyl ver-scherze- ze

In BWV 48/4 (P 109) the neumata added in mm. 34, 54, 67, and 77 of the alto part serve mainly textural and motivic functions:

Glieder wo fern hei-li - ges der See - le u. hei-li-ges

The resultant rhythmic formation ♪♫ ♫ in mm. 34 and 54 is obviously motivic, since it appears throughout the ritornello theme. The retrograde form of this rhythm in m. 77 was presumably introduced to form a rhythmic web and unbroken sixteenth-note motion with the solo oboe quotation from m. 14 of the ritornello. The voice correction, finally, in m. 67 clearly fulfills the same functions as the correction in m. 77. In the opening chorus of the same work, however, the neumatic formulas added in m. 15 of the soprano part serve a primarily expressive function, but also provide a varied sequential repetition of mm. 12–14 in mm. 14–16.

Ich e - len-der Mensch wer wird mich er - lö - - (sen)

BWV 48/1, mm. 12–16, Soprano

Considerations of text expression prompted Bach to remove a neuma on the word *sündigt* in BWV 122/2 (P 868) at the close of the first line of the aria.

O Mensch[en]   die   ihr   täg-l[ich]   sün - digt

BWV 122/2, m. 9, Bass

The final reading not only lends a rhetorically appropriate "hard" and abrupt emphasis to this affective word but is also more in keeping with the austere declamatory setting of the rest of the line.

The addition of diminution tones could also serve, as we have just seen in BWV 48/1, to present a repetition of a motif in varied form. In mm. 108–109 of BWV 33/1 (PP), too, Bach added passing tones to the cantus firmus of the sixth line of the chorale:

so that this line became a varied repetition of the fifth chorale line which had just sounded in mm. 98–102.

The correction in the oboe part of BWV 9/1 (LC), m. 3:

may be regarded as a varied repetition of the opening oboe motif in m. 1. The change was introduced perhaps not only for thematic reasons, but also to continue the sixteenth-note motion begun by the flute and first violin in the preceding measure, recalling the correction in BWV 134a/8 discussed above.

Bach's correction of the voice entrance in m. 25 of BWV 197/3 (P 91) represents both the rhythmic dissolution of a long tone and the varied repetition of an earlier passage. The voice part here enters with a slightly elaborated statement of the first measure of the opening ritornello theme:

Diminution tones were also added at times apparently to relieve the monotony of an undifferentiated rhythmic contour. The following correction of the opening motif of BWV 47/4 (P 163), "Jesu, beuge doch mein Herze," introduces passing tones in varied rhythm at the beginning and conclusion of a motif which at first proceeded almost exclusively in eighth-note motion:

The opening theme of BWV 211/10 (P 141), the concluding chorus of the Coffee Cantata, provides a further example of such a revision. The initial measures of the ritornello were originally characterized by a wooden, indeed static, even-note rhythm in the outer parts. This was relieved by introducing syncopations and shorter rhythms into both parts.[26]

BWV 211/10, mm. 1–4, Flute, Bc.

Similar considerations may have prompted the following correction in the second phrase of BWV 97/2 (NYPL).[27]

BWV 97/2, mm. 7–9, Bc.

In its corrected form the second phrase of the ritornello represents, with its eighth-note and sixteenth-note motion, a development of the quarter-note and eighth-note motion of the first phrase. It provides, moreover, a rhythmic contrast to the voice part which moves almost exclusively in quarter-notes and eighth-notes throughout the movement.

Formative Corrections of Rhythm

CONTINUO CORRECTIONS TO CREATE OR STRENGTHEN A CONTINUOUS BACKGROUND PULSE

The discussion of ornamental corrections inevitably included instances where compositional changes were doubtless motivated more by considerations of rhythmic rather than melodic factors. The preceding section, therefore, has

---

[26] See the facsimile edition.

[27] The same correction appears in the analogous measures 19–21, 43–45, 49–51, and 58–60. Measures 72–74 are the first occurrences of the figure in which the sixteenth-notes belong to the original draft and not to corrections.

already initiated a survey of formative rhythmic corrections in the arias and choruses.

It was observed above that the desire to create a continuous background motor rhythm was one of the more important motivations for the addition of diminution tones. The obvious and compelling unifying force of such a motor rhythm within a movement no doubt recommended it to the composers of the period. The problem, of course, was to prevent the device from becoming unduly conspicuous and monotonous. Bach often solved this problem by allowing the pulse to permeate several parts of the texture rather than confining it to a single voice.

The continuo line, perhaps as a logical consequence of its role as bearer of the underlying harmonic structure of a movement, plays a particularly significant role in maintaining the continuity of the structural background pulse. Further, the rhythm of the continuo is by nature usually more flexible than the rhythm of other parts. The rhythm of the vocal part is clearly determined to a large degree by the prosody of the text, while the rhythm of all melodic instruments and voices is strongly controlled by the thematic and motivic material of the movement. But the continuo part, after establishing the relatively slow pace of the harmonic rhythm, could then be rather freely manipulated. And the frequently large skips between the structural harmonic tones of the continuo could easily be filled in with passing tones and other diminution tones in order to maintain the background pulse.

In m. 20 of the bass aria "Weicht, all ihr Übelthäter," BWV 135/5 (Leipzig), for example, the continuo part was apparently corrected as follows:

The newly created rhythm | ♩ ♩ , ♫♫ | ♩ | complements the pattern | , ♫♫♩ | ♫♫ | of the Violin 1 part. And the continuo part in the first measure of BWV 28/1, the aria "Gottlob! nun geht das Jahr zu Ende" (P 92), was corrected thus:

establishing at once, together with the | ♪ , ♫♫ | pattern in the oboes, a continuous eighth-note pulse which is then maintained without interruption throughout the opening ritornello.

Again, the following corrections in mm. 5–6 of the aria "Herr, so weit die Wolken gehen," BWV 171/2 (PP), not only relieve an undifferentiated eighth-note pattern within the continuo part, but, in combination with the violin parts, form an almost uninterrupted sixteenth-note motor. The configuration serves also to integrate the three parts:

Continuo corrections in mm. 3–4 (and again in mm. 97–98) of the aria "Lasset dem Höchsten ein Danklied erschallen," BWV 66/3 (P 73), fulfill the same function, by creating, together with the  pattern in the oboes and violins, an unbroken sixteenth-note motor rhythm which persists until the cadence of m. 8.

BWV 66/3, mm. 3–4, Bc.

The continuo part in m. 44 of the tenor aria "Ihr Gedanken und ihr Sinnen," BWV 110/2 (P 153), originally maintained the rhythmic pattern of mm. 37–43 but was changed as follows, creating a rhythmic web with the voice part:

Simultaneously, the two flute parts form an almost uninterrupted sixteenth-note pulse throughout the measure, broken only by the last eighth-note of the measure; and there, of course, the sixteenth-note motion is provided by the tenor. This one measure offers an excellent example of Bach's refined treatment of the late baroque rhythmic device.

A correction in BWV 131 (PP), at the words *und viel Erlösung bei ihm* in the final chorus of the cantata, may well have been introduced for practical considerations of performance. It appears that Bach had begun to draft the bassoon line in mm. 307b–308 with the rhythm [ ] etc., as a complement to the rhythmic figure in the oboe. This reading was then placed in the violin, and the bassoon line changed to a continuous sixteenth-note pattern. The purpose of the change, presumably, was to coordinate the alternating rhythmic figures of the oboe and violin parts in these measures.

BWV 131, mm. 307–308

The following correction in the first measure of the aria "Von den Stricken meiner Sünden" from the *St. John Passion*, BWV 245/11 (P 28),

was perhaps the consequence of practical difficulties experienced with the opening rhythmic configuration of the movement:

in earlier rehearsals and performances of the work.[28]

Several other corrections that were apparently prompted by a desire to strengthen the metrical structure of a passage consist simply of a note replacing a rest on the downbeat in the continuo line. The change of the first beat of BWV 42/4 (P 55) from

to

(see the transcription on p. 169) and the correction of the rhythmic shape in

---

[28] P 28 dates from the period 1735–50 and thus represents a late stage in the history of the *Passion*. The correction seems to have been made only after the copying of the latest parts, in which it also appears as a correction, i.e., for the fourth known performance of the work—in the late 1740's.

the continuo part of BWV 94/4 (P 47/2), m. 1 from

to

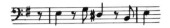

are clearly related to the correction in BWV 245/11, as is the following correction in the continuo part of BWV 205/1 (P 173), m. 1:

The introduction of an octave leap in BWV 245/11, BWV 42/4, and BWV 205/1 serves the metrical function of providing a strong downbeat accentuation to clarify the meter rather than any melodic function.

The Addition of Syncopations, Suspensions, and Anticipations

The classic method of relieving an undifferentiated or otherwise potentially monotonous or static rhythmic pattern is to introduce syncopations, suspensions, and/or anticipations into the melodic line. The effectiveness of syncopation and suspension formulas in creating powerful instabilities and tensions which carry— indeed thrust—the music forward is obvious: they form the direct rhythmic counterpart of melodic and harmonic dissonances with which, of course, they are often associated. It is not surprising, therefore, that corrections introducing such formulas are encountered rather frequently in Bach's composing scores. The addition of syncopations and suspensions is evident in the relationship between sketch and final version in Sketch No. 120. The revision of the opening theme of BWV 211/10 quoted above (p. 177) provides another instance. A few further examples, selected essentially at random, should serve to illustrate this corrective gesture.

In the Coffee Cantata, again, anticipations were introduced in mm. 98–101 of the vocal part of Movement 4. They surely were intended primarily to capture the impatience of the coffee-addicted Lieschen.

BWV 211/4, mm. 98–102, Soprano

The addition of a suspension in the Violin 1 part of BWV 51/4 (P 104) at
the conclusion of the opening ritornello not only breaks up the originally even
eighth-note motion of the theme, but forcefully propels the melodic line into
the cadence of m. 11.

BWV 51/4, mm. 10–11, Violin 1

At the same time, the correction prevents a simple rhythmic doubling between
the Violin 1 and continuo parts.[29]

Obviously related to the correction in BWV 51/4 is the following revision
in the Violin 1 part of BWV 59/1 (P 161).

BWV 59/1, mm. 12–13, Violin 1

The composer's initial concern was surely to remove the parallel unisons
between the violin part and the soprano. He achieved this simply by transposing
the fourth beat of m. 12 up a third (no doubt before he wrote the d″ at the
beginning of m. 13) which resulted in the intermediate reading (in red). Only
then, evidently, did Bach realize the possibility of having a suspension in the
second half of the measure complementing and—since it is prepared by a shorter
note-value on an offbeat—to some extent representing a diminution and intensification of the suspension in the first half of the measure. The suspension figure
added in m. 13 was presumably an outgrowth of the chain of events that had
evolved in the working-out of the preceding measure.

CORRECTIONS INTRODUCING STRUCTURAL RHYTHMIC PATTERNS
   OR ABSTRACT RHYTHMIC "DESIGNS"

In m. 14 of BWV 36/6 (P 45/2), the chorale aria "Der du bist dem Vater
gleich," Bach recast the continuo rhythm as follows:

and thereby interrupted the almost exclusive eighth-note flow of the line. But
the primary intention of the correction, no doubt, was to prepare the approach-

---

[29] Further corrections introduced to avoid such
rhythmic parallelism will be considered below.

ing cadence at the end of the first chorale phrase of the movement by retarding the prevailing rhythmic motion.

A related correction appears in the continuo part of BWV 105/1 (P 99). The alteration in mm. 79–81:

illustrates once more the interruption of a rhythmic progression in even notes, this time by the addition of diminution tones. Again, though, as in the example from BWV 36/6, the composer's primary intent presumably was to prepare and articulate the approaching cadence by changing the rhythmic motion of the supporting bass line. Unlike the correction in BWV 36/6, the rhythmic activity in the present instance is not retarded at the approach of the cadence, but rather accelerated in the manner of the age-old "drive to the cadence." Besides illustrating corrective gestures which are now quite familiar to the reader, the present example suggests another motivation for formative rhythmic corrections, which has been touched upon earlier in this chapter. The change in the continuo part of BWV 105/1 introduces a written-out stringendo which proceeds according to a clearly rational design: the three measures preceding the cadence tone are divided equally into one-and-a-half measures of half-note motion followed by one-and-a-half measures of quarter-note motion.

A surprisingly large number of rhythmic corrections succeed not merely in providing a texture with a pervasive and unifying background pulse, or in creating a melody with a varied and dynamic rhythmic profile, but also in introducing a rational—sometimes almost abstract—rhythmic design. The written-out stringendo is the most usual manifestation of such a rhythmic design. The stringendo is not simply an intellectually abstract pattern, for it produces a tangible sense of growth and progression in much the same way as do the corrections introducing varied sequences and foreshortenings. Those corrections are often associated with a stringendo effect that necessarily involved rhythmic changes.

The continuo part at the beginning of BWV 26/2 (P 47/1) was corrected thus:

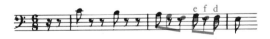

producing once more a measured stringendo, and serving again to propel the phrase forward and prepare the approaching cadence.

The addition of written-out stringendi is not only encountered in continuo parts. In the opening ritornello theme of the aria "Der Tag, der dich vordem gebar" from BWV 36c (P 43/2), the rhythmic effect of the correction in m. 5 of the violin line:

is to introduce a gradual acceleration of motion driving to the cadence in m. 9. The activity of the *Fortspinnung* portion of the ritornello theme thus proceeds, in the final reading, through the following "plateaus" of rhythmic motion:

m. 5	mm. 6b–7a	mm. 7b–8a

before the acceleration is finally restrained in the last quarter of m. 8, in order to settle into the cadence formula:

at the beginning of m. 9.

In mm. 9–10 of the duet "Gott, ach, Gott, verlaß die Deinen nimmermehr," BWV 79/5 (P 89), Bach introduced eighth-note motion into the violin part as follows.

BWV 79/5, mm. 4–12, Violin

The correction serves (1) to create, in combination with the continuo part, a background eighth-note continuum, (2) to represent an embellished and transposed variation of mm. 5 and 7 of the theme, and (3) to introduce, once again, a clearly calculated stringendo drive to the cadence in m. 12.[30]

The extensive revision of the first eight measures of BWV 214/1 (P 41/2),

[30] The passage was changed as follows in the parody version of the movement, the duet "Domine Deus" from the *Mass in G major,* BWV 236 (Darmstadt).

The new reading, a "delayed" correction (analogous changes appear in every statement of the theme with the exception of the final ritornello), provides further illustration of the removal of tone repetitions, and of the introduction both of nonharmonic and chromatic tones.

the chorus "Tönet, ihr Pauken," unquestionably provides the most remarkable correction concerned with the introduction of a measured accumulation of rhythmic energy. The original draft:[31]

[31] In the autograph the final version is superimposed on the original draft and therefore has not been considered a separate "sketch" nor included in Volume II. A facsimile of this page of the autograph score is printed in NBA I/36, p. ix; the transcription of the draft is reproduced here from NBA I/36, KB, pp. 84–85.

besides agreeing with the final reading of the passage in regard to key, orchestration, and general character, bears a number of obvious similarities as well in
regard to the choice of melodic and rhythmic motifs assigned to each instrumental group. While the large-scale rhythmic conception of these eight measures
underwent a drastic transformation in the revision, the draft was clearly not
discarded because of rhythmic factors alone. The final version begins with an
exposed timpani solo which was inspired by the opening words of the chorus.
The gradual accumulation of instrumental forces and the inevitable accompanying crescendo obviously serve considerations of orchestral effectiveness. But
this orchestral crescendo is reinforced by an equally effective and dramatic
rhythmic "crescendo." The succession of ♩♫♫ | ♫ (m. 1, timpani; again, in dimi-
nution, in m. 3) followed by ♫♫. ♫ | ♪ (mm. 2 and 4, flutes), and finally the swirl-
ing thirty-second-note figures in the strings and winds in mm. 5–8 produces an
accumulation of rhythmic momentum that not only ushers in the principal

theme of the movement but reaches its climax at this entrance. The present example is clearly related in principle—and even in function—to the structural cadential stringendi described above; but it is evidently just as much the result of an unabashed desire on the part of the composer to produce an exciting *effect*, making use of all the coloristic, dynamic, and rhythmic means at his disposal, as it is the result of a formalistic concern with structure per se.

Clearly related to the "stringendo corrections" and analogous in function to the examples of varied sequential repetition found in BWV 135/3 and 33/3 are the few corrections embodying rhythmic alterations of upbeat figures. The basic principle was to vary initially identical upbeat figures of successive short phrases in order to introduce an effect of continual rhythmic intensification. The following passage from the *Deposuit* aria of BWV 243a (P 38) provides an illustration of the principle.

BWV 243a/8, mm. 1–6, Violin

The rhythmic forms of the upbeats in the final reading of the passage proceed from ♪ | ♩. (mm. 2–3) to ♪♫ | ♪ (mm. 4–5) and finally to ♪♫♫ | ♪ (mm. 6–7).[32]

Similar considerations no doubt prompted the following changes in the trumpet parts of BWV 59/1 (P 161), m. 47.

BWV 59/1, mm. 45–47, Tpt. 1–2

In addition to corrections evidently intended to introduce a rhythmic plan based on what may perhaps be called a progressive or cumulative principle, there is at least one rhythmic correction that resulted in a rather more abstract design, constituting in essence a kind of axis symmetry. The existence of such symmetrical rhythmic configurations in Bach's works is not unknown. Perhaps the most familiar example is embodied in the subject of the G major fugue of the

---

[32] The rhythmic profile of these measures in the D major version of the *Magnificat* was changed once again, and it is profitable to compare the reading of the later version with the earlier. With one exception, all the variants appear in the auto-graph of BWV 243 (P 39) with no visible evidence of correction. The exception is found in the violin line, m. 6.1–2, where the initial reading | ♩ ♩ was changed to | ♫ ♩.

Well-Tempered Clavier, Book I. The rhythmic form of the subject presents a simple ABBA symmetry:

A rhythmic pattern similar to that of the G major fugue subject emerges in the final reading of the vocal part in mm. 15–16 and 23–24 of the aria "So schnell ein rauschend Wasser schießt," BWV 26/2 (P 47/1). The passage reads as follows in the autograph.

rau - -schend Was - ser schießt

BWV 26/2, mm. 15–16, Tenor

The final rhythmic pattern:  by virtue of the exact mirroring of the "four sixteenths plus one eighth" group in the second measure, is actually more literally symmetrical than the fugue subject.[33] Here, too, as in the fugue subject, the inversion of the rhythmic figure accompanies a general reversal in the direction of the melodic line.

One final example may serve to summarize a number of the motivations governing rhythmic corrections discussed (or implied) both in this section and in earlier sections of the present and previous chapters. The initial soprano entrance in the duet "Ehre sei Gott in der Höhe," BWV 110/5 (P 153), has the following correction.

Eh - - re, Eh - - - - (re)

BWV 110/5, m. 5, Soprano

That is, the rhythmic form of the first half of the measure was changed from ♪♬♬♪♩ to ♪♩♩ ♪♩. One result of the correction is that there is now a clear contrast (or balance) of eighth-note motion in the "subject" portion with sixteenth-note motion in the "countersubject" portion of the theme. The rhythmic contrast not only provides for an effective "kinetic" release of rhythmic energy in the second half of the theme (a kinship with the stringendo principle is clear), propelled by the ♪♩ rhythm in the second quarter of the measure, but makes for a more transparent polyphonic texture in the initial imitation between the two

[33] The tied eighth-notes in the first measure prevent, of course, a completely perfect axis symmetry.

vocal parts. Finally, by removing the sixteenth-notes from the "subject," the motivic identity with the opening of the ritornello theme becomes immediately
perceptible. This deceptively modest correction thus led to the formulation of a
theme with (1) a distinctive and energetic rhythmic profile resulting from an
almost arithmetically balanced contrast of rhythmic values based on the application of the technique of written-out stringendo; and (2) a thematic subject
that is well suited for imitative treatment.

CORRECTIONS TO REPRESENT DIFFERENT RHYTHMIC "PLANES"
IN DIFFERENT VOICES

One of the principal effects of the correction in BWV 110/5 just described
was that the imitative entrance of the tenor part in the second half of m. 5 was
made more distinct as a result of the contrast in rhythm between the eighth-note
motion of the subject and the sixteenth-note motion of the countersubject taken
up by the soprano.

BWV 110/5, m. 5, Soprano, Tenor

(The rhythmic contrast of the two parts is reinforced by the melodic contrast
between the basically disjunct subject and the basically conjunct countersubject.)

Strict rhythmic differentiation of simultaneously sounding parts is obviously
a relatively simple yet highly efficient means of producing a transparent polyphonic texture, and Bach often made use of it. We have seen such rhythmic
relationships between subject and countersubject in the present study in the fugal
expositions of BWV 65/1 (pp. 134ff.), and BWV 75/1 (pp. 139f.).

But rhythmic contrast between voices is, of course, by no means a characteristic
peculiar to polyphonic textures. The archetypal homophonic style traditionally
relies on an emphatic differentiation between a relatively quick moving melody
and a supporting accompaniment which proceeds in considerably slower note
values.

In certain works by Bach, however, the rhythmic differentiation of parts has
been refined to such an extent that it seems to have been elevated to a principle
of an almost metaphysical character, in which each of the constituent parts of
the musical texture is associated with a particular note-value and represents as
it were a specific rhythmic plane. As a result, a kind of hierarchy of voices and

rhythmic values emerges. The opening measures of the *St. John Passion* provide perhaps the most vivid and elaborate application of this principle. The accompaniment comprises (1) an unbroken sixteenth-note turn figure in the violins representing the smallest rhythmic unit of the complex; (2) eighth-note motion in the violas as well as in the cello and bassoon contingents of the continuo; and (3) half-measure articulation represented with a ♩ ♪ ♩ ♪ pattern in the organ and violone superimposed on the eighth-note pulse of the cellos and bassoons,[34] while the thematic suspension motives in the flutes and oboes create a predominantly quarter-note motion above this elaborate background.[35]

There are corrections in several cantata autographs that result in a similar hierarchical representation of different rhythmic strata in different voices, although never to the extent of the *St. John* introduction, and apparently as a secondary effect, accompanying changes made primarily for other reasons.

The Oboe 2 part in BWV 109/5 (P 112), m. 52, originally moved together with the first oboe in parallel sixths, but was changed to the present eighth-note reading, so that in the final version the first oboe proceeds in unbroken sixteenths, the second oboe in eighths, and the continuo in quarter-note motion while the voice part sustains a long tone.

BWV 109/5, mm. 52–53

The change was probably precipitated by a desire to underscore the reentrance of the ritornello theme in m. 53 (which is characterized by parallel motion between the two oboes) with an abrupt change in texture. But the resultant texture of m. 52 is quite reminiscent of the rhythmic architecture of the *St. John* introduction.

The general principle of creating rhythmically independent lines does not normally take the extreme form of assigning each voice its own unit of motion so that the part moves exclusively—for longer or shorter stretches—in an uninterrupted stream of, say, eighth- or sixteenth-notes. In the corrections familiar to this writer, Bach usually achieved this rhythmic individuality of parts simply

[34] The instrumental indications on the first page of the score suggest that the rhythmic differentiation among the continuo instruments was introduced as a correction. See Appendix I.

[35] This remarkable construction was pointed out to me by Arthur Mendel.

by abandoning what may be called a rhythmic doubling of parts and replacing it with a texture in which each of the voices has its own rhythmic identity—usually associated with a characteristic melodic or motivic figure. Thus in the opening chorus of the E♭ *Magnificat,* BWV 243a (P 38), m. 52, the violins and violas originally had | ♩. |, suggesting that Bach at first intended to have the strings essentially duplicate the rhythm of the oboes in the ensuing passage. He immediately decided instead to introduce rising arpeggio figures in the strings with the rhythmic form |♩ ♪ ♫♫|♩ ♪ ♫♫|♩ etc. This created yet one more rhythmic plane within the passage, in addition to the held notes in the oboes, the running sixteenths and ♪ ♪♪ patterns in the chorus, and the |♫ ♪♪|downbeat accents in the continuo. It will be noted that here, too, separate layers of note-values have emerged to some extent in the four measures, mm. 52–56; for the strings, together with the continuo, produce in effect an eighth-note plane, opposing the sixteenth-note motion of the chorus.

By changing the reading of the second violin and viola parts from ♩. to ♩. ♫♫ in m. 96 of BWV 173a/4 (P 42/2), Bach added a fifth rhythmic configuration to this measure, supplementing the

mordent or trill figure	♩⌒♫♫♩. ♫♫	in Flute 1
held note	♩.	in Flute 2
rising sixteenth-note run	♫♫ ♫♫ ♫♫	in Violin 1
descending eighth-note scale	♪ ♫♫♫♫	in the Bc.

Like the example from the *Magnificat* and earlier examples (pp. 183–186 above), the correction was presumably intended primarily to furnish a climactic accumulation of rhythmic activity and textural density at the approach of the cadence (m. 97), which in the present case is also a major structural caesura, marking the end of the second strophe of the aria (the D major section).

It is not surprising that corrections such as those just discussed, which are clearly designed to add "dimension" or "depth" to a straightforward homophonic texture by increasing the rhythmic independence and individuality of the constituent voices, often led to a momentary rhythmic polyphony. The continuo part in m. 99 of BWV 138/5 (P 158), the aria "Auf Gott steht meine Zuversicht," at first simply marked the downbeat: |♩ ♪ ♪| before it was changed to |♩ ♪ ♫♫|♩ ♪ ♫♫|♩ etc., thereby literally forming a rhythmic stretto with the |♪ ♫♫♩|♪ ♫♫♩|♪ pattern in the second violin and viola parts.

Similarly, the continuo part in m. 25 of BWV 119/3 (P 878) appears as follows in the autograph:

Bach apparently had begun to write the accompaniment rhythm prevalent throughout the movement, but then decided to introduce a rhythmic imitation with the oboe parts thus:

Oboe 1
Oboe 2
Bc.

A lengthy revision of the continuo rhythm in the opening fourteen measures of BWV 48/6 (P 109) once again introduces an additional rhythmic plane into a homophonic texture. The continuo line originally had for the most part the same rhythm as the Violin 1 part in these measures, duplicating the characteristic rhythm in mm. 1–2, 4–5, 7–8, 10–11, 13–14 and agreeing with the Violin 1 rhythm in m. 6. After writing m. 14, Bach changed the continuo rhythm to an exclusively even progression of quarter-notes. The correction this time, however, was presumably intended to provide a natural support and foil for the dotted rhythms and syncopations of the theme.[36]

CORRECTIONS ALTERING PHRASE STRUCTURE

The discussion of Sketches Nos. 28, 83, 127, and 139 in the preceding chapter has already emphasized the great flexibility of phrase structure and phrase length in Bach's style. It is therefore not surprising that the composing scores of the arias and choruses contain numerous examples of added or deleted beats, measures, or groups of measures which alter the structure of a particular phrase, and often substantially affect the formal proportions of an entire movement. Additions and deletions of measures which were apparently motivated primarily by considerations of large-scale harmonic or formal design will be discussed in later sections of this chapter. The corrections described below affect directly only the proportions and internal structure of a single phrase or theme.

In the chorale aria "Der Gott, der mir hat versprochen," BWV 13/3 (P 45/4), m. 40 in the Violin 1 part was originally followed by what is now mm. 41b–42a:

---

[36] A correction of the viola part in m. 1 from the rhythm of the two violin parts to the rhythm of the continuo strongly suggests that Bach first composed the outer-voice framework of the ritornello through m. 14, then began to fill in the inner parts in a homorhythmic texture. Presumably after completing the inner parts of m. 1, Bach decided to revise the rhythm of the continuo and corrected the entire part through m. 14 before he proceeded with the composition of the second violin and viola parts.

The original barring was continued through m. 43. Then the original barlines were crossed out, the new half-measure (m. 41a) written down in the available space at the bottom of the score page:

and the succeeding measures rebarred. The extra half-measure and the concomitant shift in the metrical structure of the passage were perhaps introduced simply to permit the next chorale line in mm. 42–44 to begin and end on a downbeat. The correction may thus be related to the rebarrings in the simple chorale settings discussed on pp. 74–75 above.

Again, the interpolation of the half-measure 17b in the Violin 1 part of BWV 113/2 (PP)

Mm. 17ff.

and the consequent rebarring of the following measures was most likely intended to allow the cadence tone to fall on the downbeat of m. 20 and to have the reentry of the ritornello theme start on the same part of the measure that it does at the beginning of the aria.

Bach at times inserted a measure in order to emphasize a significant word or passage of the text by repetition. The interpolated sequential repetition in mm. 33b–34a of BWV 51/3 (P 104):

must have been intended primarily to create a rhetorical emphasis of the words *deine Kinder* at the conclusion of the B section of the aria. And the present mm.

10b–11a of BWV 206/5 (P 42/1) were no doubt inserted to illustrate the word *ruft* in the following manner:[37]

The desire for "rhetorical" emphasis, but of a purely musical nature, no doubt motivated the insertion of the present m. 2 in the opening ritornello of BWV 42/6 (P 55). The first measure was originally followed by the third measure. Bach then entered the second measure in the free space on two staves after the conclusion of the preceding recitative:

Bach's primary concern here, in a way analogous to the genesis of BWV 214/1, was to create an accumulation of activity and tension, this time by prolonging the opening tonic harmony and by introducing in the violin part the repeated figure which centers on the fifth degree of the scale, and, in m. 3, ultimately is released melodically to the climactic a″ and rhythmically into an uninterrupted flow of sixteenth-notes. As in BWV 214/1, the correction has orchestral and textural ramifications, since the new measure introduces as well an imitative repartee between the violins and the continuo. It is by no means unambiguous how the thirteen-measure ritornello, which is clearly constructed according to the *Fortspinnung* model,[38] is to be subdivided. It is just this am-

[37] See NBA I/36, KB, p. 131, for the precise reading in the autograph.

[38] See the terminology developed in Dürr 1951, pp. 105ff.

biguity—or absence—of phrase structure which enables Bach to insert an extra measure into the theme so casually.

A similar corrective gesture can be observed in the opening ritornello of BWV 43/3 (P 44/6), where mm. 2–3 were interpolated between mm. 1 and 4 of the violin part.[39]

Nowhere, however, is the ease with which Bach could alter the length and structure of phrases more clearly demonstrated than in the composing score of BWV 57/1 (P 144), the aria "Selig ist der Mann." Apparently Bach had at first composed the movement as far as the present m. 69 to the text of the first two clauses only. Then, for whatever reason, he decided to work the third clause, *denn, nachdem er bewähret ist,* into the composed passages, and in order to do so had to interpolate new measures. Thus m. 48, for example, was originally followed by m. 50 with a setting of the word *Selig* and was corrected as follows.[40]

Mm. 47ff., Bass

Similarly, mm. 56–60 and 62–69 originally had the *Selig* text, and the text correction involved the interpolation of mm. 55 and 61. (Measure 70 was also added, together with a retexting of mm. 71–82. In this latter instance, however, the original reading of the text is not legible.)

There were occasions though, where the interpolation of new measures seems to reflect a concern for the proportions created between adjacent phrases. The opening phrase of the aria "Hört, ihr Völker," BWV 76/3 (P 67), was at first

[39] See NBA I/12, KB, p. 209.
[40] The new text, which is superimposed on the original text in the autograph, has been placed above or below it here for the sake of legibility.

one measure shorter than the present reading. The violin part appears approximately thus in the autograph:[41]

The interpolation extends the opening phrase from approximately two-and-a-half to three-and-a-half measures; the entire ritornello in the final reading is seven measures long.

The beginning of BWV 108/5 (P 82) was similarly corrected. What is now m. 3b originally followed directly upon m. 2a in all parts. The Violin 1 part, for example, appears thus in P 82:

The added measure was written on the bottom of the page. The Violin 1 part reads:[42]

The three-measure antecedent phrase of the final reading is followed by a five- (2 plus 3) measure *Fortspinnung,* creating an eight-measure ritornello theme.

Corrections of Harmony

It was suggested in Chapter IV that the simple four-part chorale settings constitute the most appropriate genre for a study of corrections of a purely "grammatical" nature, i.e., corrections concerned with the basic mechanics of the eighteenth-century "contrapuntal-harmonic technique" such as voice leading, chord-tone doubling and spacing, and so on. Accordingly, grammatical corrections were considered at some length in the discussion of the chorale autographs. Individual examples were analyzed and general tabulations of such corrections

---

[41] The continuo part for the original melody was drafted before Bach decided to insert the new measure. Several minor corrections in the violin part are not legible and have not been represented in this example. The movement appears in the autograph on a 5-stave system, indicating that

Bach evidently intended at first to set the aria for a complete string ensemble. The added measure of the violin part is entered on the staff of what would have been the Violin 2 part.

[42] See also NBA I/12, KB, p. 70.

in a selected number of chorale settings were presented. It is hardly necessary to pursue a survey of corrections of "harmony" in the textbook sense any further here. In fact, the literally tens of thousands of single-note corrections scattered throughout the autograph scores of arias and choruses (particularly those in inner and purely accompanimental parts) which would have to be evaluated in such a survey make the project prohibitively difficult—if not altogether impossible—without the aid of a modern computer. The following pages, therefore, will be concerned with harmonic corrections of a more "compositional" nature.

CONTINUO CORRECTIONS TO CLARIFY OR STRENGTHEN
HARMONIC PROGRESSIONS

The discussion of the bass line of four-part chorales has already called attention to the obvious dual role of the continuo part as an exposed melodic voice and as the foundation for the harmonic structure of the movement. The continuo, of course, has the same melodic and harmonic responsibilities in arias and choruses.

Preceding sections of the present chapter have considered numerous continuo corrections which served mainly to enhance the melodic or rhythmic effectiveness of the original line or too fulfill structural criteria of motivic unity or rhythmic continuity. The following corrections evidently served primarily to strengthen the harmonic function of the continuo.[43]

The last note in the continuo part of BWV 71/5 (P 45/1), m. 8 was corrected from f♯ to d:

thus introducing an "harmonic" leap of a fourth which at the same time breaks up a succession of five parallel tenths between the alto and continuo based on a static neighbor-tone figure:

---

[43] Obviously, since any change of pitch in this part has both melodic and harmonic implications, it is not really possible to consider "melodic" or "harmonic" continuo corrections in complete isolation. But this same dilemma has been encountered already in the discussions of melody and rhythm and will be encountered again.

The leap of a fourth was again introduced in BWV 52/3 (P 85), m. 9, to emphasize the harmonic motion in the middle of the measure:

perhaps as a kind of prior compensation for the $^6_3$ position cadence on the downbeat of m. 10. The latter was presumably designed to avoid an anticipation of the perfect cadence at the conclusion of the ritornello in m. 13.

Similar corrective gestures are apparent in the third trombone part of the motet *O Jesu Christ, mein's Lebens Licht*, BWV 118[1] (PP), mm. 12–16:

In mm. 6–7 of BWV 65/1 (P 147) the continuo was changed by the introduction of falling sevenths from a purely "melodic" ascending scalar line into a more "functional" bass in order to emphasize the harmonic progression of fifths underlying the passage:

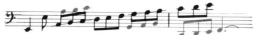

The interval of the falling seventh has, of course, great melodic effectiveness as well as harmonic significance.[44]

Without question the most extraordinary and extensive continuo corrections of the kind under consideration here are found in the autograph score of the Weimar cantata *Tritt auf die Glaubensbahn*, BWV 152 (P 45/3). Although the manuscript, in general (like almost all pre-Cöthen autographs) is relatively "clean" and could be taken for a fair copy, the continuo line in Movements 2, 4, and 6 is quite heavily corrected. The extensive revisions of the continuo in these three movements, while occasionally serving melodic or rhythmic functions, are mainly concerned with strengthening the harmonic effectiveness of the line by replacing stepwise motion with harmonic skips. To indicate the extent and nature of the revisions, both the original and final readings of the continuo part in Movement 2 will be reproduced here in their entirety.[45]

---

[44] See also pp. 163f. above.

[45] The original reading is partially erased but still, for the most part, quite legible. Uncertainty arises only in measures where quarter-note motion may have been replaced by eighth-note figures. The new reading is in a darker, blacker ink, which is observable also in the continuo corrections in the other two movements. This fact, and also the substitution (made with the same black ink) of ♮ for ♭ before the tone f in m. 35, suggests that the revision was made considerably—perhaps years—later. See NBA I/14, KB, p. 106, in regard to Bach's early notation of accidentals.

The fundamentally melodic conception of the original continuo reading,

BWV 152/2, mm. 1–2 (Oboe transposed to e minor)

with its almost defiant independence of the other parts (note the grotesquely harsh clash of minor seconds at the beginning of m. 2 and analogous measures between the continuo and oboe) leads one to speculate that Bach, at this stage in his career, had perhaps not yet fully assimilated the modern, i.e., late baroque, idiom of functional tonality and that his musical language was to a large degree still influenced by the more strictly linear and contrapuntal traits characteristic of German music of the preceding generation. But it is also possible that the first version of the continuo represents an experiment in linear part-writing that proved to be less than completely successful and was therefore replaced with a more clearly accompanimental, harmonic, bass line.

Numerous corrections in the continuo part of Movement 4 of the same cantata serve to strengthen the harmonic character of the line, and introduce diminution tones to break up sequences, provide occasional motivic references, and/or maintain the motor rhythm of the movement.

BWV 152/4, Mm. 3–4 (also mm. 16, 39–40)

BWV 152/4, m. 7 (cf. m. 1)

As in Movement 2 the continuo was revised after the entire movement was completed.

In the sixth movement, continuo corrections again serve the rhythmic function of relieving undifferentiated quarter-note motion by adding eighth-note figures:

or serve melodic-harmonic functions by introducing skips and arpeggio figures into passages which originally proceeded predominantly in stepwise motion:

While numerous corrections of both pitch and rhythm discussed in the course of this chapter—and particularly in the present section—served either directly or indirectly to strengthen the approach to and articulation of cadences, Bach did, on at least one occasion, weaken a cadential gesture in order to secure a formal nuance. The outer instrumental parts of the aria "Herr, deine Güte reicht," BWV 17/3 (P 45/5), were corrected in m. 50 as follows:[46]

The correction replaces a perfect cadence in the middle of the measure with an imperfect cadence, weakened further by the addition of a suspension figure in the Oboe (Violin) 1 part. The purpose of the correction was evidently to avoid any emphatic confirmation of the return to the tonic and further to disguise this return, just as the soprano inconspicuously reintroduced the opening ritornello theme in the preceding measure. (This reintroduction coincides with the actual arrival at the tonic.) The final vocal section of the aria thus proceeds without any significant interruption until the full cadence of m. 59. This cadence, together with the entrance of the instrumental postlude consti-

---

[46] In the autograph this movement has the heading *Aria à 2 Hautb*. The scoring in BG, however, is for two violins.

tutes, as it were, the "official" return to the tonic and the conclusion of the movement.

CHANGES OF CADENTIAL GOALS AND OTHER REVISIONS AFFECTING GENERAL TONAL STRUCTURE

Approximately 25 corrections[47] in the Bach autographs result in the change of a cadential harmony or otherwise represent a revision in the harmonic direction of a particular passage. The significance of such changes for the overall tonal design of an aria or chorus depends, of course, on the structural position and importance of the corrected passage or cadence within the movement. The following corrections, for example, which entail the substitution of deceptive cadences for perfect authentic cadences have little effect on the larger harmonic plan of the movements concerned.

The tenor part in BWV 208/4 (P 42/3), mm. 33–34, was corrected thus:

The deceptive cadence, along with the concomitant text repetition and one-measure extension of the final phrase of the B section were therefore an (immediate) afterthought.

The continuo line of the *Deposuit* aria from the E♭ version of the *Magnificat*, BWV 243a/8 (P 38), mm. 47–48, originally outlined a perfect cadence.

Readings 1 and 2

Reading 3

Bach may have planned at first to have the final ritornello enter in m. 48 but then decided to append the vocal epilog of mm. 48–54, the introduction of a deceptive cadence in that case serving, as in BWV 208/4, to extend the final vocal passage of a major section of the movement. This time, however, the presumed extension involved not one measure but the addition of a complete seven-measure phrase.

---

[47] Again I prefer not to give a precise figure.

A correction in the Violin 1/2 line of BWV 75/3 (P 66), m. 64, suggests that here, too, the deceptive cadence and—by analogy with the preceding examples—the ensuing vocal epilog before the final ritornello of the A section were not part of Bach's original plan. The Violin 1/2 line (written on one staff in the autograph) was changed:

The original reading would have corresponded to the Violin 2 part in the first measure of the aria and recreated the tonic G major context of the opening ritornello, instead of the present e minor reading.[48]

Such corrections obviously do not represent any basic tonal reorientation of the passages to which they belong. Rather they merely postpone the arrival at the originally intended harmonic goal by interpolating essentially parenthetical clauses of greater or lesser extent—again an avoidance of the inevitable and expected. Interpolations of this kind can be considered diminutions in a figurative sense, expanding the temporal dimensions and thus, to some degree, the "form" of the movement.

The substitution of a c minor sonority for an E♭ major sonority at the beginning of the first instrumental interlude in the chorale chorus "Meine Seele erhebt den Herrn," BWV 10/1 (LC), mm. 18–19:

has perhaps more harmonic-structural significance than the preceding examples. The basic harmonic outline of the interlude in mm. 19–28 is now II-V-I in B-flat major, rather than IV-V-I, so that the dominant is approached by the skip of a fourth rather than by a step. The ultimate effect of the correction on the tonal organization of the passage, however (let alone on the movement as a whole), is negligible. Considerations of chordal color rather than of harmonic structure may have motivated the correction. Bach perhaps wished mainly to avoid repeating at once the quite ornamental E♭ harmony introduced as a plagal inflection in the first half of m. 18.

The following correction in the autograph of the d minor aria "Bald zur Rechten, bald zur Linken," BWV 96/5 (P 179), represents a more substantial

---

[48] There is no correction in the continuo part in this measure, which perhaps indicates that Bach entered the parts in the measure from "top to bottom"; an illegible smudge in the tenor part on the third beat may indicate the removal of a quarter-rest.

alteration of harmonic structure. The Oboe 1 part in mm. 3–4 at the first cadence of the opening ritornello reads:

The first phrase of the theme was presumably to cadence on F, perhaps as part of a I-III, V-I ground plan for the eight-measure period instead of the present design: I-IV, IIb-V-I. The turning back on the f''♮ with an f''♯ in the final reading is doubtless an illustration of the zig-zag *verirrter Schritt*. It is therefore quite likely that the correction was primarily melodic in origin, although it involved a complete recasting of the cadential framework of the ritornello.

On the other hand, Bach simplified the harmonic plan in the opening ritornello of BWV 9/1 (LC). As mentioned above (p. 152), the flute part in mm. 11–16.1 was originally written one tone lower than the present reading, thus creating a subdominant A major region after the dominant cadence in mm. 10–11. This was eliminated in the final version of the ritornello, which has the cadential plan:

	I—V	V—	V$_7$	I
Mm.	1–11	11–16	16–17	18–24

The tonal framework of a movement is significantly affected, of course, when a correction serves either to introduce or prevent a modulation. As Alfred Dürr points out,[49] in the Eb *Magnificat*, the autograph for the violin part in m. 24 of the *Et exsultavit* aria, BWV 243a/2 (P 38), at first had the same reading as m. 4. Bach, therefore, must have intended to repeat at least the first four measures of the opening ritornello literally, before he decided to interrupt the quotation at this point in order to lead the passage to the dominant, in which key the ritornello is then repeated.

Mm. 23–26, Violin 1

The continuo correction in m. 42 of the *Deposuit* aria from the same work:

however, prevents the tenor part, which cites mm. 19–22 in mm. 39–42, from repeating the earlier modulation to the relative major (mm. 23–28), and redirects the passage to the tonic for the concluding portion of the movement.

[49] NBA II/3, KB, p. 50.

Now it is most likely that Bach from the first had intended to introduce the modulation to the dominant somewhere in the opening vocal section of the *Et exsultavit,* and to secure the tonic in the concluding vocal section of the *Deposuit.* Therefore, the corrections just described in all probability do not reflect so much a revision of the original tonal design of these arias—as it would at first appear—as simply a belated decision regarding the precise point where the planned change in harmonic direction should begin.

There are other corrections as well which reveal the composer's efforts to create a modulation or transition smoother than that provided in the original reading of a passage, but which do not represent a belated decision to introduce the modulation. The Violin 2 part, for example, in m. 8 of BWV 51/4 (P 104) was corrected as follows:

The change cancels not only the sharp signs, and D major context of the measure, but also the real imitation of the Violin 1 part, in order to prepare more smoothly the return to the tonic at the end of the ritornello in m. 11.

Bach reworked the bass answer in the fugal exposition of BWV 76/1 (P 67), mm. 72–77, on the words *Es ist keine Sprache noch Rede* in order to avoid an overly abrupt cadence on the dominant, simply by preparing the "modulation" two measures earlier and thus avoiding the excessively strong subdominant orientation of the original real answer.

Mm. 67–72, Tenor

Mm. 72–77, Bass[50]

The desire to create a smooth harmonic transition called forth the interpolation of five measures in the autograph score of BWV 44/6 (P 148). The B section

---

[50]The corrections of the bass part appear in P 67 in a darker ink than the rest of the autograph and were apparently entered at a relatively late date—after the earliest copies of the score had already been prepared. The NBA I/16, KB will no doubt consider the history of this passage in detail. The revision also called forth dense corrections in the tenor and continuo lines, which render the original readings only partially legible.

of the aria originally began after the fermata in m. 33 with what is now the passage beginning with the upbeat to m. 39, scored (as is the present mm. 34ff.) for soprano and continuo alone. Even before completing the section, Bach had apparently decided to insert the new measures 34–38; for after he had completed f. 5v of the autograph with the present m. 51a, he began the next folio, f. 6r, with the interpolated measures, and only thereafter wrote the closing passage of the B section with mm. 51b–54.[51] The addition of a string accompaniment in the present m. 39 presumably belongs to the same corrective gesture as the interpolation of mm. 34–38. The new measures provide a gradual transition from the close of the A section in B♭ to the g minor area of the B section. The proportions of the final version of the movement are:

Ritornello	A section	Ritornello	B section
8 measures	17 measures	8 measures	21 measures

That is, the additional measures in this instance served to upset rather than create an arithmetical correspondence between the two vocal sections—an indication that the interpolation was intended primarily (if not exclusively) to fulfill an harmonic function.[52]

A genuine change of harmonic goal, however, may well be evident in the *Alleluia* finale of BWV 51 (P 104). The correction again affects an imitative answer and to a limited extent can be considered a reversal of the corrective gesture in BWV 76/1. Considerations of dramatic coloristic effect as well as tonal design presumably motivated the following correction of the trumpet part in m. 44:

The reentrance of the opening subject of the movement in the tonic (mm. 41ff.) at the conclusion of the instrumental interlude apparently was to be answered conventionally by the soprano in the dominant. The final reading presents an unexpected and abrupt turn to the subdominant which is underlined by the sudden change in tessitura from the climactic c‴ in the trumpet to the low register of the entering voice. This tessitura change is accompanied of necessity by a *subito piano* effect.

Most frequently, substantial harmonic corrections affecting the basic tonal structure of the entire movement are concentrated in the middle sections of da-capo arias. The following correction in the bass part at the conclusion of the

---

[51] See the description in NBA I/12, KB, pp. 259–260.

[52] In contrast, see the discussion of BWV 40/7, below.

A section of the D major aria "Auf, auf mit hellem Schall," BWV 128/3 (PP), m. 60:

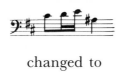

changed to

indicates that Bach originally must have had a different tonal design in mind for the B section, which at first was clearly to begin in b minor. The E_7 harmonization in the final version of m. 60 ultimately resolves through a deceptive cadence to f-sharp minor in m. 62. The middle section concludes in m. 71 in the key of b minor, so that the overall harmonic structure of the aria is essentially I V∥III VI∣I rather than I V∥VI ?∣I.

Similarly, the opening measures in the voice part (mm. 73–75) of the B section of BWV 206/3 (P 42/1), the A major aria "Schleuß des Janustempels Türen," were for the most part at first written one tone lower than the present reading. The middle section, therefore, probably was to begin in e minor rather than the more conventional submediant of the final version.[53]

The decision to conclude the B section of the f-sharp minor aria "Capital und Interessen," BWV 168/3 (P 152), with an anticipation of the tonic was apparently an afterthought. The original reading of mm. 119–122, although not completely decipherable, is legible enough to indicate that the phrase originally cadenced in c-sharp minor—the same key in which the B section had begun and the A section had ended. In the final reading there is a deceptive cadence on D in m. 122 which leads—as in BWV 243a/8 and 75/3, discussed above—to a repetition of the final line of the text in the manner of an epilog.

A correction in m. 191 of BWV 194/10 (P 43/3), the F major duet "O wie wohl ist uns geschehn," suggests that the concluding vocal epilog of the B section was an afterthought and motivated by considerations of the general harmonic design of the movement. The bass part reads:

(Thron)   und   Haus schüt - tert

BWV 194/10, mm. 190–191

[53] The original reading is reproduced in NBA I/36, KB, p. 129. The suggestion there (p. 167) that this correction may indicate that the movement was based on a preexistent model is hardly convincing. The autograph in this movement is relatively heavily corrected throughout and is clearly a composing score. See KB, pp. 128ff. and p. 148 above.

The passage in mm. 191–199 leads the harmony from B♮ to d minor before the da-capo. The principal tonal goals of the final reading of the movement are:

	A section			B section				
	I	V	I	I	III	IV	VI	DC
Mm.	1	54	90	145	160	176	199	

Bach apparently had no clear tonal plan in mind for the middle section of the G major da-capo aria "Ätzet dieses Angedenken," BWV 207/7[54] (P 174), before he began actual composition. A rejected reading for mm. 75–79[55] reveals that the composer at first planned to have the B section begin in a minor but immediately transposed the reading down a fourth. The concluding tonality of the section was uncertain as well. The continuo part originally had defined a cadence on b in mm. 118–120 which was then changed to the present e minor reading. But the first reading may have been entered inadvertently; for, as Sketch No. 138 (a continuation sketch for mm. 118–120 of the alto part) makes clear, Bach did have an e minor cadence in mind before he had written the first continuo reading on the following page of the autograph.

An interpolation in the B section of BWV 40/7 (P 63), the tenor aria "Christenkinder freuet euch," brought about major changes in both the formal and harmonic designs of the aria. The complete seven-measure passage, mm. 29b–35a, was at first omitted in the autograph. After the d minor cadence of the orchestra on the first beat of m. 29, the tenor entered on the second beat with the repetition of the opening vocal passage, marking the beginning of the A′ section of the aria. The tenor and continuo lines of m. 29 appear as follows in the autograph.

Mm. 28bff.

The additional measures, in which only the voice and continuo are active, were entered on the bottom two staves of ff. 9v–10r of the autograph, and an indication for seven measures rest was inserted in the orchestral parts of m. 29 in the

[54] As to the numbering of the movements in this cantata, see the note to Sketch No. 137 in Volume II.

[55] Reproduced in NBA I/38, KB, pp. 56f. See also Schünemann 1935, p. 7.

body of the score. The interpolation represents an expansion of the tonal architecture of the movement from

$$
\begin{array}{ccccccc}
\text{A} & \text{B} & \text{A}' & & \text{A} & \text{B} & \text{A}' \\
\text{I—V}\,|\,\text{(V)—VI}\,|\,\text{I} & & & \text{to} & \text{I—V}\,|\,\text{(V)—VI—IV}\,|\,\text{I}
\end{array}
$$

and also the addition of a second vocal exposition of the B section text, increasing
the length of the B section from nine to sixteen measures. As a result, the three
sections of the movement (excluding the opening and closing ritornelli) are
approximately equal in length (c. 15, 16, and 14 measures respectively).

Corrections of Form

FUNDAMENTAL CHANGES OF FORM

Corrections of "form," in the most common meaning of that term, are practically nonexistent in the composing scores of the vocal works. This is hardly
surprising, since the form of the text and/or cantus firmus melody, i.e., the
preexistent material, used in an aria or chorus essentially determined the basic
musical form of the movement. A fundamental change of form, however, may
be evident in the original source material for the aria "Es kommt ein Tag" from
Cantata No. 136. Although there is no extant autograph score for the cantata,
two autograph score fragments for the alto aria are preserved together with the
original parts of the composition (St 20, Part No. 16). One of these fragments,
containing mm. 29–39, i.e., the presto middle section with the following two
measures of the aria, is clearly the composing score for this section. The second
fragment is a fair copy of the same measures. There are bracket-like indications
over the first and last measures of both fragments which reveal that the passage
is most probably an insert for the lost autograph score. The existence of the
fragments strongly suggests that the aria was originally in binary form—m. 28
followed directly by m. 40—but was later recast as a ternary aria in "free
da-capo" form. Since one of the original parts for the cantata—a non-transposed
continuo part with thorough bass figures throughout (Part No. 13)—was written
out at first without mm. 29–39 (so that these measures had to be inserted
subsequently with the same bracket indications that appear in the composing
score fragment), it is clear that the composition of the middle section of the
aria was considerably delayed. The fact that Bach prepared a fair copy of the
insert suggests, furthermore, that the lost autograph score was itself a fair copy.

It seems likely that the insertion of the presto section was not a compositional
correction of purely musical origin but was connected with a change in the
text—probably the addition of the lines set in this section. That is, the change

in musical form probably was dependent on a change in the form of the text stanza.[56]

The autograph of the chorus "Unser Mund sei voll Lachens," BWV 110/1 (P 153), contains a less substantial correction of form. The movement is based on the *Ouverture* of the fourth Orchestral Suite, BWV 1069; a choral part has been worked into the allegro portion of the French-style overture. Although a comparison of BWV 1069 and BWV 110/1 reveals several significant variants of a formal nature,[57] only one of these appears as a correction in the cantata autograph. The opening *Grave* section of the movement, which is to be repeated in the suite, was originally to be repeated in the cantata as well. Measure 24 was at first written out in P 153 in two readings representing first and second endings. Bach subsequently decided, however, to omit the repetition and crossed out the first ending.[58]

Corrections in the autograph scores of the arias "In Jesu Demuth kann ich Trost," BWV 151/3 (Coburg), and "Phoebus, deine Melodei," BWV 201/9 (P 175), suggest at first that Bach had originally intended to compose both movements as strict da-capo arias before he decided to set them in "free da-capo" form. In the composing score of BWV 151/3 Bach had at first written *DC* in the alto part and drawn a double bar in each part after the conclusion of the B section in m. 68. He had similarly entered a *DC* indication in the oboe d'amore line of the "Phoebus" aria at the beginning of m. 53. In each instance, however, Bach realized—i.e., remembered—"immediately" that a complete and literal repetition of the A section would not be possible, since the section in each movement concluded in the dominant. In both cases, then, Bach from the first had planned to compose the arias in "free da-capo" form. The *DC* indications after the B sections in the two scores were without doubt set down absent-mindedly. In any event, though, even if the change had represented a compositional correction, the change from strict to free da-capo form would have reflected not so much a generic change of form as simply an harmonic modification of one and the same form.[59]

---

[56] See BG 28, p. xxx, where it is suggested that BWV 136 is a parody of a lost model, and that the model for the alto aria did not have the middle presto section. NBA I/18, KB, p. 137, acknowledges this possibility but has found no evidence that would help identify the model. W. H. Scheide suggests further in his unpublished monograph "Bach Achieves His Goal. His First Year of Regular Church Music Following the Leipzig Lutheran Calendar," that the aria is perhaps a parody of a (binary?) aria from a lost Cöthen work. The insert, according to both Rust's and Scheide's arguments,

was written to accommodate the old music to the structure of the new five-line text. I am grateful to Mr. Scheide for an opportunity to read his hypothesis.

[57] Summarized in NBA I/2, KB, pp. 68–70.

[58] The reading of the rejected measure is printed in NBA I/2, KB, p. 96.

[59] From the strictly musical point of view it could be argued that free and strict da-capo are not really one and the same form, since the free da-capo with its harmonic plan I-V ‖ X-I ‖ is more binary than ternary. But this, again, is a strictly musical point

INTERPOLATIONS AND DELETIONS OF VOCAL MOTTOES AND
INSTRUMENTAL INTERLUDES

In sum, then, there are apparently no instances of a freely inspired transformation of form in the composing scores. BWV 110/1 is definitely and BWV 136/3 very likely based on an earlier work which had a different form from the parody. The original *DC* indications in the arias from BWV 201 and 151 surely represent no more than momentary lapses of attention.

There are, however, numerous corrections which introduce modifications or refinements—but no basic transformations—of the initially chosen (or predetermined) form of an aria or chorus. The cadential revision in m. 50 of BWV 17/3 (discussed on pp. 201f.) may be recalled in this connection. The symmetrical melodic correspondence introduced at the conclusion of the BWV 175/2 ritornello (see p. 167) is another formal touch. Bach's interest in such symmetrical design is more dramatically illustrated in the opening French-overture chorus, "Preise, Jerusalem, den Herrn," BWV 119 (P 878). The bass and soprano entrances in mm. 67–68, at the conclusion of the 12/8 allegro section were at first based on the final line of the text: *Er schaffet deinen Gren[-zen Frieden]*. They were corrected as follows:

In the final version the allegro section is thus rounded off by a repetition of the theme with which it began. This entire movement is thereupon rounded off with an abbreviated reprise of the introductory *Grave*.

On several occasions Bach decided as an afterthought to introduce a vocal "motto" at the beginning of the A section of an aria. In BWV 170/5 (P 154) Bach had written the word *drum* after *leben* at the end of m. 9. The composer evidently had intended at first to set the entire opening line of the text in mm. 8ff. before he decided on a motto introduction of the voice, with a completion of the phrase in the orchestra.

A multiple correction in the soprano part of BWV 179/5 (P 146), mm. 13–14, while not altogether legible, reveals clearly enough that the motto-like detach-

of view. The generic form of the da-capo aria is
determined by the structure of the text—and this
is always ternary.

ment of the first two words of the text, like the true motto of BWV 170/5, was an afterthought. The reading of the passage appears approximately as follows in the autograph.

Reading 1

Readings 2 and 3

A related correction, but of greater formal significance than the two just described, is found at the beginning of the alto aria "Mit allem, was ich hab und bin," BWV 72/2(b)[60] (P 54). Measure 59 of Movement 2(a), the final recitative portion of the total form-complex Recitative-Arioso-Recitative-Aria, originally ended thus:

and was followed directly by the instrumental passage beginning with the upbeat to what is now m. 64. That is, the aria originally had begun conventionally with an instrumental ritornello. Sometime after he had written out the ritornello, Bach decided on a vocal introduction to the movement based on the first two lines of the aria text, which complete the sentence with which the recitative had ended.[61] As a result of the insertion of this four-measure *Themenkopf* motto as mm. 60–63, the opening ritornello now functions as a *Fortspinnung* of the motto in the voice. Such a transformation of function—an opening passage changed to a continuation—has been encountered before in the discussion of Sketch No. 28 in Chapter VI. In contrast to the vocal mottoes in BWV 170/5 and 179/5 which did not result in the interpolation of new measures (since in both movements the motto is *eingebaut* into the opening ritornello), the present correction does entail such an interpolation. It is an expansion of the original dimensions

---

[60] Concerning the numbering of the movements in this cantata see the note to Sketches Nos. 47 and 48 in Volume II.

[61] Since there was no room to insert the vocal passage between the end of the recitative and the beginning of the ritornello—m. 59 ends one system

and m. 64 begins the next on f. 6r of the autograph—the new measures were entered on the bottom of the preceding page of the score: the alto part on the last staff of f. 5v, and the continuo part below it in tablature.

of the movement, reminiscent of the added vocal epilogs and sections described earlier in this chapter in the discussion of corrections affecting tonal structure.

While the interpolation of such vocal passages is infrequent, a converse corrective gesture—the interpolation of instrumental interludes—is quite common. The interruptions of the opening vocal passages in BWV 170/5 and 179/5, in fact, can be regarded as the subsequent formation of vocal mottoes and as the (implicit) interpolation of instrumental interludes. They are perhaps best considered as special instances of the latter. There are at least 25 arias and choruses in addition to BWV 179/5 and 170/5 in which instrumental interludes were created as an afterthought. The corrective gesture is clearly a formal articulation or punctuation of the text and also, where the interlude is a true interpolation increasing the length of the movement, another manifestation of the tendency toward expansion and elaboration which we have seen operating repeatedly throughout this study.

Corrections resulting in the creation of an instrumental interlude appear for the first time in the aria "Der Zeiten Herr hat viel vergnügte Stunden," from the Cöthen cantata *Die Zeit, die Tag und Jahre macht*, BWV 134a (Paris). Measures 49–50 originally read as follows:[62]

This reading was crossed out and replaced with the final version:

Bach thus planned at first to extend the first vocal phrase of the B section by repeating the final words of the text line but then decided rather on a brief punctuating interlude, which, as in the case of the vocal mottoes in BWV 179/5 and 170/5, entailed no real addition of extra measures but simply the elimination of the vocal part. In mm. 58–59 of the same aria the decision to have a brief interlude was again an afterthought.[63] The belated insertion of interludes between the lines of the concluding chorale of BWV 105 (P 99) has already been described (pp. 73f. above). In two other movements of this cantata one observes

[62] The transcription is reproduced from NBA I/35, KB, p. 76.

[63] *Ibid.*, p. 76.

similar corrective gestures. In the opening chorus at m. 29 it is clear (although the precise pitches are not legible) that Bach at first had begun a new set of imitative choral entries directly after the cadence on the downbeat of the measure. The first few notes in the soprano and alto parts were then smudged out, and the present two-measure orchestral interlude was substituted.[64]

Two instrumental interludes were subsequent additions in the soprano aria of the same cantata. Both serve to punctuate the text and extend the dimensions of the movement. In mm. 21b–22 the words *indem sie sich* were at first entered beneath the soprano staff but were immediately smudged out.[65] This correction, of course, can once again be considered the invention of an opening motto, as well as the introduction of an interlude.

In mm. 74ff. the decision to add an interlude between the last line of the A section and the beginning of the B section was not so immediate. The soprano part in mm. 74–77 appears thus in the autograph:

so   wird   ein   ge - äng-stigt Ge - wi - ß[en]

i.e., precisely the same material is presented with which the soprano enters in m. 78 of the final version. Here the "added" nature of the interlude is considerably clearer than in the examples discussed so far.

The one-measure rest in the vocal part and the concomitant instrumental interlude in m. 4 of the bass aria "Ihr Kleingläubigen, warum seid ihr so furchtsam," BWV 81/4 (P 120), were once again an afterthought. The autograph reveals that Bach originally had planned to repeat the opening text line immediately:

Ihr Kl[ein]gläu-bi - g[en] war - um seyd ihr so furcht-sam

The correction serves the rhetorical purpose of allowing the question posed by the biblical text to "resound," as it were, answered only by the continuo figure which defines a full cadence in preparation for the reentry of the voice.

It is absolutely clear from the layout of the autograph that the continuo *Kopfmotiv* in m. 24 of the *Quia fecit* aria from the E♭ *Magnificat*, BWV 243a/5

[64] See the facsimile in BG 44, Plate 37.   [65] See BG 44, Plate 38.

(P 38), is an interpolated measure. Measures 23bff. of the original score read thus:

The ritornello *Themenkopf* was entered after the aria was completed in the free space to the right of the final measure:

The added interlude in m. 24, together with the opening ritornello, the brief interlude in m. 13, and the final ritornello statement, mark the principal harmonic stations of the movement: B♭ (m. 9), F (m. 13), d minor (m. 24) and B♭ (m. 30).

As in the *Quia fecit* aria, the two-measure orchestral interlude in mm. 69b–71a of BWV 102/1 (P 97), preceding the imitative entrances in the chorus on the words *Sie haben ein härter Angesicht,* is clearly an interpolation. Insert indications similar to those in BWV 243a/5 appear in P 97 at the beginning of the present m. 72 and correspond to indications at the beginning of an insert on the bottom of the same score page (f. 3v) containing the orchestral parts for mm. 70 and 71.[66]

[66] The remaining examples of interpolated instrumental interludes known to me are:
BWV 24/1 (P 44/4), mm. 78–79
BWV 48/6 (P 109), mm. 66b–69a
BWV 243a/3 (P 38), m. 10
BWV 135/5 (Leipzig), m. 99
BWV 87/1 (P 61), m. 24
BWV 128/4 (PP), mm. 36–38
BWV 175/4 (P 75), mm. 74b–75a
BWV 151/3 (Coburg), m. 27–29
BWV 43/9 (P 44/6), mm. 50-51 and 55–56
BWV 19/5 (P 45/8), mm. 104–106
BWV 56/3 (P 118), m. 65
BWV 55/1 (P 105), mm. 113–115
BWV 204/8 (P 107), mm. 37–40

BWV 82/1 (P 114), mm. 124–125
BWV 198/1 (P 41/1), mm. 19–20
BWV 171/4 (PP), mm. 36b–40a
BWV 201/7 (P 175), mm. 126b–127a
BWV 201/11 (P 175), mm. 40–41
BWV 97/6 (NYPL), mm. 34–35
For BWV 198/1, mm. 19–20, see the transcription in NBA I/38, KB, p. 106. Professor Werner Neumann, the editor of this volume, calls Bach's original omission of an interlude a *Versehen;* but in the light of the evidence presented on these pages, it seems equally likely that upon arriving at m. 19 Bach had not yet decided to separate the second and third lines of text by an interlude.

It must also be mentioned that on a few occasions Bach may have decided against an instrumental interlude in favor of a continuation of the vocal passage. Thus the following correction in the soprano part of BWV 77/3 (P 68), m. 33,

(Ge-)bot er-ken - [nen]   und

is a strong indication that Bach at first had intended an interlude to follow upon the conclusion of the text line *Laß mich doch dein Gebot erkennen*. And the original version of BWV 206/5 (P 42/1),[67] mm. 27–29, suggests that Bach had planned to write a relatively long interlude after the planned F♯ cadence in m. 27. In the final reading there is a semi-cadence at this point, and, after a measure's rest, the tenor reenters. It is possible, though, that the harmonic change in m. 27, which postpones the perfect cadence on F♯ until m. 32, was the determining corrective gesture, and that Bach had planned to write a vocal *Einbau* in the rejected reading but crossed it out before he wrote in the voice part. Speculation becomes completely idle at this point.

The Addition of Bridge Passages

A common correction of an essentially formal nature entails the subsequent addition of small transitional passages or bridges between phrases or sections. It was mentioned at the conclusion of Chapter VI that Bach occasionally did not write in the bridge passage between two phrases until the second phrase (or at least part of it) had already been written down. In the examples cited in Chapter VI, Bach evidently was at first completely uncertain how he would fill the lacuna between the phrases, and therefore momentarily left the space blank. He may have planned to compose a bridge passage from the first, but it is just as conceivable that he had considered having a rest rather than a transition. In over thirty instances, however, corrections in the autograph reflect not momentary uncertainty but a definite—although perhaps immediate—change of mind regarding the treatment of the gap between the end of one phrase and the beginning of the next. With few exceptions Bach decided to replace a rest or long note with an active transition figure in order to avoid a break in rhythmic motion and a wooden juxtaposition of phrases or sections.

In the aria "Wirf mein Herze, wirf dich noch," BWV 155/4 (P 129), the thirty-second-note scale figure connecting the conclusion of the B section with

---

[67] Transcribed in NBA I/36, KB, p. 132.

the final ritornello (m. 48) apparently was an afterthought, since it is entered in the autograph in a lighter shade of ink than that of the rest of the manuscript:

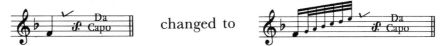

changed to

Again, in BWV 94/2 (P 47/2), the continuo part in m. 12 originally had a half-note on D, corresponding to the cadential half-note at the conclusion of the ritornello in m. 4. The connecting sixteenth-note run was therefore an after-thought. Similarly, the cadential tones in mm. 8, 16, and 88 in the Oboe 1 part of BWV 109/5 (P 112) originally had been written as |♩.| (in mm. 88–89 as |♩.|♩♪♪|) before Bach decided to carry the rhythmic flow forward with the figuration in the final readings of these measures.

The addition of a connecting sixteenth-note figure in the continuo part of BWV 105/1 (P 99), m. 47, between the adagio and allegro sections of this chorus helps establish the precise tempo relation between the two sections as $C♩ = ₵♩$ (cf. m. 57, etc.):[68]

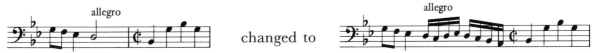

changed to

At times the new transitional figure resulted in a minor change in the following phrase. The added transition in the organ part of BWV 188/4 (Fragment), mm. 47b–48a, altered the first note of the ritornello theme as follows:

and in BWV 215/7 (P 139) the upbeat to the ritornello theme in the flute part, m. 38, was embellished thus:

The simple principle involved in these corrections hardly needs to be further illustrated.

In BWV 173a/6 (P 42/2), however, addition of a transitional bridge figure between the final vocal phrase of the A section and the following ritornello

---

[68] There are, of course, two changes of tempo here: in m. 47, third beat, the change is marked by the word *allegro;* in m. 48, first beat, by the change of time signature.

quotation is actually part of a corrective gesture intended to separate two phrases which were originally dovetailed (mm. 47–49):

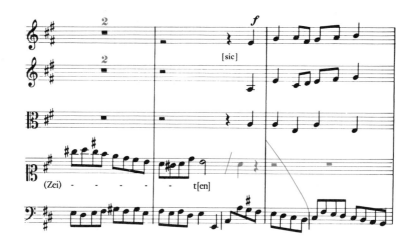

The bridge figure in this case is an interpolated measure, and the correction, accordingly, represents a basic change in the phrase structure of the complete passage.[69]

Similarly, in BWV 243a/B (P 38), the troping chorus "Freut euch und jubiliert," Bach rejected his initial intention to introduce the new text phrase *zu Bethlehem gefunden wird* in the soprano part of m. 17, which would have overlapped with the conclusion of the preceding section of the chorus. The composer decided rather to lead the first section to a full cadence on the dominant in m. 19, followed by a complete caesura before introducing the new phrase in m. 20.[70]

In BWV 194/10 (P 43/3), on the other hand, the two oboes originally had a measure's rest in m. 160, so that a complete silence followed upon the a minor cadence at the beginning of the measure. In the final reading, the oboes enter on this downbeat with the opening motif of the ritornello, thus creating an elision of the two phrases.

Corrections of Orchestration and Texture

Changes in Basic Scoring

Corrections regarding the choice of instruments to be used in a movement are relatively infrequent in the autograph scores. The basic orchestration of a planned vocal composition was no doubt strongly influenced by such practical considerations as the availability of particular instruments and the ability of the performers at Bach's disposal at any given time. The specific instrumentation

[69] See also the description of this correction in NBA I/35, KB, p. 127.

[70] See NBA II/3, KB, pp. 50, 63.

of individual movements within a new work was surely determined further by the character of the text and the affective connotation associated in the period with particular instruments.[71] It is therefore understandable that Bach almost always had a clear idea of the scoring of a vocal work before he began to write down the composition. When the composer did revise his initial choices, the corrections reveal that the revisions were usually made before actual composition had begun. The changes for the most part are reflected in a correction in the listing of instruments on the title page of the autograph score, in the general heading of the work or of a movement, or in a contradiction between such listings and the actual instrumentation of the work. There seem to be 28 corrections of this kind, 13 of which pertain to works written after 1730, i.e., after the overwhelming majority of Bach's vocal works had been composed. (See Appendix I for a list of the corrected headings and titles. With the exception of BWV 30a, all the scores listed from the *Easter Oratorio* [BWV 249] on are revision copies of parody compositions or fair copies of earlier compositions; and within this group of scores the headings are not corrected but simply incomplete.) The transverse flute is the instrument most frequently forgotten or omitted in these headings.[72] While general haste and inadvertence may explain some of these omissions, one is strongly tempted to assume that Bach could not take the availability of the transverse flute or a competent player for granted in the dozen years from c. 1733 to c. 1745.

Additional evidence of revisions in the general instrumentation of an individual movement is provided by corrections in the score layout of the movement: changes in the number of staves allotted for a score system, or corrections of the clef on a particular staff. Consider the following instances. The entire aria "Hört, ihr Völker," BWV 76/3 (P 67), is entered for the most part on 5-stave systems in the autograph.[73] The inclusion of two treble clefs and one alto clef respectively on the upper three staves of some of these systems makes it clear that the composer at first intended to set the movement for a full string ensemble. Since he retained this layout for the entire movement, Bach probably did not

---

[71] Terry 1932 offers speculations about what these associations were for Bach, but his study is weakened by its total dependence on the printed BG edition. Such a study, to be effective, would have to take into account the external circumstances surrounding the composition, premiere and later performances of each work, and would have to be based on an examination of the original source material and other available documentary evidence, and on an investigation of the contemporary literature on *Instrumentenkunde* and the *Affektenlehre*.

[72] In BWV 213 and 215 the heading corrections involved the elimination of this instrument.

[73] P 67, ff. 6v–7v. Since there are only nineteen staves on ff. 6v–7r, the bottom system on each of these pages has only four staves. The last system of the movement—on f. 7v—also has only four staves, since the rejected draft of the opening movement—Sketch No. 50 (q.v.)—was already written on staves 10–19.

abandon this plan until he had drafted the principal parts (first violin, soprano, and continuo) for the complete aria and returned to the beginning of the movement in order to fill in the second violin and viola parts. Only then, it seems, did Bach decide on the present scoring and write the heading *Violino solo* above the first system.

The presence of a bracket embracing five staves in the first system of the autograph of BWV 197a/6 (Morgan Library) reveals that the composer momentarily planned a five-part texture for the movement.[74] The change of orchestration here, though, in contrast to that in BWV 76/3, was "immediate"— made even before the clefs for the planned 5-stave system were written in.

The fact that Bach wrote out the opening measures (mm. 1–14a) of BWV 28/1 (P 92) on 5-stave systems is a strong indication that he had planned the movement without either the wind or the string section, or that he had intended to have both sections play throughout the movement in strict unison. Before completing the opening ritornello, however, he decided to have independent string and wind choirs and consequently wrote out the remainder of the movement on 8-stave systems. The implicit correction here, in contrast to the score-layout corrections in BWV 76/3 and 197a/6, is purely coloristic. There is no change in the number of real parts in BWV 28/1: the original five-part texture is retained throughout the aria, for the strings and oboes play either in unison or in alternation.

It has already been shown on the basis of clef changes that the inclusion of an obbligato trumpet part in the rejected draft of BWV 43/7 was an afterthought. Similarly, clef corrections in the first system of BWV 138/1 (P 158) suggest that the decision to employ oboe d'amore parts (and perhaps the decision to precede the choral entrance with a tenor solo) was an afterthought.[75] And the clef change (from treble to alto) in the first three systems of BWV 177/3 (P 116), reveals that Bach had considered some instrument other than the oboe da caccia for the obbligato.[76]

There is no doubt that Bach had planned to have a horn in BWV 67/6 (P 95). Not only was a staff allotted for the horn on each of the first four pages

---

[74] See the facsimile in NBA I/2, p. viii, and the description in NBA I/2, KB, p. 40. See also the brackets in Sketches Nos. 42 and 142 and the discussion on pp. 150f.

[75] The clefs were corrected from

Treble		French Violin
Treble		French Violin
Alto		Treble
Soprano	to	Treble
Alto		Alto
Tenor		Tenor
Bass		Bass

[76] Accordingly the heading *Versus 3—Hautbois da Caccia solo / e Soprano* must have been written down after at least some part of the movement had already been composed.

of the movement (mm. 1–36), but Bach in fact composed a horn part for the opening ritornello:

which he then crossed out, entering rests in the horn staff for the following 3/4 ritornello (mm. 10–25).[77]

On the other hand, the figurative Violin 1 part of the troping chorus *Gloria in excelsis Deo* from the E♭ *Magnificat,* BWV 243a/C (P 38), did not belong to the original conception of the movement. It is not written together with the rest of the score for the chorus, but entered on a spare staff, partly beneath the movement (on f. 15v) and partly after the concluding measures (f. 16r). The part was clearly added after the movement was otherwise completely composed.

Bach changed his original intention in regard to the vocal assignment of a movement in only twenty instances. (See Appendix II for a description of these changes.) This number includes recitatives as well as arias and choruses; and with the exception of just three movements (BWV 58/1, BWV 82/1, and BWV 244/36) these changes, like most changes of instrumentation, were made during the earliest stages of composition—at the time the first systems of the new movements were drawn, before actual notation of the music itself had begun.

Changes in the Number of Independent Parts

Corrections in the score layout of a movement obviously testify to changes in the number of parts as well as changes in the instrumentation of the movement. This was abundantly clear from the revisions of BWV 76/3, 197a/6, 67/6, and 243a/C just discussed. At times, though, Bach altered the number of real parts while retaining the original instrumentation. The first system of BWV 176/5 (P 81), for example, contains five staves in the autograph. Each oboe has an independent staff, although the identical melody is entered in each part. The remainder of the movement is written on a 3-stave system throughout. Bach evidently had planned at first to have three independent oboe parts before he decided on unison performance. The words *tutti gli Oboe in unisono* in the heading of the movement were doubtless a later addition.[78] Similarly, the first five systems of BWV 215/7 (P 139) have four staves each in the autograph. The upper two staves of the first system (f. 16r) have the identical flute theme; in the remaining

---

[77] In the following 4/4 section the horn staff was left blank (mm. 26–36), and it does not appear in the remainder of the movement.

[78] See Appendix I.

four systems (f. 16v) the second staff is blank (except for cue notes in mm. 10 and 19).[79] The unison writing for the two flutes and the basic three-part texture of the aria were therefore an afterthought.[80] These corrections represent in a sense an inversion of the corrective gesture in BWV 28/1 in which the original texture was preserved but the orchestration revised. In the arias BWV 176/5 and 215/7 the original instrumentation was retained but the texture changed.

Corrections of detail in several composing scores reveal similar reconsiderations of the number of real parts, but on a considerably smaller scale—affecting a particular passage rather than an entire movement. In BWV 26/2 (P 47/1), the tenor aria "So schnell ein rauschend Wasser," the violin part in m. 8.1–3, at first doubled the flute parts, thus following the pattern of intermittent doubling established in mm. 5–7 (employed here perhaps to illustrate the shimmering surface of the water), reminiscent of the doubling technique used in BWV 28/1. The final violin reading, consisting of repeated eighth-notes which are continued in the next four measures, increases from two to three the number of real parts in the last phrase of the ritornello.

Rests were replaced with notes in the viola part of BWV 132/1 (P 60), mm. 26, 33, and 42, as follows:

The revision introduces a countervoice in the viola which forms an imitative pattern with the continuo, complementing the imitative work between the oboe and violins based on the opening ritornello motif. The texture of the passage is thus increased to include two groups of imitating voices.[81]

Mm. 25–27

[79] See also the notation of the unison Violin 2 part in BWV 61/1 (P 45/6) described in NBA I/1, KB, p. 10.

[80] The oboe d'amore part printed in NBA I/37—but not in BG 34—which doubles the soprano throughout the movement in strict unison, is not indicated at all in the autograph score. It is a later (autograph) addition entered in the original Oboe 1 part. See NBA I/37, KB, pp. 51–52.

[81] The last note in the oboe part of mm. 26 and 27 is corrected. The original reading of m. 26.6 is

There were rests, too, in the two oboe parts of BWV 215/1 (P 139), mm. 190–191, before Bach realized the possibility of weaving in an extra pair of imitative voices; and the string unison part of BWV 24/1 (P 44/4) at first was silent in mm. 76–78, thereby underlining the return to the A′ section of the aria by duplicating the pause in mm. 9–10. Bach then chose, however, to introduce an imitative answer of the ritornello motif in mm. 75–76 of the continuo part. All these corrections provide further evidence of Bach's general propensity to embellish and elaborate his original ideas.

Changes in Textural "Style"

Changes in texture were most usually accomplished not by changing the number of real parts but by changing the nature of the relationship existing between the given number of parts, i.e., by introducing changes from various degrees of homophony to various degrees of polyphony.

A few abandoned drafts for opening ritornelli reveal that Bach recast the general textural style of a chorus or aria on several occasions. He rejected his initial plan to open the chorus "Die Himmel erzählen die Ehre Gottes," BWV 76/1, in a strict polyphonic style with simultaneously sounding paired imitative entrances in the chorus and oboes (Sketch No. 50). The final version begins more conventionally with a free-polyphonic instrumental ritornello based on less sophisticated *Stimmtausch* and antiphonal techniques. The first line of the Psalm text is then presented by the solo bass, and this entrance is followed by a homophonic *Choreinbau* worked into the ritornello material. While it is perhaps idle to speculate about Bach's first conception of the movement as a totality, it seems reasonable to assume that he decided to reject a setting of the first section in fugal style in order to create a contrast with the permutation fugue in the second section on the words *Es ist keine Sprache noch Rede* (mm. 67ff.). In essence, the final version separates the elements which had originally appeared simultaneously and presents them somewhat transformed: the oboe figuration of the draft becomes the theme of the orchestral introduction; the bass fugue subject becomes the "responsorial" motto. As we have already seen in comparing other rejected drafts for initial themes with the final versions, many elements contributing to the basic character of the movement remain constant; here they are the key, orchestration, and general nature of the thematic material.

Assuming that Sketch No. 69 is a tentative notation for the aria "Gott, dem der Erdenkreis zu klein," BWV 91/3 (an assumption supported by the key and meter, as well as by the range and number of the parts, and the general

unclear (f″?); the original reading of m. 27.6 was apparently as here (g″). The double clef of the oboe part in the autograph may have occasioned one or both of these corrections.

dominant-to-tonic fall of the opening motif), then it is evident that Bach at first conceived the ritornello in a homophonic, melody-dominated style. Sketch No. 71 then represents an intermediate stage in the evolution of the theme, reflecting a change of mind regarding the texture (here in imitative polyphony) but also establishing the exact profile of the opening motif. The basic texture of the final version is once again homophonic, but this time strongly chordal, although with a suggestion of the imitative style of Sketch No. 71. In addition, period construction replaces the *Fortspinnung* design of the melodic continuation in Sketch No. 69.

While such basic changes in the textural style of a movement are infrequent, limited changes affecting the texture of a specific passage are relatively numerous. A correction in the soprano and tenor parts of BWV 42/4 (P 55), mm. 39–40, though not entirely legible, indicates nonetheless that the two voices originally entered together in m. 39 and proceeded in parallel motion. The soprano reading of m. 39 was then crossed out and replaced by a one-measure rest. Similarly, the viola part of BWV 57/1 (P 144), m. 41, originally moved in parallel sixths with the Violin 2 part. In the final version the viola part enters here with a brief countervoice in a free polyphonic style:

And at the conclusion of the A section of BWV 204/2 (P 107), mm. 90–92, Bach at first thought to reintroduce the ritornello in its original homophonic setting—with parallel thirds between the two oboes.

Mm. 90–93

The imitative treatment of the present reading (the Oboe 2 enters in m. 95) provides both a contrast to the previous presentations of the theme in the A section (mm. 1ff., 35ff., 51ff., and 86ff.), where the oboes consistently proceed in parallel motion, and an anticipation of the more polyphonic treatment of the ritornello theme by the oboes in the B section of the aria.

The revision of the barring in BWV 188/4 (P 972), mm. 12ff.,[82] reveals another

---

[82] The aria is considered the fourth movement of the cantata in Neumann 1953, where the introductory sinfonia based on the D minor Clavier Concerto, BWV 1052, is counted as the first movement. BWV, however, counts the aria as the third movement by beginning the numbering with the first aria.

instance where Bach decided on imitative writing as an afterthought. The appearance of the autograph in these measures is most likely best represented (and understood) as follows:

That is, after completing the vocal phrase in m. 12, Bach wrote out the first two measures of the following vocal phrase, beginning on the downbeat of m. 13. He then noticed the possibility of introducing an imitative treatment of the new phrase by dovetailing an organ entrance over the cadence in m. 12b. This entailed the insertion of the present m. 13a and a rebarring of the alto part. Bach presumably had intended at first to continue the figurative contrapuntal style of the first vocal phrase before he decided on the present texture, one which provides a contrast to the treatment of mm. 9–12 and obviously integrates the organ and alto parts thematically.

While the prevailing tendency in such textural corrections is to replace a relatively homophonic design with a more polyphonic one, the opposite corrective gesture is also encountered on occasion. The composing score for BWV 213/1 (P 125) contains a particularly large-scale change from an imitative to a homophonic passage. Measures 53–66 of the chorus originally read:[83]

[83] See the facsimile on the following page. Arnold Schering was the first to draw attention to this passage in Schering 1933, pp. 40–41. See also NBA I/36, KB, p. 34.

VII. Rejected Draft of BWV 213, Movement 1, mm. 53-66.
Autograph, P 125, f. 2v. By courtesy of the Deutsche Staatsbibliothek,
Berlin, German Democratic Republic

The function of the passage was to serve as a bridge leading from the subdominant cadence on B♭ in m. 52 to the dominant area. According to the rejected passage, Bach's first plan was to spin out this transition with choral entrances in free imitation over a sequential continuo pattern which expressed a variant of the circle of fifths, raising the harmonic level one tone every six measures.

Mm. 53–58:	B♭	G	E	/	A	d	g	/
Mm. 59–64:	c	A	F♯	/	B♭	e	a	/
Mm. 65–(68):	d	B	G	/	C			

The appearance of the manuscript suggests that the continuo line was written down first and the imitative choral entries entered above it, controlled by the continuo progression.

The final version of the passage replaces this free-polyphonic choral writing with an essentially homophonic *Choreinbau* worked into the following presentation of the ritornello material:

(1) mm. 53–57 are based on mm. 17–21, transposed up a third;

(2) a sequential extension follows in m. 58 leading to a cadence in m. 60 based on mm. 11–12, but, as a result of the extension, now transposed up a second and changed from a perfect cadence to a semi-cadence in preparation for

(3) a choral repetition of the opening ritornello theme in mm. 61–64, presented in the dominant.

The revised passage in mm. 53ff., then, beginning with a quotation of mm. 17ff., follows naturally upon the choral repetition of the first sixteen measures of the ritornello in mm. 37–52 (mm. 37–50 a non-transposed repetition of mm. 1–14, mm. 51–52 transposed up a third).

Bach may have decided to use the *Choreinbau* technique rather than a freely composed transitional section in order to take advantage of the unifying thematic and motivic organization inherent in the technique. Here, then, as in BWV 188/4, Bach changed the textural character of a passage to secure a higher degree of structural unity in the movement, immediately perceptible on the motivic-thematic level. But, while this unity was provided in the aria by introducing an imitative polyphonic bond between the obbligato voices, unity was best achieved in the Hercules Cantata by replacing an imitative with a homophonic, or, in any event, less polyphonic style.[84]

---

[84] Another major factor leading to the rejection of the draft may have been a desire to preserve the underlying phrase structure of the movement. Every phrase in the 240-measure chorus is four measures long or a multiple thereof. The introduction of six-measure units at m. 52 would have upset the pattern already established.

CORRECTIONS TO INCREASE INSTRUMENTAL VARIETY
AND EFFECTIVENESS

A small number of corrections in the composing scores apparently were made for purely practical reasons. The continuo part in BWV 65/4 (P 147), mm. 38–39, was raised an octave no doubt simply to permit an uninterrupted continuation of the falling motivic sequence to the tonic cadence at the conclusion of the final vocal section:

And in BWV 81/1 (P 120), m. 20, the continuo part had to be transposed up an octave to permit an unbroken scalewise descent corresponding to mm. 2–3 of the ritornello theme:

Bach surely considered exploiting the lower octave here as an illustration of the text line *schon des Todes Abgrund offen,* until he realized that this was technically impossible. In mm. 25–26, though, the composer did recognize—after a moment—the opportunity of descending into the deepest register of the continuo

BWV 81/1, mm. 24bff., Bc.

while the rest of the orchestra follows in parallel $^6_3$ chords.

More significant are the few corrections which were apparently motivated by considerations of the idiomatic effectiveness of a particular instrument. The dramatic contrast of tessitura, dynamics, and tone color produced by the change of the trumpet part in the *Alleluia* of BWV 51 (described above), for example, could be mentioned here, although this contrast was very likely a secondary effect of the decision to change the harmonic context of the entire passage. There is a similar tessitura contrast in the violin part of the aria "Starkes Lieben, das dich, großer Gottessohn," BWV 182/4 (P 103), at the conclusion of the vocal section preceding the final ritornello epilog. Bach had begun to write the accompanying violin passage in mm. 32b–35a an octave higher than the present reading, before he hit upon the idea of placing the figure on the g string:

The composer's intent here was clearly to allow the violin figuration to end on c′ and thus afford a striking change of register at the reentry of the closing ritornello. The change serves to articulate this significant juncture in the design of the movement.

A correction apparently motivated by concerns for coloristic and idiomatic instrumentation alone appears in the final movement of the Hunting Cantata, BWV 208/15 (P 42/3). The orchestration principle of the movement is based essentially on *Stimmtausch* and antiphonal alternation between the woodwind and string sections, followed by tutti performance by both groups, with occasional incorporation of the horns into the exchanges. The opening ritornello is scored as follows: the oboe phrase in mm. 1–4 is answered in mm. 5–8 by the strings; the oboe figure in mm. 9–10 is similarly followed by its repetition in the strings in mm. 11–12, with interpolations in the horns; finally the entire orchestral tutti brings the ritornello to a close in mm. 12–20.

The scheme is maintained throughout the movement. Toward the end of the B section of the chorus, however, Bach was somewhat uncertain about the succession or distribution of the thematic fragments and *Stimmtausch* elements among the groups. The string figure in mm. 97–98 was at first written in the oboes, with rests in the string parts. Then these roles were exchanged—before the oboe answer in mm. 101–102 was written down. With this correction Bach perhaps intended to vary the rather predictable succession of oboe-violin, characteristic of his treatment of this punctuating figure throughout the A section of the movement (mm. 9–12, 43–46, 67–70).

In mm. 112–120, too, the *Stimmtausch* elements in the two groups were originally interchanged: the present oboe reading was entered in the string staves and the string reading written in the oboe section.[85] This basic correction entailed several changes of detail. The most interesting of these concerns the present Violin 1-2 passage in mm. 117–120, which was at first written (for the oboes) an octave higher. Bach now took advantage of the possibility of using the g string register and wrote *8tavo tieffer* over these measures.[86] Bach may have reorchestrated the passage in order to exploit the possibility of extreme register contrasts offered by the strings: the ascent to c‴ in m. 115 and then d‴ in m. 123, with the intervening unison figure, based on the pitches

in mm. 116–120. The register contrasts, together with the increasing rhythmic

---

[85] Bach revised the orchestration simply by writing *Violini* over the oboe staves and *Hautb.* over the string section. In mm. 121ff., which begin a new page in the autograph, Bach clarified the return to a normal score layout by writing *Hautb.*

over the top staff of the system and *Violini* over the fifth staff.

[86] Further revisions and corrections in mm. 112–120 are described in NBA I/35, KB, pp. 27–28.

and polyphonic activity in the chorus, prepare a climax of rhythmic, textural, and coloristic complexity in these measures, just before the several choirs are consolidated in a strongly reinforced tutti in simple four-part texture in the final measures before the da capo.

Bach often employed coloristic means alone to set in relief the polyphonic character of a passage, or even seemingly to increase the number of independent parts. The revision of the soprano melisma in BWV 14/2, mm. 63–66 (discussed above), essentially transformed a sequential pattern in one voice into a two-part imitative pattern and thus entailed orchestral and textural changes as well as the simple elimination of a monotonous sequential chain.

The relationship between several continuation sketches and the final versions provides further examples of the principle of coloristic elaboration. The notation of the violin and alto parts of BWV 213/9, mm. 31–35, on one staff in Sketch No. 141,[87] clearly illustrates the monophonic nature of the sequential scheme beginning in mm. 29–30 of the aria. The antiphonal alternation of the opening ritornello motif between the two parts is once more a pseudo-polyphonic presentation of a single melodic line.

Sketch No. 4, similarly, suggests that Bach planned to retain the ritornello melody of the opening phrase of the aria in the trumpet part. In the final version, however, the melodic line is divided between the trumpet and the first violin.[88] And in Sketch No. 8 the Oboe 1 part in m. 10 begins by developing the melodic figure introduced in the second half of m. 9:

which then dissolves into an uninterrupted flow of sixteenth-notes for five beats. The final version interrupts this motor rhythm by dividing the sixteenth-note motion and introducing a momentary imitative exchange between the Oboe 1/Violin 1 and the Oboe 2/Violin 2 lines. The sixteenth-note figure at the beginning of m. 12 is also interrupted—this time to prepare for and articulate the approaching cadence.

Sketch No. 20 which is, no doubt, a draft of the Violin 1 (and solo) line of BWV 30a/7, mm. 19–20, records the concluding figure of an approaching cadence, here marking the end of the aria ritornello. In the final version the oboe[89]

[87] A facsimile appears in NBA I/36, p. vii.
[88] There is no mention of the oboe doubling of the violin part in the autograph.
[89] P 43/1 calls for "oboe" not "oboe d'amore."

bears the structural tones of this cadential formula, while the violin spins out the figuration for two more measures to the cadence in m. 22. The tonic b′ of m. 20 is replaced with f′♯, while the b′ is transferred to the oboe. Bach may have planned to end the ritornello in m. 20, as the sketch suggests, but then decided to add the two-measure epilog following upon a deceptive cadence. The relationship between sketch and final version illustrates a heterophonic type of textural elaboration rather than antiphonal expansion, but also illustrates once again an "ornamental" correction operating in the horizontal plane, entailing the addition of an extra two measures.

The principle of coloristic elaboration is evident not only in the sketch material but also in a number of corrections in the autograph scores. In BWV 76/1 (P 67), mm. 16–20, the oboe and violin parts are written in the autograph on two staves in the following manner:

The 2-stave notation makes plain the simple 2-voice *Stimmtausch* pattern which is the basis of the interlude. The subsequent coloristic fragmentation of the two parts—a primitive kind of *Klangfarbenmelodie* technique—seems to increase the texture from two to four real parts. (In mm. 36–38.1, 48–50, and 59–61.1 of the autograph, too, the oboe and violin parts are entered on two staves as in mm. 16–20.1.)[90]

The combination of a voice-exchange pattern with an exchange of instrumental colors takes on structural significance in the opening chorale fantasy

[90] While Bach may have written the oboe and violin parts in this way only in order to save space, it seems more likely that the decision to divide the *Stimmtausch* pattern between strings and winds was a true afterthought. The Oboe 1/Violin 1 and Oboe 2/Violin 2 lines proceed almost exclusively in unison doubling throughout the rest of the movement; also, there are unused staves in the autograph for this movement, which could have been used to accommodate independent wind and violin lines: two unused staves on the bottom of ff. 1v and 2r—the pages on which mm. 16–19 and 36–37, respectively, appear. (There is also one blank staff on the bottom of f. 2v—the page containing mm. 48–49 and 59–60.)

choruses of many chorale cantatas. When the chorale melody is in *Barform*, the movement is often constructed according to the following scheme:

Ritornello

Stollen I

| Chorale line 1 | Ritornello quotation A | Chorale line 2 | Ritornello quotation B |

Stollen II

| Chorale line 3 | Ritornello quotation A′ | Chorale line 4 | Ritornello quotation B′ |

Abgesang

| Chorale line 5 | Ritornello quotation C | Chorale line 6 | Ritornello quotation D, etc. |

Ritornello

Usually the only essential difference between ritornello quotations A and A′ or between B and B′ consists precisely in the *Stimm-* and *Klangtausch* of thematic fragments and obbligato instruments.

Within this norm Bach often found occasion to introduce further permutation relationships—between the opening ritornello and Ritornello quotation A, for example, or between the instrumental accompaniment of a line from *Stollen* I and its repetition in *Stollen* II. These additional coloristic variations were sometimes introduced as an afterthought. In BWV 33/1 (PP), for example, mm. 49–66 in the instrumental interlude following the second chorale line are based on mm. 3ff. of the opening ritornello, with a *Stimmtausch* between the oboe and violin parts. In m. 64, Bach had at first entered the present Violin 1 reading in the Oboe 1 line, this reading being identical with the Oboe 1 reading of m. 18. Since the voice exchange began in m. 49, however, it is very likely that the correction only reflects a momentary lapse of attention or confusion regarding the nature of the *Klangtausch*. In the same movement, the interlude in mm. 111–115, following upon the sixth chorale line, is based on mm. 5ff. of the opening ritornello. Here Bach at first entered the Violin 2 reading of mm. 5–6 in mm. 111–112 of the same part, before placing the reading in the Oboe 2 part to effect the *Stimm-* and *Klangtausch*.

Again the fourth chorale line (mm. 47–51) of BWV 117/1 (PP) is a literal repetition of the second chorale line (mm. 32–36) but with a coloristic exchange of the motivic figures. The exchange was apparently an afterthought. Bach had at first written the sixteenth-note arpeggio figure of mm. 47–48 in the flute parts (and rests in the violin parts), corresponding to the flute parts of mm. 32–33. He then crossed out this reading, placed it in the violin parts, and entered rests in the flute staves. In the final version of the passage, then, the succession flutes-oboes-violins of mm. 32–34 is answered by the succession violins-oboes-flutes in mm. 47–49.

Such corrections, whether they are the result of a momentary lack of attention which led to mechanical copying of the model, or are true compositional revisions, draw attention in any event to the importance of the *Klangtausch* technique in this genre. The technique, and the corrections associated with it, serve, like so many other techniques and corrections examined in the course of this chapter—and indeed throughout this study—as effective means of fulfilling the cardinal aesthetic principle: "variety within unity."

Postscript

It is perhaps permissible to conclude this study by calling attention to a remarkable change of detail affecting the final note of several movements in the earliest extant cantata autographs. The corrections, if they have any significance at all (besides the evidence they provide of Bach's almost embarrassingly painstaking attention to detail), testify to his phenomenal acoustic sensitivity, and perhaps afford some evidence concerning the acoustical conditions under which the works concerned were performed.

The last note of the aria "So du willst, Herr, Sünde zurechnen" from the Mühlhausen cantata *Aus der Tiefe,* BWV 131/2 (PP), is changed in both the oboe and continuo parts from ♩ to ♪ ', i.e., the final measure reads: |♩ '. ‖ in these parts.

In the final movement, "Das neue Regiment," from the Mühlhausen *Ratswahl* cantata, *Gott ist mein König,* BWV 71/1 (P 45/1), the concluding measures were changed as follows: the last note in the trumpet, timpani, string, oboe, bassoon, and cello parts in m. 102, and the last note of the echoing recorder parts in m. 103 were changed again from ♩ to ♪'.

But the last note of the aria "Ein Fürst ist seines Landes Pan" from the Hunting Cantata, BWV 208/7 (P 42/3), probably composed in 1713,[91] was changed in all the oboe parts and the continuo from ♩ : ‖ to 𝄽 ‖.

---

[91] See Chapter I, n. 9, above.

CONCLUSION

WE HAVE attempted in these pages to trace the typical genesis of a Bach vocal work (the genre for which revealing autograph material is most complete) from the blank sheet of paper to the structurally complete, performable composition ultimately notated in the autograph score.

The autograph score, though, does not represent the last stage of this genesis. After the original parts, which were to be used in the first performance of a work, had been prepared (written out as a rule by apprentice copyists), Bach almost invariably turned the necessity of proofreading the parts into an opportunity to enter "expression" marks (dynamic indications, slurs, trills, and other symbols of articulation and ornamentation), to add thorough bass figures in the organ continuo part, and to indicate what part or parts should be doubled and what instruments should be assigned this function. For example, the frequent reinforcement of a vocal chorale cantus firmus line with a unison horn or other brass instrument, the addition of unison wind parts to the vocal parts of a chorus in motet style, or the doubling of obbligato string parts by oboes and/or flutes were evidently often determined at this stage in the history of a work. Since such activity is tangential to the *compositional* process itself, it has been mostly neglected in this study. Occasionally revisions of a formative nature were made in the original parts (such as the increase in the number of real parts in the accompanied recitative, BWV 63/6), and attention was called to such corrections in the appropriate place.

In a real sense, however, the compositional process was never terminated. Just as Bach seems to have been unable merely to copy music without introducing some change, however minor, and just as this "inability" prevented him from preparing a perfectly "fair copy," so he was frequently reluctant merely to repeat a performance of a work at a later date. Different conditions—different performers with different relative abilities, and a new opportunity to proofread the musical material—stimulated the composer anew to revise, refine, or reject. The open-ended nature of Bach's compositional process has been described by Georg von Dadelsen in his essay, "Die 'Fassung letzter Hand' in der Musik." As von Dadelsen maintains, this approach to composition was typical for the Baroque era in general, but not at all typical for later periods. It was most emphatically not the case for Beethoven, who sometimes spent years bringing forth a composition but considered it "finished" once it had appeared in print.

Von Dadelsen's observations emphasize what should always have been self-evident: that there is no such thing as *the* creative process. In the literature of music there seems to have been a tendency to identify the creative—or, more carefully formulated, the compositional—process with that of Beethoven. This is understandable in light of the volume of source material concerning Beethoven, but it is nonetheless misleading. It helps explain the pessimistic convictions of Spitta cited in the preface to this study.

Surely the factor which most significantly determines the prevailing approach to composition in a particular era is the amount of time available to the composer to put his work together. The liveried musical craftsman of pre-revolutionary Europe was obliged to produce an enormous volume of music in the service of a patron. Our present knowledge of the Bach chronology makes clear that most of the surviving vocal works were written within a three-year period at the rate of approximately one cantata per week. We may assume that the composer had only about three days to prepare the new work: he presumably began composition on Monday and had to be done with it by Wednesday in order to allow, say, one day for the parts to be written out and two days for rehearsals.[1]

Such a circumstance suggests at first that Inspiration was more important in the baroque than in the post-revolutionary period. A composer like Beethoven enjoyed a "luxury of time" which allowed him to experiment with and assemble a large number of ideas from which he would ultimately choose the best one. Bach and his contemporaries had to invent or "discover" their ideas quickly. The hectic pace of production obviously did not tolerate passive reliance on the unpredictable arrival of Inspiration. Nor did the musical conventions and techniques or the general rationalistic mentality of the time necessitate this reliance—as long as the composer was willing to accept them. The baroque composer who subjected himself to the regimen inevitably had to be a traditionalist who willingly embraced the conventions—in Bach's case even regarding many of them as eternal verities.[2]

---

[1] Arnold Schering's reconstruction of the schedule of musical instruction at the Thomasschule in Bach's time (Schering 1936[2], pp. 32–39) reveals that only four hours per week were officially devoted to "singing lessons," i.e., rehearsals: one hour each on Mondays through Wednesdays, and another hour on Friday. Bach was obliged to be present only at the first three of these sessions. It is difficult to reconcile this schedule with what seems to have been Bach's composing schedule. We are surely able to assume that a dress rehearsal of the cantata was held on the Saturday before the Sunday performance, and, as does Schering, that Bach, in addition to the official lessons, gave private instruction to the soloists who were to perform the recitatives and arias in the new work. The fact that the formal lessons were held on Mondays through Wednesdays—precisely those days when Bach was presumably composing the work—remains problematic. Perhaps we should assume that Bach in principle composed his cantatas at a weekly rate but always more than a week in advance of the projected performance.

[2] Bach expressed his sentiments on thorough bass, for example, in his *Gründlicher Unterricht des General-Basses* (a set of rules preserved in a copy by his pupil, Johann Peter Kellner) as follows: "The thorough bass is the most perfect foundation of music, being played with both hands in such manner that the left hand plays the notes written down while the right adds consonances and dissonances, in order to make a well-sounding harmony to the Glory of God and the permissible delectation of the spirit; and the aim and final reason, as of all music, so of the thorough bass should be none else but the Glory of God and the

There has been frequent reference in this study to the techniques and stylistic conventions governing Bach's compositional activity: the corpus of melody types generated by the *Figurenlehre,* the harmonic groundplans supporting arias and choruses, the repetition and modulation schemes that control the da-capo form in its myriad manifestations, and, most significantly, the aesthetic ideal of formal and expressive unity which according to the *Affektenlehre* was to prevail in any closed number and which fathered the formulas and techniques. Once again, it is these aesthetic and practical facts of musical life in the baroque era which account for the visual appearance of the Bach autographs and, concomitantly, for the nature of his compositional process.

Spitta wrote about the Bach autographs: ". . . for an understanding of the way [a composition] was formed in the beginning, the evidence . . . tells us nothing." The preface of this volume suggested one possible reply to Spitta. Some further remarks are in order now.

The musical "depth analyses" of Sigmund Freud's Viennese contemporary Heinrich Schenker, and his followers, have made us aware of the stratified nature of musical organization and of the supreme significance of the deeper, hidden, structural levels of a composition for its tonal coherence and formal logic. But even the most heavily corrected of Bach's vocal manuscripts are rarely concerned with anything but the surface—with the "foreground" of musical events. The underlying formal design, the modulation plan, or the outer-voice framework were rarely subjected to any profound transformation. The deeper levels, "the background," of the structure must have been so self-evident, so firmly and so intuitively grasped by the composer as to be of no conscious concern to him. Accordingly, Bach's musical imagination—his Genius—was "naïve." It operated on the surface, and (like naïve listeners and even naïve music analysts ever since) was concerned about details and nuances upon that surface while the "background" took care of itself. The nature of the material gathered together in the present attempt to reconstruct the Bachian compositional process necessarily reflected the composer's "superficial" concerns and may therefore have been a disappointment for readers who—like Spitta, perhaps—may have hoped for more evidence of far-reaching changes.

In one sense, though, it is impossible to uncover "significant" material on the compositional process of any composer by studying autograph manuscripts. Hugo Riemann's conviction, cited above in Chapter VI, reaches the core of the problem: Creation is done only in the mind; something of this creation is

---

recreation of the mind. Where this is not observed, there will be no real music but only a devilish hubbub." The passage has been identified as a paraphrase from F. E. Niedt, *Musikalische Hand-* *leitung* (Hamburg, 1700). The complete Kellner document is printed in Spitta II, pp. 913ff. The quotation above is taken from David-Mendel 1966, pp. 32f.

stenographically recorded by the hand on paper under the direction of Reason. A Beethoven single-staff sketch for the entire exposition of the first movement of the "Eroica" Symphony must have been a shorthand reminder, decipherable only to the composer himself, of a dense, full-voiced, complex whole. An attempt by anyone else to understand the sketch fully is bound to be futile.

Paul Mies attempted to refute Riemann, asserting that Riemann's thesis "is in complete contradiction to the nature of the sketches, their far-reaching development from the simplest beginnings with the critical judgments in Beethoven's hand."[3]

Of course, Riemann and Mies were both right. The sketch, as Riemann maintained, has much more meaning for the composer than for anyone else; and the written gestures do not represent everything the composer heard internally. But one can say, as intimated by Mies, that the sketch, whatever more it implied for the composer than for other observers, did not imply the changes that came in the next draft, which by nature represents a new idea replacing, at least momentarily, the idea—with both its notated and unnotated constituents—of the first sketch.

We shall never know what went on in the composer's mind before he wrote down the first jottings, nor what unwritten details or dimensions accompanied them. Perhaps we can even argue that the Bach autographs tell us more about his compositional process than Beethoven's autographs and sketchbooks tell us about Beethoven's. Again, the luxury of time granted Beethoven the opportunity to carry ideas around in his head and to mull over them and evaluate them before he felt ready to commit anything to paper. Beethoven tells us this himself in a widely quoted remark he made in 1823 to the Darmstadt Capellmeister, Louis Schlösser: "I carry my thoughts about with me for a long time, sometimes a very long time, before I set them down."[4]

Bach did not have time for any such thing. The observer of a Bach composing score often has the impression that the composer began setting notes down just as quickly as he thought of them, with nothing more than the vaguest conception of what "he had in mind." If the written idea was satisfactory the first time, it remained; if it was not, it was corrected or rejected. There are composing scores in which the opening ideas contain no corrections at all and others with few or many changes, and still others which were discarded entirely and replaced with something else.

In this connection it should be remarked that Bach's pre-Leipzig composing scores convey a somewhat different impression from the Leipzig scores. In general, the opening theme or ritornello in a movement is only sparsely corrected,

[3] Mies 1925, p. 140. [4] See Thayer-Forbes 1967, Vol. II, p. 851.

if at all, and seems to have caused the composer little difficulty. The continuation of the material, though, is noticeably more heavily corrected and thus must have posed greater difficulties than the opening. The Leipzig composing scores, on the other hand, contain as a rule the greatest concentration of corrections in the opening material, after which the handwriting becomes more "hasty" and corrections more infrequent. It is thus tempting to find in the pre-Leipzig scores evidence of a youthful Bach inspired by bold inventions but somewhat detained by relative inexperience in the following development of these ideas. The appearance of the Leipzig scores, conversely, invites speculation that the mature Bach may have lost the spontaneity for such effortless thematic invention but more than compensated for it by having acquired complete technical mastery.

Beethoven's remark to Schlösser continued: "You will ask me whence I take my ideas? That I cannot say with any degree of certainty: they come uninvited, directly, or indirectly. . . ."[5] Bach's ideas in a certain sense never simply came "uninvited." They were deliberately called forth by means of the conventions: the *Figurenlehre* and so on. But, as was already remarked (Chapter II, note 12), these conventions for the most part served in Bach's case merely to set in motion his seemingly limitless imagination.

Perhaps we really do see in the Bach autographs how a work "was formed in the beginning." In general, all that did occur in the composer's mind is visible because it was put on paper immediately. The composer did not often have the luxury of time to work internally, or to be especially self-critical.

It is this last point to which the autographs of Bach, or Beethoven, or any composer, really bear witness: the degree of self-criticism the composer indulged in.

Bach's critical judgment—the "Reason" component of the creative process—seems to have been "infallible," that is, the composer as a rule recognized at once when he had found the idea or solution he was seeking. If it was not the very first idea, then it was the second. Perhaps a third proposal was necessary. This "linear" character of the inner dialog between Reason and Imagination is typical for Bach. The supreme confidence in critical judgment to which it attests was the logical product of the *Stilsicherheit* informing Bach's musical imagination, and, again, the necessary product of the scarcity of time.

It was necessary for Beethoven, on the other hand, to enact a rather elaborate drama of trial and error which was extended by the evident uncertainty of his critical judgment. The Beethoven scholar Gustav Nottebohm reproduced the sketches for the opening theme of the aria "Mir ist so wunderbar" from *Fidelio*.[6] According to the transcription, Beethoven drafted thirteen beginnings for the aria. The final version most nearly resembles the seventh of these. Bach would have

---

[5] Thayer-Forbes, p. 851.   [6] See Nottebohm-Mies 1924, pp. 68f.

recognized at once the seventh sketch as the one he was looking for and would not have continued to Sketches 8 through 13. Beethoven did not stop after writing No. 7. It was the luxury of time, the perfectionism, the extreme caution, or the relative uncertainty of judgment that prompted him to explore a large number of possibilities and to choose the best one only after all had been presented and considered.

Striking differences between the procedures of Bach and Beethoven characterize every stage in the genesis of their works well beyond the invention of the initial ideas. For Bach it is almost possible to maintain that true composition in the sense of spontaneous creation of ideas was substantially concluded with the invention of the opening theme.[7] From there on the rationalistic mechanics of the period—again, the preexistent modulation plans, the widespread use of static transposition as a modulation technique, sequential repetition, permutation and combination of constituent elements, large-scale repetition of sections via the technique of "ritornello quotation," the justification of all these compositional devices by the aesthetic of the Unity of Affect, seemingly enabled the arias and choruses to be spun out "automatically." One is reminded at this point of Bach's delightfully innocent remark: "I have had to work hard; anyone who works just as hard will get just as far,"[8] with its implication that everything in the "craft" of music is teachable and learnable. The fact that no other composer of the period, with the arguable exception of Handel, even remotely approached Bach's achievement indicates clearly enough that the application of the "mechanical procedures" was not literally "automatic" but was controlled throughout by something else—by the unfortunately (or fortunately) unanalyzable factor of artistic discrimination—taste. "Taste," a most respected attribute in the culture of the eighteenth century,[9] is an utterly individual compound of raw talent, imagination, psychological disposition, judgment, skill, and experience. It is unteachable and unlearnable.

For Beethoven the rigid constructive principles of the baroque era no longer existed. The design and content of a Beethoven sonata form was not nearly so fixed or self-evident as that of the baroque aria or J. S. Bach's permutation fugue. And in place of the baroque aesthetic of Unity of Affect, Beethoven's formal consciousness was governed by a dramatic aesthetic of dualism heavily dependent

[7] Heinrich Besseler has called attention to this aspect of the Bachian idiom in his studies of Bach's *Charakterthema*. In "Bach und das Mittelalter" Besseler wrote the following in reference to the instrumental fugues: "If the unity [of the composition] was to be musically convincing, the theme had to have the power to determine the character of the entire fugue. . . . Everything depended on the invention of the subject." Besseler 1950, p. 126.

[8] David-Mendel 1966, p. 37.

[9] Consider Joseph Haydn's famous confession to Leopold Mozart: "Before God and as an honest man, I tell you that your son is the greatest composer known to me either in person or by name. He has taste and, what is more, the most profound knowledge of composition."

on contrast effects and episodic excursions. Therefore, Beethoven could, and did on occasion, begin composition of a sonata movement by first jotting ideas for the "second" theme, an approach impossible in Bach's essentially homogeneous style.

The "rationalistic" orderliness and linearity of the Bachian (or baroque) musical mentality manifested itself elsewhere as well: just as Bach drafted the beginning of a movement first, so he began composition with the first movement and proceeded in order to the last. Beethoven often drafted the second theme of a movement before the first theme, the second movement before the first movement, and so forth. It is known that Beethoven as a rule worked on more than one composition at a time, but there is no concrete evidence that Bach ever did this.[10]

In other areas of his activity Bach adopted an approach to composition more closely resembling Beethoven's. Bach's general attitude toward his keyboard music reflects to a degree the autonomous stance of the later "artist." Works such as the keyboard suites, the *Well-Tempered Clavier,* the two- and three-part inventions, the *Art of Fugue,* although intended to serve specific and practical pedagogical purposes, were not commissioned but created by Bach on his own initiative. For much of the keyboard music the composer indeed enjoyed a luxury of time to take up a particular work only when the inclination, or inspiration, seized him.[11] These works often make use of considerably more complex compositional techniques than do the vocal works; they also depend much less on tight schematic and mechanical procedures of continuation but rather indulge frequently in the "spontaneous," "organic" generation of material. The composing scores for a few of the two- and three-part inventions contained in the *Clavier-Büchlein vor Wilhelm Friedemann Bach* are quite heavily corrected in comparison with the composing scores of the vocal works. It is more significant that very few composing scores for the keyboard works survive at all. We may assume that the composer here made use of preliminary drafts, that he worked on these compositions with an extraordinary intensity of concentration and an unusual degree of self-criticism but at a relatively leisurely pace.

The creative process, then, is obviously not a universal psychological phenomenon but one crucially affected by anything from personal attitudes toward

[10] This statement is no doubt true for Bach's regular cantata production. It is surely necessary to assume, though, that when Bach was occupied with the composition of a large-scale work he may at the same time have been composing smaller ones.

[11] The autograph of the *Orgelbüchlein* reveals that Bach did not attempt to compose the chorale preludes in their planned sequence. The continuation of the Allemande of the French Suite in G major (BWV 816) was entered in the autograph several years after the opening idea was notated. See Sketch No. 167 in Volume II.

specific genres to the aesthetic and intellectual conventions of a cultural epoch. For Bach's vocal works it was clearly the conventions that definitively shaped and limited the modes and models of creative activity.

Bach and his particular musical milieu had achieved a remarkable stability in matters of style that, once accepted, must have been quite comfortable for its practitioners. The *Stilsicherheit* reduced the need or desire to experiment, to surprise, or to be deliberately original. The autonomous musical "artist" of the post-revolutionary period (Beethoven preferred to be called *Tonkünstler* rather than *Komponist*) subjected himself to these aesthetic pressures just as willingly as the baroque composer accepted the pressures of time. And just as the baroque composer's situation was relieved by an arsenal of almost "sure-fire" techniques and forms, the later composer was afforded the compensating luxury of time: to question tradition, to be infinitely perfectionistic, to be an "artist." Beethoven laboriously raised his artworks from the banal to the sublime; Bach was content to refine his handiwork from the merely competent to the immortal.

APPENDIX I

THE FOLLOWING is a tabulation, in chronological order, of corrected headings and titles. Obvious slips of the pen or changes and omissions clearly resulting from inattention are not included.

BWV 71 (P 45/1). The heading above the first movement at first mentioned *3 Violae* (i.e., violins and violas?); the numeral was corrected to *"4."* The autograph title page, however, also mentions *3 Violae,* and this numeral is not changed. The string complement of the orchestra consists of Violins 1 and 2 and undivided violas. The obbligato violoncello part is mentioned separately in both the title page and score heading.

BWV 208 (P 42/3). The title page reads *Cantata â 4 Voci. 2 Corni di* [sic] *Caccia. 2 Violini una Viola è Cont.,* i.e., not mentioning the three oboes.

BWV 61/5 (P 45/6). The heading reads *Aria. Soprano solo. è Violoncello.*

BWV 105/1 (P 99). The instrumental indications entered above the first two staves of the score—(staff 1) *Corno. e Hautb. 1 all unisoni*; (staff 2) *Hautb 2. all unison.*—are written in a darker ink than the general heading and may be a considerably later addition.

BWV 119/1 (P 878). The heading mentions *3 Trombe è Tamburi . . . Basson . . . Violoncello . . .* although the first movement has four trumpet parts and the instrumental indication below the continuo staff reads *Violoncelli, Bassoni è Violoni / all' unisono col' Organo.* The *Violoni* are not mentioned at all in the heading.

BWV 243a/9 (P 38). Above the first staff of the movement the word *Hautb:* is crossed out and *2 Flauti* written to the right of the original designation.

BWV 67/6 (P 95). The instrumental indication above the fourth staff of the first score system is changed as follows: *Violino* (crossed out) *Corno. tacet* (the word *tacet* is written in a different shade of ink from the word *Corno.*).

BWV 26/2 (P 47/1). The heading: *Aria. Travers.*; beneath the second staff of the first system: *Violini unisoni* changed to *Violino Solo.*

BWV 103/5 (P 122). Above the second staff of the first system: *Hautb: è Violini 1 in unisono.*

BWV 128/4 (PP). The heading of the movement reads *Aria. Organo,* although the movement is scored for oboe d'amore and continuo. The heading was perhaps a mistake.

BWV 176/5 (P 81). The heading: *Aria seqtr / tutti gli Oboe* [sic] / *in unisono.* The entire reference to oboes is written in a darker ink.

BWV 88 (P 145). The heading on the first page of the autograph reads *JJ. Dominica 5. post Trinitatis Concerto à.* The instrumentation was never entered.

BWV 17/3 (P 45/5). As mentioned earlier, the movement heading reads *Aria à 2 Hautb.* The movement, according to BG, is scored for Violins 1 and 2. This scoring no doubt reflects the version in the original parts.

BWV 47/2 (P 163). The heading ends abruptly as follows: *Aria Organo è.* The movement is scored for solo organ, soprano, and continuo.

BWV 112/1 (Morgan). The general heading of the work originally read [J] *J. Der Herr ist mein getreüer Hirt. à 4 Voci. 2 Corni: 2 Hautb: 2 Violini / Viola e Cont. di JSBach.* The words *d'Amour* were then crowded in above and between the words *Hautb: 2 Violini.* Although an oboe d'amore is specifically called for in the second movement of the cantata, it is possible that Bach did intend at first to use regular oboes in the first movement to double the violins. But the introduction of a voice-leading correction as early as the fifth full measure (f'♯ changed to b in the Violin I and Oboe I staves to avoid unisons with the viola) extended the range below the register of the oboe. It is conceivable that Bach corrected the heading at the moment he made the necessary grammatical change. (See the facsimile of f. 1r reproduced as Plate VI in Morgan 1970.)

BWV 36/7 (P 45/2). The heading originally read *Aria Violino Solo e / Soprano.* The words *col Sordino* were then crowded in above and between the words *Solo e.*

BWV 213/1 (P 125). The heading: *JJ. Drama à 4 Voci. 2 Corni da Caccia.* ~~*2 Trav:*~~ *2 Hautb. 2 Violini, Viola e / Cont. di Bach.*

BWV 215/2 (P 139). The heading: *Recit. 1.* ~~*Travers.*~~ *Hautb. accomp.*

BWV 248/31 (P 32). The heading originally read *Aria Violini unison* which was changed to *Aria Violini solo* [sic]. See Sketch No. 162 and the facsimile in Volume II.

BWV 14/1 (P 879). The heading reads *2 Hautb.,* although there are only two oboes in the movement.

BWV 11/10 (P 44/5). The heading reads *Aria—due Traversieri* ~~*e due*~~ *Hautb.* *in unisono* da *Caccia Soprano e Violini con Viola in unisono.*

BWV 9/3 (LC). The heading reads *Violini* unis*Solo*Aria.

BWV 249 (P 34). The general heading of the work reads *J.J. Oratorium Festo Paschatos. à 4 Voci. 3 Trombe Tamburi, 2 Hautb. / 2 Violini, Viola, Bassono e Cont.,* although Movement 5 calls for *Travers. / ô / Violino solo* and the heading for Movement 7 reads *Aria Ten. Flauti / e Violin.*

BWV 30a (P 43/1). The general heading of the work reads *JJ. Cantata à 4 Voci. 3 Trombe Tamburi, 2 Hautb. 2 Violini, Viola e Cont.,* thus omitting the *Travers.* called for in Movement 5 and again (as *Trav.*) in Movement 11.

BWV 30 (P 44/1). The general heading of this parody of the previous cantata is even less complete, failing to mention the trumpets and timpani as well as the traverso: *J.J. Concerto. Festo Joañis. à 4 Voci. 2 Hautb. 2 Violini, Viola e Cont. / di Bach.*

BWV 197 (P 91). The general heading: *JJ. In dieb[us] Nuptiarum. Concerto à 4 Voci. 3 Trombe Tamburi. 2 Hautb. 2 Violini Viola / e Cont.* does not mention the *Bassono obligato* in Movement 6.

BWV 245 (P 28). The general heading *J.J. Passio. secūdū Joañē. â 4 Voci. 2 Oboe. [sic] 2 Violini, Viola è Cont. / di J. S. Bach* is fearfully incomplete. It does not include the *Violoncelli e Bassoni* entered above the continuo line, nor the *Org. e Violone* written below it on the first page of the score (see Chapter VII, note 34 above), nor the traversi, viole d'amour, lute, and viola da gamba parts which are called for in the other movements of the score or in the (earlier) original parts.

BWV 34 (P AMB 39). The general heading *Concerto. à 4 Voci—3 Trombe, Tamburi, 2 Oboe, 2 Violini, Viola e Continuo.* omits the two traversi parts mentioned in the instrumental indications for Movement 3.

APPENDIX II

THE FOLLOWING is a description of the changes in vocal assignment of a movement.

BWV 24/5 (P 44/4). The clef of the vocal staff is changed in the first system from soprano to tenor.

BWV 138/2 (P 158). The first system of this recitative was originally set up with soprano and bass clefs, then changed to two bass clefs, implying an immediate decision to change the voice assignment of the movement.

BWV 65/5 (P 147). The opening system of the recitative originally had an alto clef in the voice part, changed to tenor clef. This may indicate a change of mind regarding the voice assignment, but the original alto clef may also have been no more than a slip of the pen.

BWV 144/4 (P 134). The clef of the voice part in the first system of the movement was changed from soprano to tenor. (The following aria is for soprano.)

BWV 44/3 (P 148). The voice staff of this aria originally had a soprano clef in the first system of the movement, which was then changed to an alto clef.

Bach apparently had a number of changes of mind regarding vocal assignments while composing the E♭ *Magnificat:*

BWV 243a/1 (P 38). The constitution of the chorus in the first movement was apparently not at all clear to Bach when he drafted the first page of the autograph (see facsimile p. 48 above). The heading originally read ". . . *4 Voci"* and was changed to *". . . 5 Voci";* the staves of the chorus originally had one soprano, two alto, and one tenor and bass clef each, which were changed to two sopranos, one alto clef, etc. The verbal indications written to the left of the first three vocal staves were also changed apparently from *Sopr., Alto 1, Alto 2* to *Sopr. 1, Sopr. 2, Alto.* (This correction is not mentioned in NBA II/3, KB.)

BWV 243a/3. The clefs on the first system of the *Quia respexit* were treble, alto, and bass, suggesting that Bach momentarily thought of setting the movement for solo alto but immediately decided upon soprano. The second system has the final reading only.

BWV 243a/D. The first system had been drafted with two soprano and one bass clefs and then changed to one soprano and two bass clefs. Bach no doubt had a passing intention to score the duet for two sopranos and continuo. The clefs of the second system have the final reading only.

BWV 87/4 (P 61). An accompanied recitative. The clef of the vocal staff in the opening system is changed from bass to tenor. The part is written out in tenor notation indicating that the change of clef was immediate.

BWV 36c/6 (P 43/2). The opening system of the movement had been set up for alto and continuo. The alto clef was then changed to a soprano clef and *Soprano* written above it to clarify the correction.

BWV 183/4 (P 149). This aria was clearly conceived at first for alto. Throughout the first two systems (the opening ritornello) the resting voice staff has an uncorrected alto clef. In the third system (mm. 18–25a) the alto clef of the voice staff is changed to soprano clef. In the next system of the aria (mm. 25bff.) the clef is again corrected from alto to soprano and the word *Soprano* appears above the staff. The voice enters in m. 27, and there are no changes of the vocal clef thereafter.

BWV 168 (P 152). The vocal staff of the first systems of Movements 2 and 3 originally had an alto clef. In both movements the key signatures are unchanged and suit the tenor clef, thus indicating that the changes of clef and voice were immediate.

BWV 164/1 (P 121). The voice clef of the first system is changed from bass to tenor. This may reflect a change of mind concerning the assignment of the voice part, but may also mean simply that Bach was about to set up the first system (containing the ritornello) without a staff for the resting voice part—i.e., two treble, alto, bass—but then decided to represent the resting voice: two treble, alto, tenor, bass. The same decision is clearly evident in the opening systems of Movement 5 of the cantata. The first two systems of the movement comprise two staves each, with no staves for the resting voices. The third system of the page (mm. 16ff.) was also originally set up as a reduced system—treble and bass—but was changed to treble, soprano, bass, bass, as soon as Bach realized that the voices would enter in m. 19. Here there is no reason to assume that Bach revised the casting of the vocal parts.

BWV 98/3 (P 160). In the first two systems a tenor clef is corrected to soprano clef in the vocal staff.

BWV 58/1 (P 866). The entire movement is written out in the autograph as a duet for soprano and alto. After the movement the following note appears in Bach's hand: *NB diese Aria muss im Bass / gesetzt werden.* Bach may have originally intended to set the entire cantata as a *Dialogo* for soprano and alto and not soprano-bass; for he set up the first four systems of Movement 2 in advance for alto and continuo, but changed the designation to bass before he had begun to compose the movement. Therefore, the decision to change the voice assignment of the cantata was not made immediately upon completion of Movement 1 but only after the clefs of Movement 2 had been written down.

BWV 82/1 (P 114). This cantata, written four weeks after BWV 58, has the same revision of the first movement. The aria is written throughout for alto solo, but is followed by the autograph directions: *NB. Die Singstimme muss in den Bass transponiert werden.* The chronological proximity of the two cantatas and the fact that in both cases the entire movements were written out before the voice change was made suggest that external factors were responsible for the changes.

BWV 171/2 (PP). There is no staff for the voice part in the first system of the aria; in the second system, a bass clef in the vocal staff is changed to tenor. As in the case of BWV 164/1, this may indicate only that Bach had begun to lay out the second system of the movement, like the first, without a staff for the voice part.

BWV 117/3 (PP). In the first system the clef of the vocal staff is changed from soprano or bass to tenor with the word *Tenor* written to clarify the correction. If the clef was originally a bass clef, then the explanations possible are the same as those for BWV 171/2 and 164/1. Since the bracket embracing the system has been extended from three to four staves, it is in fact likelier that Bach had originally planned to omit the resting vocal staff than that he planned the aria for bass. The clef of the vocal staff in the second system, however, is rather clearly changed from soprano to tenor. Bach, then, changed his mind concerning the vocal assignment of the movement.

BWV 248/55 (P 32). Bach had entered a soprano clef in the first vocal staff of this recitative and headed the movement *Recit.* He then changed the clef to tenor and the heading to *Evangel.*

BWV 244/36 (P 25). The title for this movement, written to the left of the first system, originally read: *Aria / a / due / Violini / Viola / e / Basso / Chori / 1mi.* (The words *Trav: e Hautb d'amour 1 concordant* are written above the first staff.) The word *Basso* is corrected to *Alto,* but this correction was clearly delayed, for the clef of the vocal staff in the first three systems of the movement is changed from bass to alto, and the note-heads in the vocal part for the first 28 measures of the aria (i.e., more precisely mm. 12–28) are enlarged and raised one staff-degree and thus changed from a reading in the bass clef to the same pitches an octave higher in the alto clef.

BIBLIOGRAPHY

Musical Editions and Facsimiles

BG. *Johann Sebastian Bach's Werke.* Complete edition of the Bach-Gesellschaft. 46 vols. Leipzig, 1851–1900.

NBA. *Johann Sebastian Bach. Neue Ausgabe sämtlicher Werke.* Edited by the Johann-Sebastian-Bach-Institut, Göttingen, and the Bach-Archiv, Leipzig. Kassel, Leipzig, 1954—.

Bach, Johann Sebastian. *Ach Herr, mich armen Sünder.* BWV 135. Facsimile edition of the autograph with a commentary by Karl Straube. Leipzig, 1926.

—————. *Brandenburgische Konzerte.* BWV 1046–1051. Facsimile edition of the autograph with a commentary by Peter Wackernagel. Leipzig, 1950.

—————. *Cantata a S. è Basso* (Kaffee-Kantate). BWV 211. Facsimile edition of the autograph. Vienna, 1923.

—————. *Cantate Burlesque* (Bauernkantate). BWV 212. Facsimile edition of the autograph with a commentary by Wilhelm Virneisel. Munich, 1965.

—————. *Clavier-Büchlein vor Wilhelm Friedemann Bach.* Edited in facsimile with a preface by Ralph Kirkpatrick. New Haven, 1959.

—————. *Das Wohltemperirte Clavier.* BWV 846–869. Facsimile edition of the autograph with prefaces by Hans Pischner and Karl-Heinz Köhler. (*Faksimile-Reihe Bachscher Werke und Schriftstücke,* edited by the Bach-Archiv, Leipzig, Vol. 5.) Leipzig, 1965.

—————. *Der Geist hilft unser' Schwachheit auf.* BWV 226. Facsimile edition of the autograph with a commentary by Konrad Ameln. Kassel, 1964.

—————. *Gott ist mein König.* BWV 71. Mühlhäuser Ratswechselkantate 1708. Facsimile edition of the autograph score and of the original printed libretto with a preface by Werner Neumann. (*Faksimile-Reihe Bachscher Werke und Schriftstücke,* edited by the Bach-Archiv, Leipzig, Leipzig, Vol. 9.) Leipzig, 1970.

—————. *Ich will den Kreuzstab gerne tragen.* BWV 56. Facsimile edition of the autograph. Munich, 1921.

—————. *Inventionen und Sinfonien.* BWV 772–801. Facsimile of the autograph with commentaries by Georg Schünemann (Leipzig, 1942) and Ralph Kirkpatrick. Frankfurt am Main, n.d.

—————. *Matthäuspassion.* BWV 244. Facsimile edition of the autograph. Leipzig, 1922.

————. *Matthäuspassion.* BWV 244. Facsimile edition of the autograph with a preface by Karl-Heinz Köhler. (*Faksimile-Reihe Bachscher Werke und Schrift-stücke,* edited by the Bach-Archiv, Leipzig, Vol. 7.) Leipzig, 1966.

————. *Mein Herze schwimmt im Blut.* BWV 199. Edited by C. A. Martienssen. (*Veröffentlichungen der Neuen-Bach-Gesellschaft,* Vol. XIII, 2.) Leipzig, 1913.

————. *Messe in H-moll.* BWV 232. Facsimile edition of the autograph. Leipzig, 1924.

————. *Messe in H-moll.* BWV 232. Facsimile reproduction of the autograph with a commentary edited by Alfred Dürr. Kassel, 1965.

————. *O holder Tag, erwünschte Zeit* (Hochzeitskantate). BWV 210. Facsimile edition of the autograph with a preface by Werner Neumann. (*Faksimile-Reihe Bachscher Werke und Schriftstücke,* edited by the Bach-Archiv, Leipzig, Vol. 8.) Leipzig, 1967.

————. *The Passion According to St. John.* BWV 245. Vocal Score Edited and with an Introduction by Arthur Mendel. New York, 1951.

————. *Präludium pro Organo / cum pedale obligato / di / Joh: Seb: Bach.* BWV 544. Facsimile edition of the autograph with a commentary by Georg Kinsky. Vienna, 1923.

————. *Sei solo à Violino senza Basso accompagnato.* BWV 1001–1006. Facsimile edition of the autograph with a commentary by Wilhelm Martin Luther. Kassel, 1958.

————. *Singet dem Herrn ein neues Lied.* BWV 225. Facsimile edition of the autograph with a commentary by Walter Gerstenberg. Kassel, 1958.

————. *Sonata a Cembalo obligato e Travers. solo.* BWV 1030. Facsimile edition of the autograph with a preface by Werner Neumann. (*Faksimile-Reihe Bachscher Werke und Schriftstücke,* edited by the Bach-Archiv, Leipzig, Vol. 4.) Leipzig, 1961.

————. *Weihnachts-Oratorium.* BWV 248. Facsimile reproduction of the autograph with a commentary edited by Alfred Dürr. Kassel, 1960.

————. *Weinen, Klagen, Sorgen, Zagen.* BWV 12. Edited by Arnold Schering. Leipzig, 1926.

Chrysander 1885. Chrysander, Friedrich (ed.). *Das Autograph des Oratoriums "Jephtha" von G. F. Händel.* (*Georg Friedrich Händel's Werke. Ausgabe der Deutschen Händelgesellschaft,* edited by Fr. Chrysander, Vol. 95.) Hamburg, 1885.

Riemenschneider 1941. Riemenschneider, Albert (ed.). *J. S. Bach. 371 Harmonized Chorales and 69 Chorale Melodies with Figured Bass.* New York, 1941.

Terry 1929. Terry, Charles Sanford (ed.). *The Four-Part Chorals of J. S. Bach.* London, 1929. Reprinted with a new foreword by Walter Emery. London, 1964.

Literature

Besseler 1950. Besseler, Heinrich. "Bach und das Mittelalter." In *Bericht über die Wissenschaftliche Bachtagung der Gesellschaft für Musikforschung, Leipzig 23. bis 26. Juli 1950.* Ed. Walther Vetter and Ernst Hermann Meyer, pp. 108–130. Leipzig, 1951.

Blume 1962. Blume, Friedrich. "Umrisse eines neuen Bach-Bildes," *Musica,* XVI (1962), 169–176.

Blume 1963. English version as "Outlines of a New Picture of Bach," *Music and Letters,* XLIV (1963), 214–227.

BWV. Schmieder, Wolfgang. *Thematisch-systematisches Verzeichnis der musikalischen Werke von Johann Sebastian Bach. Bach-Werke-Verzeichnis* (BWV). Leipzig, 1950.

Congress 1961. "Bach Problems." In *International Musicological Society. Report of the Eighth Congress New York 1961,* edited by Jan LaRue. *Vol. 2—Reports,* pp. 127–131. Kassel, 1962.

Dadelsen 1957. Von Dadelsen, Georg. *Bemerkungen zur Handschrift Johann Sebastian Bachs, seiner Familie und seines Kreises.* (*Tübinger Bach-Studien,* ed. Walter Gerstenberg, Heft 1.) Trossingen, 1957.

Dadelsen 1958. ———. *Beiträge zur Chronologie der Werke Johann Sebastian Bachs.* (*Tübinger Bach-Studien,* ed. Walter Gerstenberg, Heft 4/5.) Trossingen, 1958.

Dadelsen 1961. ———. "Die 'Fassung letzter Hand' in der Musik," *Acta Musicologica,* XXXIII (1961), 1–14.

Dadelsen 1962. ———. "Eine unbekannte Messen-Bearbeitung Bachs." In *Festschrift Karl Gustav Fellerer zum sechzigsten Gerburtstag,* edited by Heinrich Hüschen, pp. 88–94. Regensburg, 1962.

David-Mendel 1966. David, Hans T., and Mendel, Arthur. *The Bach Reader. A Life of Johann Sebastian Bach in Letters and Documents.* Revised edition. New York, 1966.

Dürr 1951. Dürr, Alfred. *Studien über die frühen Kantaten J. S. Bachs.* Leipzig, 1951.

Dürr 1957. ———. "Zur Chronologie der Leipziger Vokalwerke J. S. Bachs," *Bach-Jahrbuch 1957,* 5–162.

Dürr 1958. ———. "'Ich bin ein Pilgrim auf der Welt,' eine verschollene Kantate J. S. Bachs," *Die Musikforschung,* XI (1958), 422–427.

Dürr 1962[1]. ———. "Der Eingangssatz zu Bachs Himmelfahrts-Oratorium und seine Vorlage." In *Hans Albrecht in Memoriam; Gedenkschrift mit Beiträgen von Freunden und Schülern,* eds. Wilfried Brennecke and Hans Haase, pp. 121–126. Kassel, 1962.

Dürr 1962[2]. ———. "Zum Wandel des Bach-Bildes. Zu Friedrich Blumes Mainzer Vortrag," *Musik und Kirche,* XXXII (1962), 145–152.

Dürr 1967. ———. "Bach's Chorale Cantatas." In *Cantors at the Crossroads. Essays on Church Music in Honor of Walter E. Buszin,* edited by Johannes Riedel, pp. 111–120. St. Louis, 1967.

Dürr 1968. ———. "Neues über Bachs Pergolesi-Bearbeitung," *Bach-Jahrbuch 1968,* 89–100.

Dürr 1970. ———. "Zur Textvorlage der Choralkantaten Johann Sebastian Bachs." In *Kerygma und Melos. Christhard Mahrenholz 70 Jahre,* edited by Walter Blankenburg, Herwarth von Schade, Kurt Schmidt-Clausen with the collaboration of Alexander Völker, pp. 222–236. Kassel, 1970.

Emery 1964. Emery, Walter, Review of *Festschrift für Friedrich Smend zum 70. Geburtstag.* In *Music and Letters,* XLV (1964), 167–170.

Herz 1970. Herz, Gerhard. "Toward a New Image of Bach," *Bach. The Quarterly Journal of the Riemenschneider Bach Institute,* Volume I, No. 4 (October 1970), 9–27.

Hiekel. Hiekel, Hans Otto. "Katalog der Rastrierungen in den Originalhandschriften J. S. Bachs." Unpublished manuscript. Johann-Sebastian-Bach-Institut, Göttingen, 1963.

Kast 1958. Kast, Paul. *Die Bach-Handschriften der Berliner Staatsbibliothek. (Tübinger Bach-Studien,* ed. Walter Gerstenberg, Heft 2/3.) Trossingen, 1958.

McAll 1962. McAll, May deForest (ed.). *Melodic Index to the Works of Johann Sebastian Bach.* New York, 1962.

McHose 1947. McHose, Allen Irvine. *The Contrapuntal Harmonic Technique of the 18th Century.* New York, 1947.

Marshall 1968. Marshall, Robert L. Review of J. S. Bach. *Cantate Burlesque.* Facsimile edition. In *Notes,* XXIV (1968), 573–575.

Mattheson 1739. Mattheson, Johann. *Der vollkommene Capellmeister.* Hamburg, 1739. Facsimile reproduction edited by Margarete Reimann. (*Documenta Musicologica. Erste Reihe: Druckschriften-Faksimiles,* Vol. 5.) Kassel, 1954.

Melchert 1958. Melchert, Hermann. *Das Rezitativ der Kirchenkantaten Joh. Seb. Bachs.* Frankfurt am Main, 1958.

Mendel 1959. Mendel, Arthur. "A Note on Proportional Relationships in Bach Tempi," *The Musical Times,* C (1959), 683–685.

Mendel 1960[1]. ———. "Recent Developments in Bach Chronology," *The Musical Quarterly,* XLVI (1960), 283–300.

Mendel 1960[2]. ———. "Bach Tempi: A Rebuttal," *The Musical Times,* CI (1960), 251.

Mendel 1964. ———. "More on the Weimar Origin of Bach's *O Mensch, Bewein* (BWV 244/35)," *Journal of the American Musicological Society,* XVII (1964), 203–206.

Mies 1925. Mies, Paul. *Die Bedeutung der Skizzen Beethovens zur Erkenntnis seines Stiles.* Leipzig, 1925.

Morgan 1970. *The Mary Flagler Cary Music Collection. Printed Books and Music, Manuscripts, Autograph Letters, Documents, Portraits.* The Pierpont Morgan Library, New York, 1970.

Neumann 1938 (1953). Neumann, Werner. *J. S. Bachs Chorfuge. Ein Beitrag zur Kompositionstechnik Bachs.* Leipzig, 1953. (Originally published 1938.)

Neumann 1953. ———. *Handbuch der Kantaten Joh. Seb. Bachs.* Second edition. Leipzig, 1953.

Neumann 1956. ——— (ed.). *Johann Sebastian Bach. Sämtliche Kantatentexte.* Leipzig, 1956.

Neumann 1957. ———. *Auf den Lebenswegen Johann Sebastian Bachs.* Munich, 1957.

Neumann 1965. ———. "Über Ausmaß und Wesen des Bachschen Parodieverfahrens," *Bach-Jahrbuch 1965,* 63–85.

Neumerkel 1935. Neumerkel, Otto. "Studien an Skizzen Ludwig van Beethovens. Ein Beitrag zur künstlerischen Schaffensweise." Unpublished dissertation, University of Vienna, 1935.

Nottebohm-Mies 1924. Nottebohm, Gustav. *Zwei Skizzenbücher von Beethoven aus den Jahren 1801 bis 1803.* New edition with a foreword by Paul Mies. Leipzig, 1924.

Platen 1959. Platen, Emil. *Untersuchungen zur Struktur der chorischen Choralbearbeitung Johann Sebastian Bachs.* Bonn, 1959.

Platen 1961. ———. "Eine Pergolesi-Bearbeitung Bachs," *Bach-Jahrbuch 1961,* 35–51.

Richter 1920. Richter, Bernhard Friedrich. "Der Nekrolog auf Seb. Bach vom Jahre 1754," *Bach-Jahrbuch 1920,* 11–29.

Riemann 1909. Riemann, Hugo. "Spontane Phantasietätigkeit und verstandesmäßige Arbeit in der tonkünstlerischen Produktion," *Jahrbuch der Musikbibliothek Peters für 1909,* XVI (1910), 33–46.

Rose 1959. Rose, Bernard. "Some Further Observations on the Performance of Purcell's Music," *The Musical Times,* C (1959), 385–386.

Rose 1960. ———. "A Further Note on Bach's Tempi," *The Musical Times,* CI (1960), 107–108.

Scheide. Scheide, William H. "Bach Achieves His Goal. His First Year of Regular Church Music Following the Leipzig Lutheran Calendar." Unpublished manuscript.

Scheide 1961. ————. "Johann Sebastian Bachs Sammlung von Kantaten seines Vetters Johann Ludwig Bach," *Bach-Jahrbuch 1961,* 5–24.

Schering 1925. Schering, Arnold. "Geschichtliches zur 'Ars inveniendi' in der Musik," *Jahrbuch der Musikbibliothek Peters für 1925,* XXXII (1926), 25–34.

Schering 1933. ————. "Kleine Bachstudien," *Bach-Jahrbuch 1933,* 30–70.

Schering 1936[1]. ————. "Die Hohe Messe in h-moll," *Bach-Jahrbuch 1936,* 1–30.

Schering 1936[2]. ————. *Johann Sebastian Bachs Leipziger Kirchenmusik. Studien und Wege zu ihrer Erkenntnis. (Veröffentlichungen der Neuen Bachgesellschaft Vereinsjahr 36,2).* Leipzig, 1936.

Schmieder 1939. Schmieder, Wolfgang. *Musikerhandschriften in drei Jahrhunderten.* Leipzig, 1939.

Schmieder 1950. ————. "Bemerkungen zur Bachquellenforschung." In *Bericht über die Wissenschaftliche Bachtagung der Gesellschaft für Musikforschung, Leipzig 23. bis 26. Juli 1950,* eds. Walther Vetter and Ernst Hermann Meyer, pp. 219–230. Leipzig, 1951.

Schmitz 1950[1]. Schmitz, Arnold. *Die Bildlichkeit der wortgebundenen Musik Johann Sebastian Bachs. (Neue Studien zur Musikwissenschaft,* ed. Kommission für Musikwissenschaft der Akademie der Wissenschaften und der Literatur, Vol. 1.) Mainz, 1950.

Schmitz 1950[2]. ————. "Die oratorische Kunst J. S. Bachs—Grundfragen und Grundlagen." In *Kongress-Bericht, Gesellschaft für Musikforschung, Lüneburg 1950,* eds. Hans Albrecht, Helmut Osthoff, Walter Wiora, pp. 33–49. Kassel, 1950.

Schünemann 1935. Schünemann, Georg. "Bachs Verbesserungen und Entwürfe," *Bach-Jahrbuch 1935,* 1–32.

Schünemann 1936[1]. ————. *Musikerhandschriften von Bach bis Schumann.* Berlin, 1936.

Schünemann 1936[2]. ————. "Bachs Trauungskantate 'Gott Beherrscher aller Dinge,'" *Bach-Jahrbuch 1936,* 31–52.

Schulze 1961. Schulze, Hans-Joachim. "Marginalien zu einigen Bach-Dokumenten," *Bach-Jahrbuch 1961,* 79–99.

Schulze 1963. ————. "Frühe Schriftzeugnisse der beiden jüngsten Bach-Söhne," *Bach-Jahrbuch 1963/64,* 61–69.

Schulze 1968. ————. "Johann Sebastian Bach und Christian Gottlob Meißner," *Bach-Jahrbuch 1968,* 80–88.

Siegele 1962. Siegele, Ulrich. "Bemerkungen zu Bachs Motetten," *Bach-Jahrbuch 1962,* 33–57.

Smend 1962. Smend, Friedrich. "Was bleibt? Zu Friedrich Blumes Bach-Bild," *Der Kirchenmusiker,* XIII (1962), 178–190.

Spitta I, II. Spitta, Philipp. *Johann Sebastian Bach.* 2 vols. Leipzig, 1873–1880. Fifth edition. Wiesbaden, 1962.

Spitta 1892[1]. ———. "Beethoveniana." In *Zur Musik. Sechzehn Aufsätze.* Berlin, 1892.

Spitta 1892[2]. ———. "Mariane von Ziegler und Joh. Sebastian Bach," *Zur Musik. Sechzehn Aufsätze.* Berlin, 1892.

Steger 1962. Steger, Werner. "G. H. Stölzels Abhandlung vom Rezitativ." Unpublished dissertation, University of Heidelberg, 1962.

Strunk 1950. Strunk, Oliver. *Source Readings in Music History.* New York, 1950.

Tagliavini 1956. Tagliavini, Luigi Ferdinando. *Studi sui Testi delle Cantate Sacre di J. S. Bach. (Università di Padova. Pubblicazioni della Facoltà di Lettere e Filosofia,* Vol. XXXI.) Padua, Kassel, 1956.

Terry 1932. Terry, Charles Sanford. *Bach's Orchestra.* London, 1932. Reprinted 1958.

Thayer-Forbes 1967. *Thayer's Life of Beethoven.* Revised and edited by Elliot Forbes. 2 vols. Revised edition, Princeton, 1967.

Trautmann 1969. Trautmann, Christoph. " *'Calovii Schrifften. 3. Bände'* aus Johann Sebastian Bachs Nachlaß und ihre Bedeutung für das Bild des lutherischen Kantors Bach," *Musik und Kirche,* 39. Jahrgang (1969), 145–160.

Trautmann 1970. ———. "Ansätze zu ideell-ideologischen Problemen um Johann Sebastian Bach." In *Kerygma und Melos. Christhard Mahrenholz 70 Jahre,* edited by Walter Blankenburg, Herwarth von Schade, Kurt Schmidt-Clausen with the collaboration of Alexander Völker, pp. 237–245. Kassel 1970.

Unger 1941. Unger, Heinrich. *Die Beziehungen zwischen Musik und Rhetorik im 16.–18. Jahrhundert. (Musik und Geistesgeschichte, Berliner Studien zur Musikwissenschaft,* ed. Arnold Schering, Vol. 4.) Würzburg, 1941. Reprinted 1969.

Vopelius 1682. Vopelius, Gottfried. *Neu Leipziger Gesangbuch . . . .* Leipzig, 1682.

Wackernagel 1955. Wackernagel, Peter. "Beobachtungen am Autograph von Bachs Brandenburgischen Konzerten." In *Festschrift Max Schneider zum achtzigsten Geburtstage,* ed. Walther Vetter, pp. 129–138. Leipzig, 1955.

Walther 1708. Walther, Johann Gottfried. *Praecepta der Musicalischen Composition.* Edited by Peter Benary. (*Jenaer Beiträge zur Musikforschung,* ed. Heinrich Besseler, Vol. 2.) Leipzig, 1955.

Walther 1732. ———. *Musicalisches Lexicon.* Leipzig, 1732. Facsimile reproduction edited by Richard Schaal. (*Documenta Musicologica. Erste Reihe: Druckschriften-Faksimiles,* Vol. 3.) Kassel, 1953.

Weiß 1962. Weiß, Wisso. "Die Wasserzeichen in den Bach-Dokumenten." Unpublished manuscript. Johann-Sebastian-Bach-Institut, Göttingen, 1962.

Winternitz 1955. Winternitz, Emanuel. *Musical Autographs from Monteverdi to Hindemith.* 2 vols. Princeton, 1955.

Wolff 1963. Wolff, Christoph. "Die Rastrierungen in den Originalhandschriften Joh. Seb. Bachs und ihre Bedeutung für die diplomatische Quellenkritik." In *Festschrift für Friedrich Smend zum 70. Geburtstag dargebracht von Freunden und Schülern,* pp. 80–92. Berlin, 1963.

Wolff 1968. ———. *Der Stile Antico in der Musik Johann Sebastian Bachs. Studien zu Bachs Spätwerk. (Beihefte zum Archiv für Musikwissenschaft,* ed. Hans Heinrich Eggebrecht, Vol. 6.) Wiesbaden, 1968.

Zander 1968. Zander, Ferdinand. "Die Dichter der Kantatentexte Johann Sebastian Bachs. Untersuchungen zu ihrer Bestimmung," *Bach-Jahrbuch 1968,* 9–64.

INDEX

Page references are to Volume I unless preceded by "II:".

Punctuation and orthography of all German titles and text incipits are taken from Neumann 1956. Work titles and incipits are printed in italics, while incipits of individual movements are in quotation marks. Incipits serving both as work and movement headings appear both in italics and in quotation marks.